The European Court of Justice

Edited by

GRÁINNE DE BÚRCA and J. H. H. WEILER

Academy of European Law
European University Institute

OXFORD
UNIVERSITY PRESS

OXFORD

UNIVERSITY PRESS

Great Clarendon Street, Oxford OX2 6DP

Oxford University Press is a department of the University of Oxford.
It furthers the University's objective of excellence in research, scholarship,
and education by publishing worldwide in

Oxford New York

Athens Auckland Bangkok Bogotá Buenos Aires Cape Town
Chennai Dar es Salaam Delhi Florence Hong Kong Istanbul Karachi
Kolkata Kuala Lumpur Madrid Melbourne Mexico City Mumbai Nairobi
Paris São Paulo Shanghai Singapore Taipei Tokyo Toronto Warsaw

and associated companies in Berlin Ibadan

Oxford is a registered trade mark of Oxford University Press
in the UK and in certain other countries

Published in the United States
by Oxford University Press Inc., New York

© G. De Búrca and J.H.H. Weiler 2001

British Library Cataloguing in Publication Data

Data available

Library of Congress Cataloging in Publication Data
The European Court of Justice/edited by Gráinne de Búrca and J.H.H. Weiler.
p. cm.—(The collected courses of the Academy of European Law; v. 11/2)
This collection of essays originated in a series of seminars given at the summer
courses of the Academy of European Law at the European Law at the
European University Institute, Florence in 1999.
Includes bibliographical references and index.
1. Court of Justice of the European Communities. 2. Courts—European Union countries.
I. De Búrca, G. (Gráinne) II. Weiler, Joseph, 1951– III. Series.
KJE5461.E933 2001   341.5'5'094—dc21   2001036408

ISBN 0–19–924602–5 (hbk.)
ISBN 0–19–924601–7 (pbk.)

1 3 5 7 9 10 8 6 4 2

Typeset in Garamond
by Hope Services (Abingdon) Ltd.
Printed in Great Britain
on acid-free paper by
Biddles Ltd., Guildford and King's Lynn

Foreword

This volume of essays, which focuses on the judicial system of the European Union, and more specifically on the jurisdiction and role of the European Court of Justice and Court of First Instance, originated in a series of seminars given at the summer courses of the Academy of European Law at the European University Institute, Florence in 1999. To celebrate the tenth anniversary of the Academy, the directors chose the subject of the Court of Justice as one of enduring centrality to the European political and legal system. The developments which have since taken place under the Nice Treaty further underscore the importance of re-evaluating the past, present and future functioning of the European judicial system. We are grateful to Renaud Dehousse for his work in connection with this volume as a former director of the Academy, and to Anny Bremner and Barbara Ciomei for their sterling work in all aspects of the administration of the Academy, and in particular in the preparation of these collected courses for publication. Thanks are also due to John Louth and his colleagues at Oxford University Press for their assistance at every stage.

G. de B.
J.H.H.W.

Contents

Notes on Contributors

JOXERRAMON BENGOETXEA is, since 1998, Deputy Minister for Labour and Social Security at the Department of Justice, Labour and Social Affairs of the Basque Autonomous Government, and, since 1990, Professor of Legal Theory and Jurisprudence at the University of the Basque Country. From 1993 to 1998 he served as Legal Secretary of Judge David Edward at the European Court of Justice. He holds a Ph.D. in Law from Edinburgh University, and his academic interests focus on European Community Law, the Court of Justice, the Legal Order of the EC, free movement of persons, employment, education, and social issues in the EC, as well as Legal Theory and Jurisprudence, Political Philosophy (theory of State and nationalism), and Human Rights. He has published, among other works, *The Legal Reasoning of the European Court of Justice* (1993).

ERHARD BLANKENBURG has been teaching sociology of law and criminology at the Vrije Universiteit Amsterdam since 1980. Professor Blankenburg holds a Master of Arts from the University of Oregon, a Doctors degree from Basel, and a Dr. habil. at Freiburg (Germany). After teaching sociology and sociology of law at Freiburg University 1965–70, he served as consultant with the QuickbornTeam Hamburg until 1972, as senior research fellow at the PrognosAG Basel until 1974, at the Max Planck Institut Freiburg 1974/5, and at the Science Centre Berlin until 1980. He has published on comparative legal cultures, police, public prosecutors, civil courts, labour courts, legal aid, and mobilization of law.

PAUL CRAIG, MA, BCL, FBA, QC (Hon) is Professor of English Law at St John's College, Oxford. He has been an academic at Oxford since 1976. He has also taught at a number of other Universities in Canada, Australia, and the USA. Professor Craig's academic interests are divided between public law (constitutional and administrative law), and EU law. His principal publications include *Administrative Law*, 4th edn.; *Public Law and Democracy in the UK and the USA*; *EU Law, Text, Cases and Materials*, 2nd edn., jointly with Gráinne de Búrca; and *The Evolution of EU Law*, jointly with Gráinne de Búrca. He is currently working on a book on Law, Governance, and Administration in the EU.

GRÁINNE DE BÚRCA is Professor of European Union Law at the European University Institute, Florence, and co-director of the EUI's Academy of European Law. She also taught for nine years at Somerville College, Oxford, and her research has focused primarily on the field of EU constitutional law. She is co-author with Paul Craig of the textbook *EU Law* (1998), the third edition of which is currently under preparation, and co-editor of the OUP book series Oxford Studies in European Law. Her recent publications include two books co-edited with Joanne Scott, *The*

Constitution of the EU: From Uniformity to Flexibility (2000) and *The EU and the WTO: Legal and Constitutional Aspects* (2001).

CLAIRE KILPATRICK is a Lecturer in Law at Queen Mary, University of London. She did her doctoral thesis at the EUI in Florence on the comparative utilization and conceptualization of EU gender equality norms. Part of this work was further developed in a research project now published in S. Sciarra, *Labour Law in the Courts: National Judges and the ECJ* (2001). She is one of the editors of a collection of essays on *The Future of Remedies in Europe* (2000) and co-editor of the European Developments Section of the *Industrial Law Journal.*

SIR NEIL MACCORMICK is a Member of the European Parliament (Scotland; Scottish National Party/European Free Alliance); a Member of the EP's Committees on Legal Affairs and Single Market (co-ordinator for the Greens/European Free Alliance Group); Constitutional Affairs Committee; Vice-President of the Temporary Committee (2000–1) on the Echelon Interception System; and a Vice-President of the Scottish National Party since 1999. A distinguished academic lawyer and graduate of Glasgow, Oxford, and Edinburgh Universities, he has been Regius Professor of Public Law at Edinburgh University since 1972 (leave of absence, 1999–2004); honorary Doctor of Laws from universities in several countries (Uppsala, Sweden; the Saarland, Germany; Macerata, Italy; Queen's, Kingston, Ontario; Glasgow, Scotland); foreign member of the Finnish Academy, Fellow of the Royal Society of Edinburgh and of the British Academy, Member of the Academia Europaea, and honorary QC. Author of many books and articles in legal and political theory, most recently *Questioning Sovereignty: Law State and Nation in the European Commonwealth* (1999). On 16 June 2001 Professor MacCormick was knighted in the Queen's Birthday Honours List for services to scholarship in law.

LEONOR MORAL SORIANO is Senior Research Fellow at the Max Plank Project Group on Law of Common Goods, Bonn, and Lecturer in Administrative Law at the University of Granada. She obtained her Ph.D at the European University Institute, Florence. She was Marie Curie Fellow at the Centre for Law and Society, Edinburgh, where she conducted postdoctoral research on the legal reasoning of the European Court of Justice and English courts in environmental issues. Her research interests are twofold. In the field of legal theory, she analyses the notion of coherence in legal reasoning and in particular the principle of proportionality. In the field of European Law, her research focuses on competition law and in particular on the liberalization of universal services. The results of her research have been published in a number of journals: *ARSP, Ratio Juris, Journal of Environmental Law,* and *DOXA* among others.

JO SHAW is Professor of European Law at the University of Leeds, and Director of the Centre for the Study of Law in Europe (1995–2001), having previously worked at the Universities of Keele and Exeter, and University College London. She holds a Jean

Monnet Chair in European Law and Integration. During 1998, she was EU-Fulbright Scholar-in-Residence and Visiting Professor at Harvard Law School. From September 2001 she will be Professor of European Law and Jean Monnet Chair in European Law at the University of Manchester. Her research interests fall in the fields of EU constitutionalism and EU institutions, particularly in socio-legal and interdisciplinary perspective.

HARM SCHEPEL teaches European law at Kent Law School, University of Kent at Canterbury. Previously, he was attached to the Centre for European Law and Policy at the University of Bremen and held a Marie Curie Fellowship at the Centre de Théorie Politique at the Université Libre de Bruxelles. He has published and lectured widely on the general themes of legal sociology and European integration. His current research focuses on the role of private governance regimes in integrating markets. He co-authored *The Legal Status of Standardisation in the Member States of the EC and of EFTA* (2000).

J. H. H. WEILER is Jean Monnet Professor of Law and Director of the Center for International and Regional Economic Law and Justice at New York University Law School. He is a faculty member at the College of Europe in Bruges, Belgium, and an Honorary Professor at University College London, and at the University of Copenhagen. He served as a Member of the Committee of Jurists of the Institutional Affairs Committee of the European Parliament, co-drafting the European Parliament's Declaration of Human Rights and Freedoms and the Parliament's input to the Maastricht Inter-Governmental Conference. He also served as Co-Director of the Academy of European Law in Florence. He was a member of the *Groupe des Sages* advising the Commission of the European Union on the 1996/7 Amsterdam Treaty. He is a WTO Panel Member. His most recent book is *The Constitution of Europe: Do the New Clothes Have an Emperor?* (1999).

Table of Cases

Court of First Instance

Opinions

National Cases

Table of Legislation

A. EU Legislation

Abbreviations

CAP	Common Agricultural Policy
CFI	Court of First Instance
CMLR	Common Market Law Reports
COM	Communication
EAGGF	European Agricultural Guidance and Guarantee Fund
EAT	Employment Appeals Tribunal
EC	European Community
ECB	European Central Bank
ECHR	European Court of Human Rights
ECJ	European Court of Justice
ECOSOC	Economic and Social Council
EMU	European Monetary Union
EOC	Equal Opportunities Commission
EqPA	Equal Pay Act
ETD	Equal Treatment Directive
EU	European Union
GATT	General Agreement on Tariffs and Trade
GDP	Gross Domestic Product
IAEA	International Atomic Energy Group
IBRD	International Bank for Reconstruction and Development
ICCPR	International Covenant on Civil and Political Rights
ICESCR	International Covenant on Economic, Social, and Cultural Rights
ICJ	International Court of Justice
ICRC	International Committee of the Red Cross
IDA	International Development Association
IGC	Inter-Governmental Conference
ILO	International Labour Organization
IMO	International Maritime Organization
IMF	International Monetary Fund
IRLR	Industrial Relations Law Reports
MLR	Modern Law Review
NATO	North Atlantic Treaty Organization
NGO	Non-Governmental Organization
OJ	Official Journal of the European Communities
OSCE	Organization for Security and Cooperation in Europe
SDA	Sexual Discrimination Act 1975
SEA	Single European Act
TEU	Treaty on European Union
TRIPS	Trade-Related Aspects of Intellectual Property Rights
UNCED	Rio Conference on Environmental Development

UNCTAD	UN Conference on Trade and Development
UNESCO	United Nations Educational, Scientific and Cultural Organization
WGIP	Working Group on Indigenous Populations
WHO	World Health Organization
WTO	World Trade Organization

1

Introduction

GRÁINNE DE BÚRCA

There are many reasons to reflect anew on the role and position of the European judicial branch. When attention focuses on the profound and vital developments confronting the EU both at present and over the next decade—including the prospect of substantial enlargement, and the existence of new and growing areas of highly significant EC and EU policy competence such as in the monetary sphere and in immigration and policing—it is curious how little reflection there tends to be on the possible implications for the European Court of Justice. The spotlight is firmly on the Commission, the Council, the Parliament, on the political and diplomatic structures for policy-making; insofar as attention is paid to the Court, it tends to be on the question of case-load and to be couched in fairly technical and abstract terms. And yet the exponential growth and expansion of the EU in terms of size, substance, and complexity profoundly affects the judicial branch as it does all others. The central relationship of the Court of Justice with national courts, including the constitutional and other courts of future Member States with their diverse constitutional traditions and histories, will undoubtedly undergo change and encounter new challenges. And the significant developments which have taken place within the EU, including the increasing differentiation, diffusion, and complexity of its legal and political forms and structures, inevitably must affect the values and methodology of the Court which defines and mediates the legal relations within that system.

Jo Shaw wrote in 1995 that 'an unwillingness to make the Court the centrepiece in emerging work in European Union legal studies may be in part a reaction against the dominance of Court-centred work in EC law scholarship'.[1] The comment was written in the introductory chapter to a collection of essays which sought self-consciously to explore fresh avenues and approaches to EU law and to move away from the relatively de-contextualized analysis of judicial doctrine and the concentration on the output of the Court

Thanks are due to Joseph H. H. Weiler for his comments and input.

[1] Introduction, in J. Shaw and G. More (eds.), *New Legal Dynamics of European Union* (Oxford: Oxford University Press, 1995).

of Justice which characterized much of the earlier EC law scholarship. The diversity, richness, and range of EU legal scholarship has grown over the years even since the publication of that collection of essays, as has the interest shown in the Court by EU scholars from other disciplinary backgrounds. Although there is still no shortage of case analysis nor any real question in the minds of lawyers as to the centrality and importance of the ECJ as a European legal institution and actor, there has been a greater openness within legal literature to the insights both of other bodies of scholarship and of other disciplines within European Union studies which have traditionally placed far more emphasis on legislative policy and on political rather than judicial processes. More generally, as this field of legal scholarship has matured, a greater acceptance has developed of the inadequacy of a largely court-centred approach in terms of understanding the complex fabric of EU law and policy. At the same time, however, the unusual, influential, and evolving role of the ECJ as a key legal institution within an emergent and powerful political entity has continued to generate scholarly interest and research from within the legal academic community as well as from legal practitioners and institutional actors. Apart from the continuing flow of journal articles, a number of English language monographs dedicated to the Court have appeared in the last two years,[2] as well as a number of works focusing on the relationship between the ECJ and national courts.[3] These 'later-generation' works tend to concentrate less on tracing and analysing the doctrine developed by the ECJ, they are less uncritically accepting than much of the earlier literature[4] of the validity of the claims made by the Court both about the nature and effect of EC law and about its own authority and status, and they are more frequently addressed to or emanating from scholars whose primary disciplinary training is not in law.

Apart from engaging with and developing further some of this more interesting research, a number of the essays in this book seek also to develop certain avenues of analysis which, despite the significant increase in the range and volume of literature, have not yet been fully explored. Thus they include a legal-philosophical account of the ECJ's reasoning, a sociological analysis of patterns of litigation before the Court, and an investigation of the impact and

---

[2] See e.g. R. Dehousse, *The European Court of Justice: The Politics of Judicial Integration* (London: Macmillan, 1998), H. Rasmussen, *The European Court of Justice* (Copenhagen, GadJura, 1998), and A. Arnull, *The European Union and Its Court of Justice* (Oxford: Oxford University Press, 1999).

[3] e.g. A. Slaughter, A. Stone Sweet, and J. H. H. Weiler (eds.), *The European Courts and National Courts: Doctrine and Jurisprudence* (Oxford: Hart, 1998), A. Stone Sweet, *Governing with Judges: Constitutional Politics in Europe* (Oxford: Oxford University Press, 2000), and K. Alter, *The Creation of an International Rule of Law: The European Court and National Judiciaries* (forthcoming, Oxford University Press, 2001).

[4] H. Rasmussen's 1986 thesis, *On Law and Policy in the European Court of Justice* (Dordrecht: Nijhoff, 1986), being one of the notable exceptions in this respect.

presence of gender in the Court's work and on its institutional position. Other contributions look afresh at the more topical and sometimes controversial subject of the relationship between national courts and the Court of Justice, focusing on the implicit conversation between national constitutional courts and the ECJ over issues of final authority, and on the more prosaic but fundamentally important question of the reception, use, transformation, and questioning by ordinary national courts of ECJ doctrine under the preliminary reference mechanism. Finally, focusing on contemporary institutional developments, two of the essays contemplate the likely effect on the Court of Justice and the Court of First Instance of the reforms to the judicial structure proposed during and before the 2000 Inter-governmental Conference

The essays thus partly reflect the fact that, despite the wealth of literature and the growing diversity of focus and approach, a number of perspectives remain relatively under-explored in the search for a fuller social, empirical, and theoretically grounded understanding of the contemporary role of the ECJ within the European legal and political order. There have, for example, been few attempts to appraise the methodology and output of the Court from a jurisprudential or theoretical perspective, and the field of EC law and legal scholarship has remained relatively unaffected by the rich legal-philosophical literature on adjudication. Joxerramon Bengoetxea's 1983 book was really the first significant and sustained work to adopt a legal theoretical approach to the Court's decision-making.[5] Despite this promising start, however, and although the phenomenon of European integration and the nature of the European legal order more generally has begun to attract the attention of legal theorists and of philosophers,[6] the work of the Court of Justice remains under-theorized. In this volume, however, Bengoetxea, MacCormick, and Moral question the integrity and coherence of the European legal system as interpreted by the Court, and ask whether an analysis of the Court's work lends support to the argument that the European Community is in fact a 'community of principle'. They conclude that it does, and that the idea of integration of Member States is an omnipresent and driving value which is ascribed by the Court to the whole of the EC legal system.

In contrast with the contribution by Shaw on gender and the Court, in which both the details of case law of the ECJ on sex equality and some of the broader issues on the relevance and impact of gender in the Court's case law more generally are examined, this conclusion may appear rather optimistic. The analysis in Shaw's chapter tends to suggest that she would be far from

---

[5] *The Legal Reasoning of the European Court of Justice: Towards a European Jurisprudence* (Oxford: Clarendon Press, 1993).

[6] See e.g. the work of Neil MacCormick, Jürgen Habermas, and Bert van Roermund, and collections such as the 1997 issue of the journal *Law and Philosophy* and that edited by Z. Bankowski and A. Scott, *The European Union and Its Order: The Legal Theory of European Integration* (Oxford: Blackwell, 2000).

convinced by this particular picture of judicial and legal integrity. She points to the way in which cases where the language and surface of the Court's judgments appear to reflect values such as the fundamental human right to equality and the principle of non-discrimination on grounds of sex can actually be seen to be underpinned and motivated far more strongly by the values of national sovereignty and subsidiarity (e.g. in deferring over time to the affirmative action choices made by subnational or national authorities within the framework of EC sex discrimination policy). It could be argued that this view is not necessarily inconsistent with the claim made by Bengoetxea et al., since they do not seek to argue that there are no competing principles at stake in different litigation contexts, but rather that the value of integration of national laws and of Member States is a general underlying and driving value which lends coherence to the Court's jurisprudence and to the legal system as a whole. Nonetheless, the different readings of the Court's work in the two respective chapters appear to be more fundamentally at odds with one another than this suggested reconciliation would imply. It may, for instance, be the case that different policy fields have received somewhat different treatment within the ECJ's case law, and also that different periods within the Community's five decades of history merit rather different analytical conclusions. Kilpatrick in her chapter, for example, expressly charges the Court with undermining the creation of a 'community of principle' by abandoning the implications of its principled judgments when particular kinds of governmental interest are raised. And more generally, the shift in constitutional culture within the EU over the last decade in particular, and the growth in salience of concepts such as flexibility and subsidiarity, suggest that the Court's reasoning, methodology, or even teleology can hardly have remained unaffected.[7] Shaw's suggestion that unarticulated values such as national sovereignty and subsidiarity may be animating decisions which on their face are about human rights and gender equality is persuasive, and her analysis more generally could suggest that the strength of the guiding value of integration—even if it lends theoretical coherence to the Court's jurisprudence in the earlier decades of its operation—may actually be waning.

Using the lens of gender, Shaw criticizes both the quality of the Court's judgments (in terms of reasoning by reference to principle and precedent) and its political choices, as indeed does Kilpatrick in the more specific field of remedies. Shaw's chapter, however, looks beyond the way in which gender equality as a value has affected the Court's decisions in cases concerning sex discrimination. She considers also the relevance of the overwhelmingly male composition of the Court of Justice until very recently, and the largely male

---

[7] See C. Lyons, 'Closer Cooperation and the Court of Justice', in G. de Búrca and J. Scott (eds.), *Constitutional Change in the EU: From Uniformity to Flexibility?* (Oxford: Hart, 2000), 95.

composition of the Court of First Instance, and questions the extent to which the ECJ has adapted its reasoning to accommodate the animating value of gender mainstreaming which the political institutions and particularly the Commission have adopted. Her conclusion is that the predictable structural bias within the EU system, common to any liberal legal order, and the specific constraints imposed by the constitutional relationship between the ECJ and national courts, have combined to prevent gender analysis becoming a strong and autonomous factor in the development of law and policy by the ECJ—rather than an occasional cloak for policy decisions of a different kind to confer legitimacy on itself. This particular combination has meant that the ECJ has not had a free hand to follow, for example, the lead of the Canadian Supreme Court in articulating and applying a substantive equality principle through its interpretation of the 1982 Charter of Rights. One might speculate, in pondering Shaw's conclusions, what potential impact the adoption of an EU Charter of Fundamental Rights, even as a political and non-binding declaration, might have on the interpretive strategies of the Court in the years to come.

There are other reasons too, apart from the relative neglect of certain approaches and perspectives, for choosing to place the Court of Justice once again at the centre of a collection of essays in European law. Leaving aside the vast amount of legal scholarship analysing judicial doctrine and the case law of the court in specific and often complex subject areas, the most sustained debate about the ECJ until recently has been about its 'activism', by which is meant the political implications of the policy choices made by the Court in its interpretive role.[8] However, for the first time since the decision to establish a Court of First Instance in 1988, political attention in the last year or two has been directly and seriously fixed on the European judicial branch, with the intention of proposing institutional and structural reform.[9] The reason for this move has largely been a practical one, prompted by the increasing volume of litigation before the Court which, given the imminence of geographical enlargement, seems likely only to expand further. However, the implications of the reforms, as is evident from the changes made in the Nice Treaty, go beyond largely technical matters such as the number of judges within chambers or even the abolition of the need for an Advocate-General's opinion in

---

[8] See T. Hartley, (1996) 112 LQR 95; T. Tridimas, (1997) 22 ELRev. 199; A. Arnull, (1996) 112 LQR 195, and, more recently, T. Hartley, *Constitutional Problems of the European Union* (Oxford: Hart, 1999).

[9] Despite the discussion during the 1990/1 IGC, reform of the Court was not taken seriously at the time of the Maastricht Treaty. Apart from excluding its jurisdiction from matters falling under the second and third pillars, little was done to affect the position of the ECJ and CFI at that time. See, for some of the suggestions which had been made, P. Jacqué and J. H. H. Weiler, 'On the Road to European Union: A New Judicial Architecture', (1990) 27 CMLRev. 185.

every case. They touch, as indeed one of the Commission's papers on reform of the Court system makes evident, on broader questions about the nature of the judicial role as well as the relationship of the European Court with national courts.

As is well known, the ECJ currently acts in many capacities—as an administrative court, a constitutional court, and a tribunal which deals with many specialized and technical areas of law, from taxation to company law to customs classification and intellectual property. Many of its administrative and staff dispute functions were diverted to the Court of First Instance when that body was established, but the ECJ remains a hybrid and unusual court, with an appellate jurisdiction from the CFI and a more interactive preliminary rulings jurisdiction from national courts, in addition to its own eclectic range of first instance and advisory jurisdiction. As Craig's essay demonstrates, however, some of the proposals which emerged during the debate on the future of the Court were clearly designed to strengthen its hierarchical position in relation to national courts, in a way which would transform the role which it has played to date under the all-important preliminary reference mechanism. And as Kilpatrick's chapter illustrates, this has facilitated interaction between the legal systems in a way which cannot be understood as a strictly top-down structure dominated or controlled by the ECJ, and it has, as Schepel and Blankenburg's essay demonstrates, broadened the range of litigants capable of participating in proceedings before the Court. The Commission's contribution, however, was one of the main institutional contributions to the debate on reform of the Court structure which acknowledged the more substantive constitutional implications of such reform: the political focus otherwise was largely on questions of practicability, of getting through the caseload, rather than on the methodology or the policy role of the court. To quote from the Commission's paper on reform of the Court system for the IGC, 'The intention now is to redesign the judicial system in its entirety, by dividing jurisdiction in such a way as to make the Court of Justice the genuine supreme court of the Union and to give the Court of First Instance, which would acquire autonomous status, general powers as an ordinary court.' Nonetheless, as Craig's chapter indicates, the discussion papers prepared by the Court of Justice and the Court of First Instance themselves, as well as that of the ad hoc working party chaired by Olé Dué, also focus attention on a range of options which could profoundly affect the so-called 'architecture' of the European judiciary as well as the substantive nature of its role. He identifies five key questions: first, whether the CFI will emerge as a general court of first instance; secondly, whether only one Community court should be authorized to hear preliminary references; thirdly, whether this preliminary reference system is to move to a more appellate system; fourthly, whether there is to be a shift towards decentralized judicial bodies; and finally, the relationship between such decentralized bodies and the Court of First Instance. The provisions of the Nice Treaty relevant to the ECJ and the CFI clearly affect some of these questions in a more significant way than any previous attempts at reform, and the next few years will begin to demonstrate the practical effects of those changes.

Schepel and Blankenburg's chapter, by comparison with Craig's, looks not so much to the future shape of the Court and the possible procedural avenues open to activate its jurisdiction, but focuses instead on the past and current practice of the Court, on its agency in shaping the avenues which already exist. They question whether the ECJ has sought to develop a particular constitutional role for itself as a 'citizens' court' or a participative assembly, but they conclude that, despite the self-perception expressed by some of its more vocal judges in their extra-judicial writings, the Court has resisted the various options offered by the procedural routes before it to transform itself into a more open forum of this kind. Their conclusions, based on a survey of the varieties and types of litigation coming before the Court, add an interesting dimension to the activism debate and provide concrete data of a particular kind which suggest that the more 'optimistic' predictions of the likelihood of the Court of Justice gradually emerging as a European people's court may be overstated. As they argue, even if the prospect of the assertion of a 'pan-European judicial power to emancipate civil society, rationalize administration and curb raw political power' at the behest of the citizen seems an attractive one, it is not borne out by an examination of the Court's approach to direct annulment actions, to enforcement actions by the Commission, or to the preliminary reference procedure.

Kilpatrick, indeed, points to the strategic use made by the Court of the rhetorical language of individuals' rights to pursue the interest of the effectiveness of Community law in one of the few areas in which the litigants genuinely exemplify the ordinary citizen and the humble worker—*Defrenne*, *Marshall*, *Emmott*, etc. The subject of national remedies and procedures in the field of sex equality is used in her piece to exemplify aspects of the dialogic relationship between the ECJ and national courts in exploring the applications and uses they have made of ECJ doctrine, thus exposing some possible misunderstandings of the legal developments which the Court has contributed to bringing about in this context. She does not just consider the individual actors and litigants (aided or otherwise) who mobilize the Court of Justice, but also examines the role of national courts in their capacity as mobilizers of a sort. She makes the important point too that the bilateral model of the preliminary reference procedure as 'dialogue' between two courts may more plausibly be seen, in certain policy fields at least, as a multilateral process involving many actors and an increasingly crowded stage.

Finally, in his epilogue, Weiler examines some of the principal modifications to the system introduced by Nice. The 'verdict' is mixed. Positive in terms of an agenda which has at its centre the functional problems created by a growing docket slowly overwhelming both Court of Justice and Court of First Instance. Less positive if one is willing to question the very suitability of the basic judicial architecture, which has remained essentially unchanged since inception, to a very different Community at the beginning of this century. Weiler suggests an alternative concept which may be part of the judicial Après Nice discussion.

Given its crucial role within the legal system of such a fascinating and powerful emergent polity, the Court of Justice will continue to absorb the attention of EU lawyers and scholars. Doubtless the nature and extent of this attention will continue to attract legitimate criticism from commentators who seek to broaden the focus of European scholarly research beyond the doctrinal output of the judicial branch. Nonetheless, the focus on the Court in more recent years, and in the essays included in this volume, has sought to move beyond the analysis of doctrine and beyond the simplified judicial activism/judicial restraint debate to consider the current and future role of the Court as one of the significant players within the European political and constitutional space. In an EU of twenty or thirty states with a vastly enlarged citizenry and a highly complex and differentiated legal and political system, the perception of the ECJ as a constitutional tribunal promoting the rule of law in a community of principle is likely to come under increasing strain, and the challenges facing the EU judicial system should not be underestimated.

2

Mobilizing the European Court of Justice

HARM SCHEPEL and ERHARD BLANKENBURG

I INTRODUCTION: KEEPING THE PROMISE OF AN EVER CLOSER UNION

Justice Breyer of the US Supreme Court recently described a 'movement, almost worldwide, toward the realization that people's liberty and their prosperity depend in part upon strong judicial institutions'.[1] Judges are of course likely to say that their job is important, and even more likely to say that they do not want to be interfered with while doing it. But the statement is more than self-serving rhetoric. And judicial self-confidence is not just an American phenomenon.[2] Increasingly, judges see themselves, in Antoine Garapon's suggestive formulation, as *gardiens de promesses*, keepers of promises.[3]

There are obvious possible explanations. One is the increasing 'juridification' of society. There are more laws, more legal regulation of more and more spheres of social life. There are more lawyers. People turn to law more often to regulate their relationships, to settle disputes and to bring claims formerly thought outside the realm of law altogether.[4] 'Juridification', in turn, likely leads to 'judicialization'.[5] If more and more relations are governed by law and people expect more and more legal redress for any wrong done to themselves, their interests, or even their beliefs, judges will be called upon more and more to uphold not just the law but moral standards, legitimate expectations, fairness: to keep everyone's promises.

One special brand of 'judicialization' is the spread of judicial review of legislation. Perhaps two more suggestive French phrases can illustrate the development. '*L'État sans politique*' describes the process of withering ideologies

---

[1] S. G. Breyer, 'Comment: Liberty, Prosperity, and a Strong Judicial Institution', (1998) 61 Law and Contemporary Problems 3.
[2] C. N. Tate and T. Vallinder (eds.), *The Global Expansion of Judicial Power* (1995).
[3] *Le gardien des promesses: Justice et démocratie* (1996).
[4] See e.g. M. Galanter, 'Law Abounding: Legislation around the North Atlantic', (1992) 55 MLR 1.
[5] A. Pizzorno, *Il potere dei giudici: Stato democratico e controllo della virtù* (1998).

and the disappearance of the idea of the State as a collective political project.[6] '*Le droit sans l'État*' is Cohen-Tanugi's plea for the decoupling of law and state: for law to be understood and used as an instrument for the curbing of state power, not as the mere extension of Leviathan's long arm.[7] The growth of the welfare state has led to a huge state 'apparatus', a plethora of laws, regulations, administrative decision-making. People's lives are touched upon more directly and more profoundly by faceless bureaucrats than by visionary politicians. Growing distrust of government and administration has elevated the judge into the position of 'a kind of anti-bureaucratic hero';[8] distrust of politics into the position of the keeper of the greatest promise of them all— the Constitution.[9]

The European Court of Justice has another promise to keep: the prospect of an 'ever closer union between the peoples of Europe'. From the Treaty's lofty objectives, the Court has inferred the necessity to endow Community law with 'direct effect' and 'supremacy' in a process EU lawyers are fond of calling the 'constitutionalization' of EC Law. The Court famously entertains *une certaine idée de l'Europe*.[10] That idea of Europe joins forces with 'a certain idea of law' against the backdrop of the material and moral ruin of the Second World War. The Community is a community of law, held together only by the authority of law.[11] Article 164 EC provides that 'the Court of Justice shall ensure that in the interpretation and application of this Treaty the law is observed'. Constantinos Kakouris, the most poetic of judges, deducts from this that 'the written law of the Treaty has above it Law with a capital "L", the unwritten Law, the Idea of Law. And the Court has to ensure the observance of that Law. The Idea of Law becomes the ultimate "telos" that should guide the Court.'[12] That unwritten Law, then, is found, directly or indirectly, in 'the people'. The real objective of the Community, in this light, is 'the realization of the convictions, beliefs and a certain way of life' of the peoples of Europe. The Court acts as the 'conscience' of the peoples of Europe.[13]

---

[6] M. Bouvier, *L'État sans politique* (1986).

[7] L. Cohen-Tanugi, *Le Droit sans l'État* (1985).

[8] Cf. M. Shapiro, 'The Globalization of Law', (1993) 1 Indiana Journal of Global Legal Studies 37.

[9] A sure sign of a trend: the backlash is starting. See e.g. M. Tushnet, *Taking the Constitution Away from the Courts* (1999).

[10] P. Pescatore, 'The Doctrine of Direct Effect: An Infant Disease of Community Law', (1983) ELR 155, 157.

[11] U. Everling, 'Zur Begründung der Urteile des Gerichtshofs der Europäischen Gemeinschaften', (1994) 29 Europarecht 127, 143.

[12] 'La Cour de Justice des communautés européennes comme Cour Constitutionnelle: Trois observations', in O. Dué, M. Lutter, and J. Schwarze (eds.), *Festschrift für Ulrich Everling* (1995), 629, 632.

[13] Ibid. 635.

The judges' appeal to 'the people', counter-intuitive as it may seem, has been a constant in their writing. Robert Lecourt ended his *L'Europe des juges* with the suggestion that, to 'the people', the Court's work seemed dominated by a concern with 'protection of the weak'.[14] For Federico Mancini, the effect of *Van Gend en Loos* was to 'take Community law out of the hands of the politicians and bureaucrats and to give it to the people',[15] and the measure of the Court's usefulness its capacity to hand down judgments that 'enable ordinary men and women to savor the fruits of integration'.[16] The Court positions itself as the embodiment of a new European *Volksgeist*, one that emphasizes the emancipatory power of legal rationality over (national) politics and judicial process over political debate.

The analogy of the Court's self-perception with the historical school of the nineteenth century will hardly be lost on anyone. But there is even some empirical evidence that it reflects expectations of people in Europe, unrealistic as those expectations may be. General support for values associated with the 'rule of law', however large the differences among Member States, is rather high.[17] Overall, the respect most Europeans grant to high courts is not altogether negative—next to parliaments, more is expected of these courts than of any other political bodies.[18] The visibility of the ECJ, compared to other EU institutions, is surprisingly high. Leaving aside the European Parliament (which, after all, is elected by the peoples of Europe), more people in most Member States have heard of the ECJ than they have of the Council or the Commission.[19] People 'very' or 'somewhat' satisfied with the Court's decisions range from 24 per cent in France to 61 per cent in Ireland—levels which are generally lower than satisfaction with the decisions of national high courts, ranging from 39 per cent in Portugal to 79 per cent in the Netherlands. They are very significantly lower in Denmark, Germany, Greece, and the Netherlands.

---

[14] R. Lecourt, *L'Europe des juges* (1976), 309.

[15] F. Mancini and D. Keeling, 'Democracy and the European Court of Justice' (1994) 57 MLR 175, at 183. In its contribution to the IGC, *Report of the Court of Justice on Certain Aspects of the Application of the Treaty on European Union* (Luxembourg, May 1995; http://europa.eu.int/en/agenda/igc-home/eu-doc/justice/cj_rep.html), the Court explicitly linked the doctrine of direct effect to a pre-Maastricht notion of European 'citizenship'.

[16] F. Mancini and D. Keeling, 'Language, Culture and Politics in the Life of the European Court of Justice', (1995) 1 Columbia Journal of European Law 397, at 413. The Court's press release announcing its 1998 annual report states: 'The Cases dealt with in 1998 once again demonstrate the importance of Community law in the day-to-day life of citizens of the union' (press release 18/99, 18 Mar. 1999).

[17] J. L. Gibson and G. A. Caldeira, 'The Legal Cultures of Europe', (1996) 30 Law and Society Review 55.

[18] J. L. Gibson and G. A. Caldeira, 'The European Court of Justice: A Question of Legitimacy', (1993) Zeitschrift für Rechtssoziologie 205.

[19] J. L. Gibson and G. A. Caldeira, 'Changes in the Legitimacy of the European Court of Justice: A Post-Maastricht Analysis', (1998) 28 British Journal of Political Science 63.

As a result of the constitutionalization process, the Court is set to become more visible and more likely to be drawn into political battles. The 'juridification' of the Union's political process inevitably brings with it the 'politicization' of Community law. Judicial review inevitably blurs the boundaries between adjudication and lawmaking and draws courts squarely into political debates.[20] The Court deals with politically highly sensitive issues, such as transsexuals' rights in the workplace or the rights of women in the armed forces.[21] As an institution, the Court has grown to be a constitutional review court.[22]

Constitutional review in a political system *sui generis* featuring national governments and national constitutional courts, however, cannot be quite the same as constitutional review in a single state under separation of powers. This should become obvious when we consider the limited procedural avenues that lead to the Court of Justice, the relatively small number of cases it handles, and the organizational background of litigants that mobilize it. The Court of Justice, as other courts, depends on 'demand' for its services, or at least on the ways and means it has to manipulate that demand. It needs to be mobilized. If it is now a fully fledged constitutional review court, its success will depend, on the one hand, on the comparative readiness of litigants to vent their grievances through judicial, rather than political channels; on the other, on its own ability to escape the logic of politicization through juridification.

The Court's caseload has grown steadily, if not spectacularly, over the years. Reaching 100 judgments in 1977, it had delivered 238 judgments in 1988, the year before the Court of First Instance was created to unburden the ECJ. As a step towards the Court's status as a constitutional court, that event itself, the creation of a lower court handling fact-intensive cases whose decisions are open for appeal at the ECJ, can hardly be overestimated. The CFI now handles staff cases and all direct actions brought by private parties. Nevertheless, by 1998 the Court of Justice was already back to 254 judgments. The caseload is likely to continue to grow with the new competences granted by the Treaty of Amsterdam and with enlargement a very real prospect, sparking off a debate over the future of the Courts' organization.[23] Tables 2.1 and 2.2 show the composition of both courts' caseload over the last seven years.

---

[20] Cf. M. Shapiro, *Courts: A Comparative and Political Analysis* (1981); more recently from different perspectives, e.g. G. Timsit, *Gouverner ou juger* (1995), D. Kennedy, *A Critique of Adjudication (Fin de Siècle)* (1997).

[21] See Case C-13/94, *P v. S and Cornwall County Council*, [1996] I-2143; Case C-273/97, *Angela Maria Sirdar*: [1999] ECR I-1279; Case C-285/98 *Tanja Kreil*: [2000] ECR I-69.

[22] Cf. M. Shapiro, 'The European Court of Justice', in P. Craig and G. de Búrca (eds.), *The Evolution of EU Law* (1999), 321.

[23] See 'The Future of the Judicial System of the European Union: Proposals and Reflections', submitted by the ECJ's President on 28 May 1999.

Table 2.1. Basis of action of Court of Justice judgments/opinions, 1992–1998

	1992	1993	1994	1995	1996	1997	1998
169	43	31	29	38	42	43	54
173	34	26	21	11	16	11	21
177	107	125	108	103	120	161	154
Others	26	21	30	22	16	39	25
TOTAL	210	203	188	174	194	242	254

Table 2.2. Basis of action of Court of First Instance judgments, 1992–1998

	1992	1993	1994	1995	1996	1997	1998
173	17	4	17	56	36	29	52
Staff regulations	41	43	41	34	66	51	58
Others	2	0	2	8	5	12	19
TOTAL	60	47	60	98	107	92	129

Source: Statistical information of the Court of First Instance 1997 and 1998; EC general reports on activities.

The bulk of the Court's caseload, then, is concentrated around three procedures.[24] Actions under Article 173 are brought by Member States, Community institutions, or concerned private parties, and seek annulment of measures taken by Community institutions; actions under Article 169 are brought by the Commission against Member States for failure to fulfil their obligations under the Treaty, and preliminary references under Article 177 are brought by national courts who may, and sometimes must, refer a question of interpretation of Community law to the Court of Justice if such is necessary for the resolution of a case before them. The latter now take up more than half of all cases before the Court.

The Court is hence mobilized by Member States, by the Commission, by national courts, and by economic actors affected by the Community's regulatory machine. Is it possible to construct a 'people's Europe' through law on these premises?

[24] This chapter is sufficiently backward-looking for us to be excused for using the old numbering of the Treaty. Articles 164, 169, 173, and 177 EC have now become Articles 220, 226, 230, and 234 EC, respectively.

II THE ECJ AS A KANGAROO COURT

Article 169 EC styles the Commission as the 'watchdog' of the Treaty, giving it the possibility of bringing Member States to court for failing to fulfil their duties under the Treaty. It is thus the front-door option of reviewing the compatibility of national legislation with Community law. It provides for a procedure whereby the Commission writes a 'letter of formal notice' to the Member State allegedly committing the infringement concerned giving it 'the opportunity to submit its observations'. After that, the Commission delivers a 'reasoned opinion'. If the Member State still refuses to comply, the Commission 'may' bring the matter before the Court of Justice.

The Commission deals with around 1,200 cases of suspected infringements per year.[25]

Table 2.3. Suspected infringements, by sector and Member State, 1991–1997, in absolute figures

	DG XV (III) Internal market	DG IV Competition	DG V Social Affairs	DG VI Agriculture	DG XI Environment	DG XXI Customs/ Indirect taxation	Others	Total
B	235	11	44	78	72	35	64	539
DK	75	12	13	45	53	25	49	272
D	505	24	27	151	319	32	139	1,197
EL	286	37	28	86	229	51	76	793
E	300	31	23	146	568	44	103	1,215
F	573	30	58	264	281	65	134	1,405
IRL	65	9	11	45	206	13	24	373
I	504	44	45	210	206	72	116	1,197
L	48	7	4	18	22	5	23	127
NL	154	14	20	89	49	20	56	402
P	122	7	9	55	126	18	58	395
UK	264	8	58	159	383	36	69	977
TOTAL	3,131	234	340	1,346	2,514	416	911	8,892

Except for Greece, the ranking is largely a function of the size of Member States. Looked at by sector, the picture becomes more complicated. Italy and France's high figures in agriculture seems to reflect the political strength of farmers' lobbies; the high figures for the environment for Spain and the United Kingdom, and the relatively high figures of Ireland, may be thought to reflect regulatory deficits; the opposite would then be valid for Belgium and

[25] Given the time-frame, all tables in this paper refer to the EU 12.

Table 2.4 Suspected infringements, by Sector and Member State, 1991–1997, in percentage points

	DG XV (III) Internal market	DG IV Competition	DG V Social Affairs	DG VI Agriculture	DG XI Environment	DG XXI Customs/ Indirect taxation	Others	Total
B	43.6	2	8.2	14.5	13.4	6.5	11.9	100
DK	27.6	4.4	4.8	16.5	19.5	9.2	18	100
D	42.2	2	2.3	12.6	26.7	2.7	11.6	100
EL	36.1	4.7	3.5	10.8	28.9	6.4	9.6	100
E	24.7	2.6	1.9	12	46.7	3.6	8.5	100
F	40.8	2.1	4.1	18.8	20	4.6	9.5	100
IRL	17.4	2.4	2.9	12	55.2	3.5	6.4	100
I	42.1	3.7	3.8	17.5	17.2	6	9.7	100
L	37.8	5.5	3.1	14.2	17.3	3.9	18.1	100
NL	38.8	3.5	5	22.1	12.2	5	14	100
P	30.9	1.8	2.3	13.9	31.9	4.6	14.7	100
UK	27	0.8	5.9	16.3	39	4.6	7.1	100
TOTAL	35.2	2.6	3.8	15.1	28.3	4.7	10.2	100

Source: 9th–15th annual reports on Commission monitoring of the application of Community law.

the Netherlands. High values for the internal market for Belgium, Italy, Germany, and France, and low values for Denmark and the United Kingdom, match the Single Market Scoreboard's reports on implementation deficits. For Greece and the Netherlands, respectively among the main sinners and among the star performers in the Scoreboard, a different explanation has to be found.[26]

The Commission comes to suspect infringements partly through its own detective work, partly through popular complaints. A surge in the Commission's detective work in 1988 and 1989 brought 752 and 962 cases to light, respectively; after that the numbers stabilized at around 260 cases a year. Amounts of complaints are relatively stable, with a high of 1,274 in 1990 and a low of 819 in 1996. It is estimated that 5 per cent of these complaints come from Member States, 5 per cent from individuals, and the rest from companies. When one takes this into account, one could relate the figures for Greece—a relatively closed country economically—and the Netherlands—a very open country economically—to the likelihood of exporting or importing companies being hindered in their trade.

[26] The First Single Market Scoreboard reports implementation deficits of 8.5% for Belgium and Germany, 7.6 for Italy, 7.5 for Greece, 7.4 for France, 6.5 for Luxembourg, 5.9 for Portugal, 5.4 for Ireland, 4.7 for Spain, 4.6 for the UK, 3.5 for the Netherlands, and 3.2 for Denmark.

The Commission attaches great importance to these complaints:

The large number of complaints is accounted for mainly by the growing awareness among ordinary people of the Community's importance and, in some cases, by the limited means of redress at national level or the tendency to appeal to the Commission when all national remedies have been exhausted. The Commission's complaints procedure is easily accessible, as it involves no formalities or expense. The Commission has tried to encourage its use with the aim of improving the application of Community law and at the same time fostering a real people's Europe.[27]

The role of the complainant in the procedure, however, ends with the complaint itself. The only way to grant the complainant a right to act in later stages would be to review a Commission decision not to deliver a reasoned opinion or to bring a Member State to Court under Article 173, or under Article 175 for failure to act. The Court, however, has repeatedly refused to do so.

It is clear from the scheme of Article 169 of the treaty that the Commission is not bound to commence the proceedings provided for in that provision but in this regard has a discretion which excludes the right for individuals to require that institution to adopt a specific position.

It is only if it considers that the Member State in question has failed to fulfil one of its obligations that the Commission delivers a reasoned opinion. Furthermore, in the event that the State does not comply with the opinion within the period allowed, the institution has in any event the right, but not the obligation, to apply to the Court of Justice for a declaration that the alleged breach of obligations has occurred.

It must also be observed that in requesting the Commission to commence proceedings pursuant to Article 169 the applicant is in fact seeking the adoption of acts which are not of direct and individual concern to it within the meaning of the second paragraph of Article 173 and which it could not therefore challenge by means of an action for annulment in any event.[28]

The Court is accused of demonstrating a 'failure to stimulate the growth of a necessary public interest action in EC administrative law and bring out into the open for investigation possibly suspect dealings between the Commission and other powerful actors on the transnational political scene'.[29]

The argument to maintain the Commission's much-criticized discretion[30] and resist the juridification of the procedure is to give the Commission

---

[27] The Commission's 10th Annual Report on the Monitoring of the Application of Community Law, 1993 OJ C 233/1, at 7.

[28] Case 247/87, *Star Fruit v. Commission*, [1989] ECR 291, paras. 11–13. The doctrine goes back to Case 48/65, *Luetticke v. Commission*, [1966] ECR 19. Cf Case C-87/89, *Sonito v. Commission*, [1990] ECR I-1981, Case C-29/92, *Asia Motor France v. Commission*, [1992] ECR I-3935, and Case T-182/97, *Smanor v. Commission*, [1998] ECR II-271.

[29] C. Harlow, 'European Administrative Law and the Global Challenge', in Craig and de Búrca, *The Evolution of EU Law*, 261, 270.

[30] R. Mastroianni, 'The Enforcement Procedure under Article 169 of the EC Treaty and the Powers of the European Commission: *Quis Custodiet Custodes?*', (1995) 1 EPL 535;

leeway in its pre-litigation negotiations. Infringement procedures are by their very nature intensely political, and the Commission makes every effort to avoid bringing Member States to court. A measure of this phenomenon is the fact that Article 170, which allows Member States to bring each other to court for failure to fulfil obligations under the Treaty, has only ever been used four times.[31]

As Snyder argues forcefully, the Commission as a 'repeat player' uses litigation as part of a process:

We usually think of negotiation and adjudication as alternative forms of dispute settlement. It may be suggested, however, that in the daily practice and working ideology of the Commission, the two are not alternatives but instead are complementary. The main form of dispute settlement used by the Commission is negotiation, and litigation is simply a part, sometimes inevitable but nevertheless generally a minor part, of this process.[32]

Table 2.5 reports on the whole trajectory from letters of formal notice to court proceedings.[33] It follows all procedures started with a letter of formal notice over an eight-year period. Fewer than 10 per cent of these cases were referred to the ECJ in the end; judgment was rendered in not even 4 per cent of them. The Court finds almost invariably in favour of the Commission.

When looking at the differences between Member States, one of the most striking results is the combination of a good implementation record and an extreme aversion to litigation of the Danish government. Not only is it lowest on the Commission's target list in absolute figures, it is also ranks highest in relative terms in stopping the procedure before the 'reasoned opinion'. Exactly the opposite is true for Italy, which receives the highest amount of letters in absolute figures and ranks right at the bottom as far as avoiding litigation is concerned. Belgium is a good second in absolute terms and a proud litigation-happy first in relative terms. The Portuguese administration's delaying tactics in responding to the Commission's letters and opinions gives a cynical twist to its success in avoiding litigation.[34] No such easy explanations are available for the UK's aversion to litigation.

J. P. Gaffney, 'The Enforcement Procedure Under Article 169 EC and the Duty of Member States to Supply Information Requested by the Commission: Is There a Regulatory Gap?', (1998) 25 LIEI 117.

[31] Belgium v. Spain, Spain v. UK, Ireland v. France, and France v. UK. The UK does not seem to consider the procedure even in the painful 'beef war' with France.

[32] F. Snyder, 'The Effectiveness of European Community Law: Institutions, Processes, Tools and Techniques', (1993) 56 MLR 19, 30.

[33] For the step from suspected infringements to letters of formal notice the differences between the Member States level out, with Luxembourg, Portugal, and Italy receiving far more letters than might have been expected and France far less.

[34] Over 1996, Portugal took 166 days to respond to letters of formal notice and 237 days to respond to reasoned opinions. The EU 15 average was 108 and 114, respectively. Data from the first Single Market Scoreboard.

Table 2.5. Article 169 procedures started in 1988–1994, followed through different stages

	Letters	%	Reasoned opinion	%	Referral to ECJ	%	ECJ	%	In favour of Member States
Total	6,473	100	2,381	36.8	613	9.5	238	3.7	18
B	541	100	230	42.5	80	14.8	41	7.6	3
DK	323	100	32	9.9	3	0.9	2	0.6	0
D	539	100	208	38.6	54	10	21	3.9	3
EL	691	100	320	46.3	82	11.9	32	4.6	2
E	597	100	202	33.8	44	7.3	26	4.4	2
F	560	100	177	31.6	48	8.6	14	2.5	3
IRL	450	100	153	34	44	9.7	20	4.4	0
I	797	100	413	51.8	138	17.3	55	6.9	4
L	438	100	165	37.6	51	11.6	8	1.8	0
NL	446	100	114	25.6	24	5.4	12	2.7	1
P	645	100	268	41.6	36	5.6	2	0.3	0
UK	446	100	99	22.2	9	2	5	0.4	0

Source: 9th–15th annual reports on Commission monitoring of the application of Community law.

Were the Commission to make use of litigation more frequently, it would run the danger of having the Court's judgments prescribe its policy. 'Juridification' of the process would create a shadow over every step of the procedure and, paradoxically, 'politicize' relations between the Commission and the Member States. The Commission plays it safe. Rather than risking a principled decision of the Court, it strikes a deal. In the few cases in which it invokes the Court in infringement procedures, its success rate is so high as to make the ECJ look like a kangaroo court—being the baby in the pouch of the mother, it has to follow wherever the Commission goes.

III THE ECJ AS A FORUM FOR INTER-INSTITUTIONAL DEBATE

Under Article 173, Member States and Community institutions can seek the annulment of Community measures without any need to show a legitimate interest in doing so. In one of its most controversial lines of case law, the Court has rewritten the first paragraphs of Article 173 to include the European Parliament both in the list of Community institutions whose acts can be challenged and in the list of 'privileged applicants'.[35] In *Les Verts* it famously held:

[35] The whole saga is well told in R. Dehousse, *The European Court of Justice* (1998), 97 ff.

the European Economic Community is a Community based on the rule of law inasmuch as neither its Member States nor its institutions can avoid a review of the question whether the measures adopted by them are in conformity with the basic constitutional charter, the Treaty.[36]

It then argued that the Parliament had been omitted from the list because it had no powers to adopt measures 'intended to have legal effects vis-à-vis third parties' in the original version of the Treaty. Since it now had those powers, 'an interpretation of Article 173 of the Treaty which excluded measures adopted by the European Parliament from those which could be contested would lead to a result contrary both to the spirit of the treaty as expressed in Article 164 and to its system'.[37] The Parliament went on to claim active standing under Article 173. In *Comitology*,[38] it was denied. A year and a half later, in *Chernobyl*, the Court changed its mind and held:

The absence in the Treaties of any provision giving the parliament the right to bring an action for annulment may constitute a procedural gap, but it cannot prevail over the fundamental interest in the maintenance and observance of the institutional balance laid down in the Treaties establishing the European Communities.
    Consequently, an action for annulment brought by the parliament against an act of the Council of the Commission is admissible provided that the action seeks only to safeguard its prerogatives and that it is founded only on submissions alleging their infringement.[39]

Whereas Hartley singles out *Chernobyl* as a clear example of 'changing the law while supposedly interpreting it';[40] Bengoetxea reads the case as a fine last chapter of a Dworkinian chain novel.[41] Strong appeals to the closing of the 'democratic deficit' are an essential part of the Court's reasoning. With the Parliament granted a right to seek review of legislative measures, the Court now has control over the Council's choice of legal basis and hence over the Parliament's involvement in the policy process. Both *Les Verts* and *Chernobyl* are now codified in the Treaty.

    The danger of the procedure is, obviously, the 'jurifidification' of the Union's policy process, not only for those cases brought by Parliament but also for those brought by Member States which are outvoted in the Council, where the latter can decide by qualified majority. Table 2.6 brings together all litigation under the first paragraph of Article 173 over the last ten years.

    A few caveats are in order. Litigation against the Parliament typically involves either budget votes or decisions regarding its seat. Spanish litigation

---

[36] Case 294/83, *Parti Ecologiste 'Les Verts'*, [1986] ECR 1339, para. 23.
[37] Ibid. paras. 24 and 25.
[38] Case 302/87, *European Parliament v. Council*, [1988] ECR 5615.
[39] Case C-70/88, *European Parliament v. Council*, [1990] ECR I-2041, paras. 26–7.
[40] T. C. Hartley, *The Foundations of European Community Law*, 4th edn. (1998), 79.
[41] J. Bengoetxea, *The Legal Reasoning of the European Court of Justice* (1993), 105 ff.

Table 2.6. Applications for annulment, privileged applicants, 1989–1998

	Commission	Won	Council	Won	European Parliament	Won
Commission	X	X	13	6	0	0
Council	0	0	X	X	2	2
European Parliament	2	0	16	7	X	X
B	7	0	0	0	0	0
DK	2	0	0	0	0	0
D	12	5	4	1	1	0
EL	12	3	1	0	0	0
E	12	3	1	0	0	0
F	19	11	1	0	1	1
IRL	3	0	0	0	0	0
I	22	4	1	0	0	0
L	0	0	0	0	1	0
NL	7	3	1	0	0	0
P	2	1	3	0	0	0
UK	3	1	4	1	0	0
Member States	101	31	22	2	3	1

Data compiled by the authors from the ECR.

against the Council includes four 1992 cases where it sought the annulment of Regulations fixing fishing quotas. Most importantly, nearly half of all Member State actions against the Commission involve the annual ritual of protesting against the Commission's decisions on the clearance of accounts presented by Member States in respect of the European Agricultural Guidance and Guarantee Fund (EAGGF). These account for both Danish cases, 2 out of 3 Irish cases, 10 out of 12 Greek cases and 13 out of 22 Italian cases.

Another good portion, 22 cases, consists of Member States' disagreement with Commission decisions on state aids. For Spain, these take up 7 out of 12 cases. For Italy, they take up 6 out of 22, for France, 4 out of 19. Germany, far and away the primary victim of the Commission's disapproval, has only brought 3 cases. It is reasonable to suppose that Germany's reluctance to bring the Commission to Court in state aid cases is part of a strategy of cooperation in light of the vast amount of notified schemes after reunification.[42] In only

---

[42] In 1994–7, the Commission had 'no objection' to 578 out of 752 German notified schemes. Where it opened an official procedure, it gave 25 positive and 16 negative decisions. For France, the figures are 142 out of 192, and 8 positive and 5 negative decisions. For Spain, 265 out of 313, 8 positive and 5 negative; for Italy, 190 out of 262, 16 positive and 9 negative. Data from the 24th and 28th Commission reports on competition policy.

one case did a Member State take the step of seeking the annulment of the Commission's approval of another Member State's aid.[43]

In so far as litigation against the Council involves policy issues, Table 2.6 clearly shows the Court unwilling to find in favour of Member States. Whereas the Parliament wins almost half of its cases against the Council, Member States win less than one in ten.

IV THE ECJ AS A REGULATORY COMPLAINT BOARD

Natural and legal persons can only institute proceedings against 'a decision addressed to that person, or against a decision which, although in the form of a regulation or a decision addressed to another person, is of direct and individual concern to the former'.[44] The procedure thus allows a review of the Community's regulatory machine. The Court has refused to turn Article 173 into a vehicle of popular action for constitutional review from early case law on. In *Plaumann* it devised a test to identify the class of people entitled to standing:

Persons other than those to whom a decision is addressed may only claim to be individually concerned if that decision affects them by reason of certain attributes which are peculiar to them or by reason of circumstances in which they are differentiated from all other persons and by virtue of these factors distinguishes them individually just as in the case of the person addressed.[45]

It later devised a test to determine what constitutes a 'sham' regulation:[46]

The possibility of defining more or less precisely the number or even the identity of the persons to whom a measure applies does not in any way imply that it must be regarded as being of individual concern to them, as long as it is established that such application takes effect by virtue of an objective legal or factual situation defined by the measure in question.[47]

---

[43] Case 56/93, *Belgium v. Commission*, [1996] ECR I-723, was brought against a decision to allow Dutch aid.

[44] Exhaustively, A. Albors-Llorens, *Private Parties in European Community Law* (1996).

[45] Case 25/62, *Plaumann v. Commission*, [1963] ECR 106.

[46] 'The objective of that provision is in particular to prevent the Community institutions from being in a position, merely by choosing the form of a regulation, to exclude an application by an individual against a decision which concerns him directly and individually; it therefore stipulates that the choice of form cannot change the nature of the decision.' Cases 789 and 790/79, *Calpak v. Commission*, [1980] ECR 1949, para. 7.

[47] Case C-131/92, *Arnaud v. Council*, [1993] ECR I-2573; Case C-264/91, *Abertal v. Council*, [1993] ECR I-3265; Case C-209, P *Buralux v. Council* [1996] ECR I-615. The Court's reference to Case 123/77, *UNICME v. Council*, [1978] ECR 845, is valid only for the first part of the paragraph.

Thus, if the legal affects the measure produces concern certain categories of persons 'envisaged generally and in the abstract',[48] the Court will consider the measure a general rule of Community law against which no possibility of review is open.

Even if the Court has indicated at times a willingness to relax the criteria in certain circumstances,[49] its recent decision in *Greenpeace* should put to rest hopes that Article 173 can be used as a vehicle for public interest litigation. The Court repeated that applicants whom the contested decision concerns 'in a general and abstract manner' are not 'individually concerned'. The same applies, then, to associations who claim to represent such applicants.[50] An exception to its strict conditions lies in those areas where the applicants have certain rights in the procedure leading up to the contested decision.

In *COFAZ*, the Court generalized from earlier case law and held:

where a regulation accords applicant undertakings procedural guarantees entitling them to request the Commission to find an infringement of Community rules, those undertakings should be able to institute proceedings to protect their legitimate interests.[51]

The reasoning extends to participation in consultation and negotiation processes leading up to decisions.[52] It is only logical, then, to accord standing to collective interest groups and trade associations, for obvious reasons the Commission's preferred partners in the legislative process. In a state aid case, the Court therefore held:

It is undisputed that CIRFS, an association whose membership consists of the main international manufacturers of synthetic fibres, has pursued, in the interest of those manufacturers, a number of actions connected with the policy of restructuring that sector. In particular, it has been the Commission's interlocutor with regard to the introduction of the discipline and its extension and adaptation. Furthermore, during the procedure prior to these proceedings, CIRFS actively pursued negotiations with the Commission, in particular by submitting written observations to it and by keeping in close contact with the responsible departments.

---

[48] Cases 789 and 790/79, *Calpak v. Commission*, [1980] ECR 1949; Case C-209/94 P, *Buralux v. Council*, [1996] ECR I-615.

[49] See e.g. Case 11/82, *Piraiki-Patraiki v. Commission*, [1985] ECR 207; Case 294/83, *Parti Écologiste 'Les Verts'*, [1986] ECR 1339; Case C-152/88, *Sofrimport*, [1990] ECR I-2477; Case C-358/89, *Extramet v. Council*, [1991] ECR I-2501; Case C-309/89, *Codorniu*, [1994] ECR I-1853.

[50] Case C-321/95 P, *Stichting Greenpeace v. Commission*, [1998] ECR I-1651, paras. 27–30.

[51] Case 169/84, *COFAZ v. Commission*, [1986] ECR 391. Cf. Case 26/76, *Metro v. Commission*, [1977] ECR 1875. Cf. B. Vesterdorf, 'Complaints Concerning Infringements of Competition Law within the Context of European Community Law', (1994) 31 CMLR 77; C. Kerse, 'The Complainant in Competition Cases: A Progress Report', (1997) 31 CMLR 77.

[52] Case 264/82, *Timex v. Council*, [1985] ECR 849 (anti-dumping).

The position of CIRFS in its capacity as negotiator of the discipline is therefore affected by the contested decision. It follows that the application is admissible as far as CIRFS is concerned.[53]

The Court of First Instance circumscribed the conditions for standing of associations and discussed the advantages of having a trade association bring a complaint:

The Court considers that an association of undertakings may claim a legitimate interest in lodging a complaint even if it is not directly concerned, as an undertaking operating in the relevant market, by the conduct complained of, provided however, first, it is entitled to represent the interests of its members and, secondly, the conduct complained of is liable adversely to affect the interests of its members. Moreover certain procedural advantages accrue to the Commission as a result of the right of associations of undertakings to lodge complaints in defence of the interests of their members collectively, in that the risk that the Commission will receive a large number of complaints criticizing the same conduct is reduced.[54]

The next logical step is then to allow standing to associations in an action against a Commission decision denying them the status of 'interested party'.[55] Public interest litigation, then, is possible only if the interest grouping concerned can show that it participated in the process leading up to the adoption of the measure.[56]

The Court's relaxing of requirements in these cases has an obvious democratic appeal. Granting private parties who have participated or at least had the right to participate in the policy process the right to seek review of the acts adopted arguably goes a long way to improve and monitor the democratic content of decision-making at Community level.[57] In that sense, there is a

[53] Case C-313/90, *Comité International de la Rayonne et des Fibres Synthétiques (CIRFS) v. Commission*, [1993] ECR I-1125, paras. 29 and 30, with reference to Joined Cases 67, 68, and 70/85, *Van der Kooy v. Commission*, [1988] ECR 219. Cf. Joined Cases T-447, 448, and 449/93, *AITEC v. Commission* [1995] ECR II-1971.

[54] Case T-114/92, *BENIM v. Commission*, [1995] ECR II-147. The Court of First Instance had already entertained proceedings brought by two consumer organizations against a rejection of complaint without discussing the matter of standing in Case T-37/92, *BEUC and NCC v. Commission*, [1994] ECR II-285. The procedural rights of the association do not automatically extend to its members: 'While the extension of the right to bring proceedings to associations defending the interests of their members may offer procedural advantages, the participation of such associations in the administrative procedure cannot relieve their members of the need to establish a link between their individual situation and the action of the association.' Case C-70/97 P, *Kruidvat v. Commission*, [1998] ECR I-7183, para. 23.

[55] Case T-84/97, *BEUC v. Commission*, [1998] ECR II-795.

[56] In *Greenpeace*, both the Court of First Instance and the Court of Justice implied as much. Cf. Case T-583/93, *Greenpeace v. Commission* [1995] ECR II-2205, and Case C-321/95 P, *Greenpeace v. Commission*, [1998] I-1651.

[57] An upbeat assessment is H. P. Nehl, *Principles of Administrative Procedure in EC Law* (1999).

parallel with the Parliament cases discussed above. The Court draws the line, however, where litigants turn to the Court to strike down general rules of Community law on *substantial* grounds of incompatibility with the Treaty.

The Court's conservatism with regard to private parties has attracted much criticism.[58] Rasmussen offers a fairly straightforward political explanation for the Court's contrasting treatment of Parliament on the one hand and private parties on the other: Parliament can be counted on to be 'pro-integration'; private parties seeking the annulment of Community measures are by definition 'anti-integration'.[59] In the Court's defence, a number of arguments can be put forward. First, rather obviously, there is the matter of the text of Article 173.[60] If one disregards the letter of the first part of the Article in the Parliament cases, however, that argument is not as strong as it may appear at first sight. Another argument is the fact that constitutional review of legislative acts is by no means 'a tradition common to the Member States'.[61] Another is fear of a litigation flood.[62] In *Greenpeace*, Advocate-General Cosmas used some dazzling arithmetic to illustrate the danger:

I believe that a relaxation by the Court, to the extent sought, of the criteria of admissibility could be abused and lead to aberrant consequences. Natural persons without locus standi under the fourth paragraph of Article 173 of the Treaty could circumvent that procedural impediment by setting up an environmental association. Moreover, whilst the number of natural persons, that is to say citizens of the European Union, however high it may be, none the less remains limited, the number of environmental associations capable of being created is, at least in theory, infinite.[63]

Tables 2.7–2.10 report litigation of unprivileged applicants under Article 173 over the last nine years.[64] The difficulty here is that the competence to hear different kinds of actions has been passed over to the Court of First Instance gradually. From October 1989 the CFI hears staff cases and actions against

---

[58] See e.g. C. Harlow, 'Toward a Theory of Access to the Court of Justice', (1992) 12 YBEL 213; A. Arnull, 'Private Applicants and the Action for Annulment under Article 173 of the EC Treaty', (1995) 32 CMLR 7.

[59] H. Rasmussen, *The European Court of Justice* (1998), 198 ff.

[60] Or rather, the contrast with the more liberal wording of the equivalent Article in the ECSC Treaty.

[61] F. Schockweiler, 'L'Accès à la justice dans l'ordre juridique communautaire', (1996) 4(25) Journal des Tribunaux: Droit européen 1, 6.

[62] Ibid.

[63] Case C-321/95 P, *Greenpeace v. Commission*, [1998] ECR I-1651, para. 117 of the Opinion.

[64] As for the nationality of applicants, the table could be seen as a follow-up to C. Harding, 'Who Goes to Court in Europe? An Analysis of Litigation against the European Community', (1992) 17 ELR 105. For a recent analysis of the CFI's part of this caseload, see M. C. Reale, 'Il tribunale di primo grado delle comunità europee: un'analisi sociologico-giuridica' (Ph.D, EUI, Florence, 1998). The most striking difference with Harding is the new French predominance at the cost of German applicants.

Table 2.7. Applications for annulment, unprivileged applicants, Court of First Instance, 1990–1998

	v. Commission	v. Council	Total
Total	256	22	278
Inadmissible	38	5	43
Dismissed	106	13	119
Measure (partly) annulled	112	4	116

B	DK	D	EL	E	F	IRL	I	L	NL	P	UK	Others	Total
24	2	35	2	7	52	4	28	4	30	10	35	45	278

Table 2.8. Applications for annulment, unprivileged applicants, Court of Justice, 1989–1994

	v. Commission	v. Council	Total
Total	77	25	102
Inadmissible	12	4	16
Dismissed	35	18	53
Measure (partly) annulled	30	3	33

B	DK	D	EL	E	F	IRL	I	L	NL	P	UK	Others	Total
8	1	8	3	7	15	1	9	0	9	7	3	31	102

Commission decisions on competition law. In June 1993 all actions brought by natural legal persons were transferred to the CFI, with the exception of anti-dumping cases. The latter were brought to the CFI in March 1994. CFI judgments can be appealed at the ECJ; from the little experience so far, the success rate is barely over 20 per cent.

The overall success rate of unprivileged applications for annulment is around 40 per cent, with a high of 55 per cent for competition cases and lows of under 10 per cent for anti-dumping and CAP and fisheries cases.

Two areas seem to overlap. First, there is a preponderance of applicants from bigger Member States; second, there is a north–south divide. The only case that cannot be explained by either one of these is Portugal. The explanation there is simple: fifteen out of seventeen cases are directed against Commission decisions concerning grants under the European Social Fund.

Relative comparisons of government and private litigation under Article 173 shows Spanish and Greek private parties far less willing to go to the ECJ than their governments; the same, if to a far lesser degree, holds true for Italy.

Table 2.9. Applications for annulment, nationality unprivileged applicants and subject matter, 1989–1998, Court of First Instance and Court of Justice

	B	DK	D	EL	E	F	IRL	I	L	NL	P	UK	Others	Total
Total	32 (8.4)	3 (0.8)	43 (11.3)	5 (1.3)	14 (3.7)	67 (17.6)	5 (1.3)	37 (9.7)	4 (1.1)	39 (10.3)	17 (4.5)	38 (10)	76 (20)	380 (100)
Competition	15 (8.3)	2 (1.1)	24 (13.3)	0 (0)	7 (3.9)	35 (19.4)	1 (0.6)	14 (7.8)	4 (2.2)	23 (12.8)	0 (0)	22 (12.2)	33 (16.7)	180 (100)
State aids	4 (12.5)	1 (3.1)	1 (3.1)	0 (0)	3 (9.3)	9 (28.1)	1 (3.1)	4 (12.5)	0 (0)	2 (6.2)	0 (0)	7 (21.9)		32 (100)
Anti-dumping	2 (4.2)	0 (0)	5 (10.4)	1 (2.1)	1 (2.1)	6 (12.5)	0 (0)	2 (4.2)	0 (0)	0 (0)	0 (0)	2 (4.2)	29 (60.4)	48 (100)
CAP + fisheries	3 (7.3)	0 (0)	5 (12.2)	1 (2.4)	3 (7.3)	10 (24.4)	2 (4.9)	6 (14.6)	0 (0)	6 (14.6)	2 (4.9)	1 (2.4)	2 (4.9)	41 (100)
Others	8 (10.1)	0 (0)	8 (10.1)	3 (3.8)	0 (0)	7 (8.9)	1 (1.3)	11 (13.9)	0 (0)	8 (10.1)	15 (19)	6 (7.6)	12 (15.2)	79 (100)

Percentages in brackets.

Table 2.10. CFI judgments on applications for annulment appealed before the ECJ, 1994–1998

Member States	B	DK	D	EL	E	F	IRL	I	L	NL	P	UK	CEC	Others	Total
Brought	3		5		2	7	1	3	2	2	4	4	5	4	32
(Partly) won						3				1	1			2	7

Data compiled by the authors from the ECR. Joined cases are counted separately; in case of several complainants in one case we took the admittedly arbitrary decision to count only the first party named.

The opposite seems valid for the Netherlands, Belgium, Germany, and the UK. The sheer volume of French private litigation makes it true as well for France. The Danes, Irish, and Luxembourgers remain at the fringes, whether in private or in public.

By far the largest single subject for private litigation against Community institution consists of competition law. Table 2.11 takes a closer look.

Table 2.11. Unprivileged applications for annulment of competition measures, ECJ (1989–1993) and CFI (1990–1998)

	B	DK	D	EL	E	F	IRL	I	L	NL	P	UK	Other	Total
Inf.	12	2	21		3	19	1	12	1	12		19	30	132
Proc.			2	4		2				3		1	1	13
Subtotal	12	2	23	7		21	1	12	1	15		20	31	145
Won	6	1	15		3	10		7		6		11	23	82
Rej.	3		1			7		2	3	5		1	2	24
Ex.						7				3		1		11
Subtotal	3		1			14		2	3	8		2	2	35
Won	1					5		2	3			2	2	15
TOTAL	15	2	24	7		35	1	14	4	23		22	29	180
%														100

Inf.: Commission decisions finding an infringement of competition law and (usually) imposing a fine or refusing an exemption.
Proc.: Procedural matters: Commission decisions requesting information or decisions to enter the premises of companies to conduct on-site searches.
Rej.: Commission decisions rejecting complaints against competitors or deciding not to act upon them.
Ex.: Commission decisions granting exemptions to competitors or allowing mergers under the Merger Regulation.
Data compiled by the authors from the ECR.

It divides competition law litigation into two main categories: actions against decisions addressed to the applicant, and actions against decisions concerning competitors. Whereas practically all Belgian, German, Italian, British, and Spanish litigation concerns the former category, the French and the Dutch are disproportionately concerned with the Commission's handling of their complaints against competitors, or with the Commission's lenience towards these competitors.

Private litigation attacking state aid measures can be divided along the same lines, into decisions addressed to the applicant and decisions directed at competitors. The one German case was brought by the victim of a Commission decision prohibiting aid, as was one of the two Dutch cases. For France, this constellation was present in only one of nine cases, the other eight being divided equally over decisions allowing aid to French and foreign competitors (of which two were against Dutch competitors). All seven British cases were brought against decisions allowing aid to foreign competitors, of which four were against French competitors. The same is true for three out of four Belgian cases, two of which were against Italian competitors.

V THE ECJ AS A CONSTITUTIONAL REVIEW COURT

Functionally, the infringement procedure is the front-door route to review the compatibility of national legislation with Community law; Article 173 the vehicle for reviewing the constitutionality of Community measures. The Court has elevated the preliminary reference procedure to the functional equivalent of both.

In *Van Gend en Loos* the Court 'gave Community law to the people' by introducing the principle of direct effect. It held:

A restriction of the guarantees against an infringement of Article 12 by Member States to the procedures of Articles 169 and 170 would remove all direct legal protection of the individual rights of their nationals. There is the risk that recourse to the procedure under these articles would be ineffective if it were to occur after the implementation of a national decision taken contrary to the provisions of the Treaty.

The vigilance of individuals concerned to protect their rights amounts to an effective supervision in addition to the supervision entrusted by Articles 169 and 170 to the diligence of the Commission and the Member States.[65]

Through a series of judgments, including the indirect effect given to Directives in *Marleasing*,[66] the Court has built up a judicial liability system to enhance the effectiveness of private enforcement of Community law.[67] That development culminated in *Francovich*, where it established as a 'principle of Community law'

[t]hat the Member States are obliged to pay compensation for harm caused to individuals by breaches of Community law for which they can be held responsible.[68]

The Maastricht Treaty amended Article 169 by introducing the power to fine Member States for not complying with judgments finding infringements. In Mancini's estimate, however,

---

[65] Case 26/62, *Van Gend en Loos*, [1963] ECR 10.

[66] Case C-106/89, *Marleasing*, [1990] ECR I-4135 established that national courts are to interpret provisions of national law which conflict with Community law in such a way as to make them consistent. Cf. Case C-344/92, *Wagner Miret*, [1993] ECR I-1911. But see Case C-168/95, *Luciano Arcaro*, [1996] ECR I-4705. The Court confirmed its refusal to give horizontal direct effect to Directives in Case C-91/92, *Paola Faccini Dori*, [1994] ECR I-3325.

[67] See Snyder, above n. 32, 40 ff.

[68] Joined Cases C-6/90 and C-9/90, *Francovich and Bonifaci v. Italy*, [1991] ECR I-5337, para. 37.

Francovich gave to Article 169, and thus to the power of review over national legislation, claws and teeth that are far sharper and more incisive than those concocted by the authors of the Maastricht Treaty.[69]

Similarly, the Court has advertised the preliminary reference procedure as a vehicle to compensate for its less than generous treatment of private applicants under Article 173. It held in *Rau*:

It must be emphasized that there is nothing in Community law to prevent an action being brought before a national court against a measure implementing a decision adopted by a Community institution where the conditions laid down by national law are satisfied. When such an action is brought, if the outcome of the dispute depends on validity of that decision the national court may submit questions to the Court of Justice by way of a reference for a preliminary ruling, without there being any need to ascertain whether or not the plaintiff in the main proceedings has the possibility of challenging the decision directly before the Court.
The possibility of bringing a direct action under the second paragraph of Article 173 of the EEC Treaty against a decision adopted by a Community decision does not preclude the possibility of bringing an action in a national court against a measure adopted by a national authority for the implementation of that decision on the ground that the latter decision is unlawful.[70]

The Court reduced its generosity in *TWD*, where it held that an action in national court is not possible once the time-limits for a direct action under Article 173 have expired.[71] The application of that principle, however, seems limited to cases where admissibility under Article 173 is not in doubt. For measures of a general nature, then, the preliminary reference is still the advised route.[72] The Court used the same reasoning in *Greenpeace*, suggesting that its rights are fully protected in proceedings before the national courts 'which may, if need be, refer a question to this Court for a preliminary ruling under Article 177 of the Treaty'.[73]

---

[69] F. Mancini and D. Keeling, 'From CILFIT to ERT: The Constitutional Challenges facing the European Court', (1991) 11 YBEL 1, 10.

[70] Joined Cases 133 to 136/85, *Walter Rau*, [1987] ECR 2289, paras. 11 and 12. Cf. Case 216/82, *Technische Universität Hamburg*, [1983] ECR 2271.

[71] Case C-188/92, *TWD Textilwerke Deggendorf*, [1994] ECR I-833.

[72] The Court in *TWD* distinguished that case from *Rau* in the fact that in the latter cases the plaintiffs had brought actions under Article 230; it distinguished *TWD* from *Technische Universität Hamburg* in the general nature of the measure in the latter case. Cf. F. Mancini and C. Curti Gialdino, 'Brevi noti in tema di abuso del processo comunitario', (1998) Rivista di diritto europeo 245, 251.

[73] Case C-321/95 P, *Stichting Greenpeace v. Commission*, [1998] ECR I-1651. As AG Cosmas points out in para. 74 of his Opinion, the proceedings before national courts in this case could hardly substitute for the protection that would have been available had the Court of First Instance granted standing.

If a Community measure is attacked before a national judge, the Court has made it clear that the national court *must* use the preliminary reference procedure before declaring the measure invalid:

Since Article 173 gives the Court exclusive jurisdiction to declare void an act of a Community institution, the coherence of the system requires that where the validity of a Community act is challenged before a national court the power to declare the act invalid must also be reserved to the Court of Justice.[74]

Rasmussen has argued strongly that the Court closed down Article 173 to force applicants through the door of Article 177 in an ambition to become a Federal Appellate Court.[75] Crude as his analysis may be, he may feel heartened by Judge Mancini's dismissal of Article 173 as 'strategically less important' in the making of a European constitution.[76]

All roads to review, then, seem to lead to national courts and the preliminary reference procedure.[77] The success of this mechanism for judicial cooperation is quite extraordinary. The first lonely preliminary reference arrived in Luxembourg in 1961. Their numbers have been growing steadily since, from 37 in 1971, 109 in 1981, 186 in 1991, to 264 in 1998. They now account for well over half the cases brought before the Court of Justice. Table 2.12 shows the division of references over courts of different Member States over the last ten years.

Table 2.12. Article 177 references, 1989–1998

B	DK	D	EL	E	F	IRL
181	49	510	34	118	244	17
(9.3)	(2.5)	(26.1)	(1.7)	(6)	(12.5)	(0.9)

I	L	NL	P	UK	Total	
380	19	192	31	177	1,952	
(19.5)	(1)	(9.8)	(1.6)	(9.1)	(100)	

Percentages in brackets.
Source: Statistical information of the Court of Justice 1998.

---

[74] Case 314/84, *Foto-Frost*, [1987] ECR 4199, para. 17.

[75] H. Rasmussen, 'Why Is Article 173 Interpreted against Private Plaintiffs?', (1980) 5 ELR 112.

[76] Mancini and Keeling, above n. 69, 8. Another strong endorsement of the preliminary reference procedure rather than Article 173 for review of general rules of Community law is P. Nihoul, 'La recevabilité des recours en annulation introduits par un particulier à l'encontre d'un acte communautaire de portée générale', (1994) 30 RTDE 171.

[77] See generally e.g. D. Anderson, *References to the European Court* (1995) and M. Jimeno Bulnes, *La cuestión prejudicial del Artículo 177 TCE* (1996).

In the search for an explanation of these differences, Alec Stone Sweet and his collaborators have correlated national patterns of preliminary references with population, number of foreign EU residents and other plausible variables. The near-perfect match they found was with absolute values of intra-EU exports. From the match, they then constructed an elegant transaction-based theory of European integration. They model a 'dynamic and relatively autonomous system of mutual influence' of three variables: transnational economic activity will create a need for transnational dispute resolution and coordinative rules. To the extent that European institutions—especially the ECJ and the Commission—respond to this demand, new case law and legislation will feed back into society and will fuel increased transnational activity in ever more areas.[78]

The model fits nicely with the court's self-styled role as the liberator of European civil society. For a legal sociologist, it poses some important questions.[79] The theory implies that legal systems are automatically 'triggered' by social demand, and that this triggering effect occurs evenly across the different Member States with their vastly different legal cultures. This 'conveyer belt' theory of social demand and legal change[80] has, however, proved unable to explain differences in litigation rates between the Netherlands and Germany, arguably the two countries closest in socio-economic conditions in the Union. The case has thus been made that the explanation lies not in social 'demand' but in the supply side—in the relative availability of legal infrastructure.[81]

Furthermore, one could seriously doubt whether the demand comes from 'transnational activity'. As would be expected, the penetration of Community law in national legal and economic systems increasingly means that Community law will be invoked for purely internal matters. It also means that an increasing proportion concerns civil litigation and even criminal prosecution, and not just administrative litigation.

---

[78] A. Stone Sweet and T. Brunell, 'The European Court and the National Courts: A Statistical Analysis of Preliminary References, 1961–95', (1998) 5 Journal of European Public Policy 66. Cf. Stone Sweet and Brunell, 'Constructing a Supranational Constitution: Dispute Resolution and Governance in the European Community', (1998) 92 American Political Science Review 63; A. Stone Sweet and J. Caporaso, 'La Cour de Justice et l'intégration européenne', (1998) 48 Revue française de science politique 195, and 'From Free Trade to Supranational Polity: The European Court and Integration', in W. Sandholtz and A. Stone Sweet (eds.), *European Integration and Supranational Governance* (1998), 93.

[79] This section draws heavily on H. Schepel, 'The Mobilisation of European Community Law', in J. Brand and D. Strempel (eds.), *Soziologie des Rechts: Festschrift für Erhard Blankenburg* (1998), 443.

[80] See e.g. L. M. Friedman, *The Legal System: A Social Science Perspective* (1985).

[81] E. Blankenburg, 'The Infrastructure for Avoiding Civil Litigation: Comparing Cultures of Legal Behaviour in the Netherlands and West Germany', (1994) 28 Law and Society Review 789. Cf. E. Blankenburg (ed.), *Prozessflut?* (1988).

Table 2.13. Transnational nature of conflict before national courts

	1965	1970	1975	1980	1985	1990	1995
Purely internal	0	3	11	13	35	46	53
Transnational	6	26	34	64	75	66	59
Total	6	29	45	77	110	112	112
% transnational	100	89.7	75.6	83.1	68.2	58.9	52.7

Data compiled by the authors from the ECR, table previously published in H. Schepel, 'The Mobilisation of European Community Law', in J. Brand and D. Strempel (eds.), *Soziologie des Rechts—Festschrift für Erhard Blankenburg* (1998), 443, to which we refer for methodological notes.

From the breakdown into sectors established by Stone Sweet the 'demand' seems to depend in some cases on social conditions. Belgium brings many social security cases, Italy few. Most of the Belgian cases, however, involve Italian immigrants. In large part it depends on national regulatory structures. German courts bring relatively few cases in competition law, France many. Germany brings relatively few cases on environmental law, Italy many. The UK predictably brings many cases concerning social provisions.

On the 'supply side', the procedure depends crucially on the acceptance of supremacy of Community law by national judges. Theories abound about why they would seem to have done so.[82] For the judges themselves, it is the sheer brilliance of its judgments that ensured not only acceptance but admiration.[83] A more modest variation is plain formalism, the *per se* compliance pull of a dialogue conducted in 'legalese'. The more cynical offer is judicial empowerment—national judges finding themselves in unthought of positions of power to review and recast national law and policy. Karen Alter's version is inter-court competition, compliance resulting from contingent struggles between different layers and branches of the judiciary.[84] Her theory has the considerable advantage of being able to explain why some courts did not, and do not, accept supremacy.

Two contrasting mechanisms seem to be at work. On the one hand, where, in countries such as Ireland and Spain, the proportion of cases brought by courts of last instance diminishes, the argument could be made that obedient

---

[82] For overviews see K. Alter, 'Explaining National Court Acceptance of European Court Jurisprudence: A Critical Evaluation of Theories of Legal Integration', in A.-M. Slaughter, A. Stone Sweet, and J. H. H. Weiler (eds.), *The European Court and National Courts: Doctrine and Jurisprudence: Legal Change in Its Social Context* (1998), 227, and J. H. H. Weiler, *The Constitution of Europe* (1999), 195 ff.

[83] C. N. Kakouris, 'La Mission de la Cour de Justice des communautés européennes et l' "ethos" du juge', (1994) (4) RAE 35, 37.

[84] Alter, above n. 82, 241 ff. She elaborates in 'The Creation of an International Rule of Law in Europe' (1999), MS.

Table 2.14. Nature of proceedings before national court

	1965	1970	1975	1980	1985	1990	1995
Administrative	3 (50)	26 (89.6)	42 (93.3)	57 (74)	84 (76.4)	84 (75)	71 (63.4)
Civil	3 (50)	3 (10.3)	2 (4.4)	13 (16.9)	21 (19.1)	17 (15.2)	27 (24.1)
Criminal	0 (0)	0 (0)	1 (2.2)	7 (9.1)	5 (4.5)	11 (9.8)	14 (12.5)
TOTAL	6 (100)	29 (100)	45 (100)	77 (100)	110 (100)	112 (100)	112 (100)

Percentages in brackets.
Data compiled by the authors from the ECR.

Table 2.15. References brought by Courts of Last Instance, 1961–1998

	B	DK	D	EL	E	F	IRL	I	L	NL	P	UK	Total
1961–93													
Total	303	48	857	32	28	465	28	319	32	406	10	162	2,690
High courts	46	10	258	3	20	57	22	59	20	238	3	14	750
% of total	15.2	20.8	30.1	9.4	71.4	12.2	78.6	18.5	62.5	58.6	30	8.5	27.9
1994–8													
Total	94	30	256	21	93	129	9	263	10	87	21	107	1,120
High courts	24	4	77	6	18	15	3	32	3	47	15	19	263
% of total	25.5	13.3	30.1	28.6	19.4	11.6	33.3	12.2	30	54	71.4	17.8	23.5

Source: Statistical information of the Court of Justice 1998 and EC general reports on activities.

lower courts have begun to refer questions to the ECJ after the principles of supremacy and direct effect of Community law have been accepted by high courts. On the other hand, where, in countries such as Belgium, Portugal, and the UK, the proportion increases one can hypothesize reluctant high courts being forced into obedience in part by activist low courts.

Depending as it does on the voluntary submission of questions by lower national courts, and an unsanctionable duty for courts of last instance to refer, the development of judicial cooperation has been a matter of gaining trust. One of the ways of doing this has been to organize judicial visits to the Court in Luxembourg.[85] Apparently, they help. Says Lord Denning: 'I would pay tribute to the work of the European Court at Luxembourg. I have been there. I have met the judges. They are of the highest quality.'[86]

Another way has been the 'unlimited patience' with which the Court answered the questions referred to it in the early years of the Community.[87] Faced with the repeated request to rule on the compatibility of a provision of national legislation with Community law, the Court will 'reformulate' the question such as to give a ruling on the 'interpretation' of the Treaty. Asked by an Italian court in *Costa v. ENEL* whether the nationalization of an electricity company was allowed under Community law, the Court held:

> The Court has the power to extract from a question imperfectly formulated by the national court those questions which alone pertain to the interpretation of the Treaty. Consequently a decision should be given by the Court not on the validity of an Italian law in relation to the Treaty, but only upon the interpretation of the abovementioned Articles in the context of the points of law stated by the Giudice Conciliatore.[88]

The judge is thus 'led hand in hand as far as the door'.[89]

Even with national courts uniformly accepting the supremacy of Community law, the use of national judicial systems in direct correlation with demand created by transnational activity would seem at odds with well-known differences not only in the efficiency of national judicial systems and the litigiousness of societies, but also with differences in legal ideology.[90] Table 2.16 correlates the different procedures with various variables.

---

[85] Around 10,000 people visit the Court each year. In 1995 they included 831 national judges. See R. Dehousse, *The European Court of Justice* (1998), 139. Cf. I. Maher, 'National Courts as Community Courts', (1994) 14 LS 226, 233–4.

[86] *What Next in the Law* (1982), 301.

[87] F. Mancini, 'The Making of a Constitution for Europe', (1989) 26 CMLR 599, 606.

[88] Case 6/64, *Costa v. ENEL* [1964] ECR 592. Cf. P. Demaret, 'Le Juge et le jugement dans l'Europe d'aujourd'hui: la Cour de Justice des communautés européennes', in R. Jacob (ed.), *Le Juge et le jugement dans les traditions juridiques européennes* (1996), 303, 312 ('ce rappel est devenu de pure forme et ne trompe personne').

[89] Mancini, above n. 87.

[90] See V. Gessner, A. Hoeland, and C. Varga (eds.), *European Legal Cultures* (1996).

Table 2.16. Litigation rates under different procedures correlated with selected variables

	B	DK	D	EL	E	F	IRL	I	L	NL	P	UK
Suspected infringements	32	11	84	52	85	100	19	84	0	22	21	67
Article 169	73	0	36	57	45	23	34	100	11	19	0	9
Article 173: Member States	27	5	73	55	55	91	9	100	0	32	18	27
Article 173: private parties	45	0	63	3	17	100	3	53	2	56	22	55
Article 177	33	7	100	3	20	46	0	74	0	35	3	13
Population	12	6	100	12	48	71	4	69	0	19	11	72
GDP	11	7	100	5	24	66	3	54	0	16	4	61
Intra-EU exports	42	9	100	0	22	60	0	47	–	42	6	45
Salience of ECJ	57	50	76	3	13	24	45	0	100	20	17	8
Satisfaction with ECJ	39	77	46	6	14	0	100	21	85	81	16	97
Satisfaction with national high court	19	97	86	28	17	4	48	9	17	100	0	67
Support for the rule of law	44	100	55	0	36	65	18	36	29	88	1	87

Rankings are expressed in rounded percentage points with the highest value set at 100 and the lowest at 0.

Data on population, GDP, and intra-EU exports are drawn from *European Economy*. Data for the salience of the ECJ and satisfaction with ECJ and national high courts comes from J. L. Gibson and G. A. Caldeira, 'Changes in the Legitimacy of the European Court of Justice: A Post-Maastricht Analysis', (1998) 28 British Journal of Political Science 63. Data for the support for the rule of law comes from Gibson and Caldeira, 'The Legal Cultures of Europe', (1996) 30 Law and Society Review 55, on the basis of disagreement expressed with the statement: 'It is not necessary to obey a law you consider unjust.'

If we take at face value the functional equivalence between the preliminary reference and the infringement procedure for the review of national legislation we could compare the two sets of data. That hypothesis yields results more or less consistent with the little we know about national legal cultures. Germans are relatively more willing to go through the judicial system, the French relatively more willing to follow the administrative route of complaining at the Commission. The hypothesis would also provide an alternative explanation of the very low figures of preliminary references originating from, say, Greece; rather than in low levels of transnational activity, the key might then be thought to lie in the low levels of trust in judicial institutions. Cynicism about national judicial institutions may then also be a better explanation for Greece's relatively high figures in suspected infringements than Greek lack of support for the 'rule of law', as hypothesized by Gibson and

Caldeira.[91] They suppose a correlation between compliance with Community law and popular levels of support for values associated with the rule of law. The theory would be valid for the Netherlands, Denmark, and Italy, but could never explain France and the UK. Grand theories are unlikely to explain the intricacies of different national patterns of mobilization of Community law; lots of very thick description might.

The Court has always characterized the relationship with national courts as one of cooperation based on a clear separation of functions, where the Court of Justice 'helps' the national court concerned to solve the case at hand. Over time, the relationship has changed from, as Craig and de Búrca have it, *horizontal* and *bilateral* to *vertical* and *multilateral*.[92] The Court denied national courts the power to declare Community acts invalid in *Foto-Frost*. There, it held that

[t]he main purpose of the powers accorded to the Court by Article 177 is to ensure that Community law is applied uniformly by national courts. That requirement of uniformity is particularly imperative when the validity of a Community act is in question. Divergences between courts in the Member States as to the validity of Community acts would be liable to place in jeopardy the very unity of the Community legal order and detract from the fundamental requirement of legal certainty.[93]

The other side of the coin is that national courts are effectively enlisted as 'Community courts', obliged to give 'full force and effect' to Community law. In *Simmenthal* the Court held that the effectiveness of Article 177

[w]ould be impaired if the national court were prevented from forthwith applying Community law in accordance with the decision or the case-law of the Court.
    It follows from the foregoing that every national court must, in a case within its jurisdiction, apply Community law in its entirety and protect rights which the latter confers on individuals and must accordingly set aside any provision of national law which may conflict with it, whether prior or subsequent to the Community rule.[94]

Depending on one's interpretation of the case, the Court's ruling in *CILFIT* could be added to this centralizing case law. There, the Court on the one hand established an *acte clair* exception to the duty to refer for courts of last instance in cases where the correct application of Community law is 'so obvious as to leave no scope for any reasonable doubt as to the manner in which

---

[91] Gibson and Caldeira, above n. 17.
[92] P. Craig and G. de Búrca, *EC Law* (1995), 400.
[93] Case 314/84, *Foto-Frost*, [1987] ECR 4199, para. 15.
[94] Case 106/77, *Simmenthal*, [1978] ECR 629. Cf. Case 213/89, *Factortame* [1990] ECR I-2433. Cf. e.g. A. Barav, 'Omnipotent Courts', in D. Curtin and T. Heukels (eds.), *Institutional Dynamics of European Integration: Essays in Honour of Henry G. Schermers* [vol.] *II* (1994), 265, and C. N. Kakouris, 'Do the Member States Possess Judicial "Autonomy"?', (1997) 34 CMLR 1389.

the question raised is to be resolved'.[95] On the other hand, it placed such a long list of conditions on the exception as to make it virtually impossible to consider the application of Community law 'obvious'.[96] Countering criticism,[97] Judge Mancini sees the case as the result of an 'acute understanding of judicial psychology' and explains the Court's strategy:

By granting supreme courts the power to do lawfully that which they could in any case do unlawfully, but by subjecting that power to stringent conditions, the Court hoped to induce the supreme courts to use willingly the 'mechanism for judicial co-operation' provided by the Treaty. The result is to eliminate sterile and damaging conflicts and to reduce the risk that Community law might be subject to divergent interpretations.[98]

The procedure has been an enormous success for the Court, not just in quantitative terms but in qualitative terms as well. It wholeheartedly invited and welcomed references—*any* references—in the beginning, and constructed grand principles of Community law thanks to rather petty cases brought to it by national courts: *Van Gend en Loos* and *Costa v. ENEL* were spectacular only for the concepts of supremacy and direct effect, not because of the intrinsic injustice rectified. Article 177 is especially suited for lawmaking; the Court's duty to abstain from deciding on compatibility but rather to limit itself to an 'interpretation' of the Treaty gives it the opportunity to 'say the law' in the abstract, without actually resolving a dispute.[99] In sheer volume of cases the procedure threatens, as it has for a decade or so, to become a victim of its own success.[100] Over time, both trends have reversed: from abstract lawmaking to dispute resolution, and from an open-ended invitation to docket control.

---

[95] Case 283/81, *CILFIT*, [1982] ECR 3415, para. 16.

[96] The national court must be 'convinced that the matter is equally obvious to the courts of the other Member States and to the Court of Justice'; further, it must bear in mind that Community law is drafted in several equally authentic languages, that Community law uses concepts 'which are peculiar to it' and have different meanings in different national legal systems, and that provisions of Community law should be interpreted in the light of Community law as a whole, 'regard being had to the objectives thereof and its share of evolution'. Ibid.

[97] Cf. A. Arnull, 'The Use and Abuse of Article 177', (1989) 52 MLR 622.

[98] Mancini and Keeling, above n. 69, 5. The same argument was made by H. Rasmussen, 'The European Court's *Acte Clair* Strategy in *CILFIT*', (1984) 9 ELR 242.

[99] Dehousse, above n. 35, 77. One favourite tactic of the Court is what Hartley describes as the 'gradual introduction of a doctrine'—establishing the doctrine subject to various qualifications, maybe even finding a reason why it should not apply in the case at hand, and then slowly whittling away the qualifications and 'revealing' the full extent of the doctrine. Cf. Hartley, above n. 40, 79. Another one is such a generous use of the *obiter dictum* that it has now become the object in its own right of scholarly scrutiny; cf. Charrier, 'L'*obiter dictum* dans la jurisprudence de la Cour de Justice des communautés européennes', (1998) 34 CDE 79.

[100] For early warnings, see T. Koopmans, 'La procédure préjudicielle: victime de son succès?', in F. Capotorti et al. (eds.), *Du droit international au droit de l'intégration: Liber amicorum Pierre Pescatore* (1987) 347, and H. G. Schermers et al. (eds.), *Article 177 EEC: Experiences and Problems* (1987).

Allegedly, the trend has been away from general principles to substantive justice in the specific case for quite some time now. Judge Everling wrote in the mid 1980s:

However, in the course of the seventies the Court of Justice seems to have become increasingly cautious about laying down general principles and has concentrated to a greater extent on the problem to be solved in the individual case. In any event that is clearly the trend today. The reasons for this are open to various conjectures. On the one hand there is the increasing complexity of the facts of cases, which makes it ever more difficult to foresee the effects of judgments in the context of the obscure interaction of provisions of Community law and provisions of national law. On the other hand, the cause may lie in the changes in the composition of the Court, that is to say in the arrival of judges from the common law tradition schooled in case law and inclined to a pragmatic approach and in the gradual introduction of a new generation of Judges. Finally it would seem that the general lack of political direction also plays a part. The Court is no longer able to rely on a general unconditional will to integrate.[101]

The recent toughening up of admissibility requirements could be seen as the procedural extension of the trend. Over the last eight years or so, the Court has started to refuse to entertain questions put to it—much to the dismay of commentators who fear that the Court may be 'alienating' the national judiciary and attacking the spirit of co-operation which made the procedure such a success.[102]

In *Telemarsicabruzzo* the Court held:

It must be pointed out that the need to provide an interpretation of Community law which will be of use to the national court makes it necessary that the national court define the factual and legislative context of the question it is asking or, at the very least, explain the factual circumstances on which those questions are based.[103]

In *Max Mara* it added that

The information provided and the questions raised in decisions making references must not only enable the Court to give helpful answers but must also give the

---

[101] U. Everling, 'The Court of Justice as a Decisionmaking Authority', in Michigan Law Review Association (ed.), *The Art of Governance: Festschrift zu Ehren von Eric Stein* (1987), 156, 163.

[102] D. O'Keeffe, 'Is the Spirit of Article 177 Under Attack? Preliminary References and Admissibility', (1998) 23 ELR 509; Anderson, 'The Admissibility of Preliminary References', (1994)14 YBEL 179; C. Barnard and E. Sharpston, 'The Changing Face of Article 177 References', (1997) 34 CMLR 1113. Less preoccupied, G. Tesauro, 'The Effectiveness of Judicial Protection and Co-operation between the Court of Justice and National Courts', (1993) 13 YBEL 1; and R. Joliet, 'Coopération entre la Cour de Justice des communautés européennes et les juridictions nationales', (1993) *Journal des tribunaux: Droit européen* 2.

[103] Joined Cases C-320/90, C-321/90, and C-322/90, *Telemarsicabruzzo*, [1993] ECR I-393, para. 5.

Governments of the Member States and other interested parties the opportunity to submit observations.[104]

In 1996 the Court published a 'note for guidance on references by national courts'.[105] Perhaps strengthened by its having done everything to aid national courts in drafting a decent order of reference, the Court has grown quite confident in rejecting references on these grounds,[106] even if it will generally find a way around its own strictness if it wants to.[107] In line with Everling's argument, the reason for the Court's insistence on being fully briefed may well be thought to be its reluctance to start off on a course the consequences of which it cannot safely predict. 'There must be a significant risk that it will commit itself to a line of reasoning which will subsequently prove unfruitful or even embarrassing.'[108]

The Court resists turning the procedure into a continuous deliberative assembly of lawyers, judges, and litigants. In its *Foglia* decisions in the early 1980s, it considered its task under Article 177 to be 'not that of delivering opinions on general or hypothetical questions but of assisting in the administration of justice in the Member States'.[109] It insisted, in *Foglia*, on a 'genuine dispute',[110] declining jurisdiction 'to reply to questions posed within the framework of procedural devices arranged by the parties in order to induce the Court to give its view on certain problems of Community law which do not correspond to an objective requirement inherent in the resolution of a dispute'.[111] *Foglia* was heavily attacked,[112] and the Court kept it in the closet for a while[113] until it was resurrected in *Meilicke*.[114] It also declines jurisdiction over cases that have been settled in the meantime, not impressed by the

---

[104] Case C-307/95, *Max Mara Fashion*, [1995] ECR I-5083, para. 7.

[105] Court of Justice, Proceedings no. 34/96.

[106] Recently, see Case C-422/98, *Colonia*, [1999] ECR I-1279; Joined Cases C-28/98 and C-29/98, *Charreire*, [1999] ECR I-1963, and Case C-325/98, *Anssens*, [1999] ECR I-2969.

[107] See e.g. Case C-316/93, *Vaneetveld*, [1994] ECR I-736; Case C-125/94, *Aprile*, [1995] ECR I-2919; and Case 18/97, *van der Kooy*, [1999] ECR I-483.

[108] Barnard and Sharpston, above n. 102, 1150.

[109] Case 244/80, *Pasquale Foglia v. Mariella Novello ('Foglia II')*, [1981] ECR 3045, para. 18. Cf. Case 149/82, *Stephanie Robards*, [1983] ECR 171, para. 19.

[110] Case 104/79, *Pasquale Foglia v. Mariella Novello ('Foglia I')*, [1980] ECR 745.

[111] Case 244/80, *Foglia II*, [1981] ECR 3045, para. 18. Cf. Case C-83/91, *Wienand Meilicke*, [1992] ECR I-4871, and Case C-343/90, *Manuel José Lourenço Dias*, [1992] ECR I-4673.

[112] Cf. e.g. A. Barav, 'Preliminary Censorship? The Judgment of the European Court in *Foglia v. Novello*', (1980) 5 ELR 443, and G. Bebr, 'The Existence of a Genuine Dispute: An Indispensable Precondition for the Jurisdiction of the Court under Article 177 EEC Treaty?', (1980) 17 CMLR 525

[113] The Court accepted jurisdiction over arguably 'fabricated' cases in e.g. Case 46/80, *Vinal*, [1981] ECR 77, Case 261/81, *Walter Rau*, [1982] ECR 3961, and Case C-150/88, *Parfümerie Fabrik 4711*, [1989] ECR 3891.

[114] Case C-83/91, *Meilicke*, [1992] ECR I-4871.

argument that the questions posed 'are of such importance that they go beyond the dispute between the parties'.[115] Even if there is arguably a trend, the Court has fallen under suspicion of not taking the 'orchestration' argument or the 'hypothetical questions' argument very seriously when there are important cases to decide. *Faccini Dori*, *Bosman* and *Lecerc-Siplec* are examples.[116]

Whereas it could be argued that the Court's procedural case law is really a form of concealed docket control,[117] in its substantive case law the reverse could be happening. In *Keck*, the Court considered it necessary to 'clarify' its case law on the free movement of goods, limiting the scope of Article 30, 'in view of the increasing tendency of traders to invoke Article 30 of the treaty as a means of challenging any rules whose effect is to limit their commercial freedom'.[118]

Be that as it may, weeding out fabricated and hypothetical cases does nothing to alleviate the Court's burden of genuine but excruciatingly boring cases. As Mancini admitted, 'if the Court ever acquires the power to indulge in agenda-setting, the customs classification of shoes and sandals will not be high on the agenda'.[119]

Advocate General Jacobs lost patience not with the customs classification of shoes and sandals, but with that of pyjamas and nightdresses. In his Opinion in *Wiener*, he discussed the value of the Court's definition of 'pyjama':

The fact that there is now such an interpretation does not preclude new disputes. In turn, those disputes could always be characterized as raising a new question of interpretation. Parties might for example raise the question: 'Is it significant in assessing whether certain sets of garments are clearly intended to be worn mainly in bed as

---

[115] Joined Cases C-422/93, 423/93, and 424/93, *Teresa Zabala Erasun*, [1995] ECR I-1567, para. 26. Cf. Case C-314/96, *Ourdia Djabali*, [1998] ECR I-1149.

[116] Case C-91/92, *Paola Faccini Dori*, [1994] ECR I-3325; Case C-415/93, *Bosman*, [1995] ECR I-4921; and Case 412/93, *Leclerc Siplec*, [1995] ECR I-179. See Barnard and Sharpston, above n. 102, at 1144 on 'sexy cases'.

[117] That explicitly, O'Keeffe, above n. 102.

[118] Joined Cases 267/91 and C-268/91, *Keck and Mithouard* [1993] ECR I-6097, para, 14. On *Keck* as docket-control, cf. e.g. S. Weatherill, 'After *Keck*: Some Thoughts on How to Clarify the Clarification', (1996) 33 CMLR 885 ('Keck was doubtless intended to empower national courts to dismiss far-fetched attempts to deploy internal market law which were clogging up the Community judicial system', at 885) with J. H. H. Weiler, 'The Constitution of the Common Market Place: Text and Context in the Evolution of the Free Movement of Goods' in Craig and de Búrca, *The Evolution of EU Law*, 349 ('We should, I think, give more credit to the Court. If the doctrine is justified on its merits, your alarm at an increase in case load should be directed at the phenomena that give rise to the increase, not to the doctrine. You do not address a growing flood of murder cases by changing the definition of murder', at 370).

[119] F. Mancini, 'The US Supreme Court and the European Court of Justice' in N. Emiliou and D. O'Keeffe (eds.), *Legal Aspects of Integration in the European Union* (1997), 7.

pyjamas that those garments carry pictures or drawings suggesting beach and holiday scenes?' The national court might be persuaded to refer that question to this Court as a further question of interpretation of the sub-heading 'pyjamas'. On the approach which it has hitherto adopted, the Court would attempt to give a specific reply to that question.

I do not consider that it is appropriate, or indeed possible, for the Court to continue to respond fully to all references which, through the creativity of lawyers and judges, are couched in terms of interpretation, even though the reference might in a particular case be better characterized as concerning the application of law rather than its interpretation.[120]

His solution is to suggest self-restraint to national judges. The Court of Justice 'could perhaps give some informal guidance and so encourage self-restraint by the national courts in appropriate cases'. The Court itself could, in certain areas, declare 'that it has substantially performed its task of uniform interpretation, in that the essential principles or rules of interpretation have been set out sufficiently to enable national courts to decide matters themselves'.[121] In policy papers, it is now talking of the introduction of 'filtering systems'—for all practical purposes a form of *certiorari*.[122]

VI CONCLUSION

A Court that wants to engage in lawmaking usually transforms its courtroom into a legislative assembly—allowing class actions, public interest litigation, popular constitutional complaints, *Brandeis* briefs. The most striking feature of the ECJ's case law is that it has resisted all of these. It has refrained from turning Article 173 into a vehicle of general constitutional review of Community measures on substantive grounds. In spectacular fashion for Parliament, and rather less impressively for private parties, it has, however, actively explored the possibilities the action carries with it to protect the procedural rights of those involved in the Community policy process. For constitutional ambitions, however, the procedure is of limited use only, and the Court must be relieved to leave a large part of it to the Court of First Instance. The Court has been content to be used as a stick behind the door by the

---

[120] Case C-338/95, *Wiener v. Hauptzollamt Emmerich*, [1997] ECR I-6495, paras. 16 and 17. The Court did of course answer the question put to it, ruling that 'nightdresses' are 'under garments which, by reason of their objective characteristics, are intended to be worn exclusively or essentially in bed'.

[121] Ibid., paras 20–21.

[122] *Certiorari* is advocated by T. Kennedy, 'First steps towards a European Certiorari', (1993) 18 ELR 121, and Rasmussen, *The European Court of Justice* (1998), 158 ff. *Contra* e.g. T. Koopmans, 'The Future of the Court of Justice of the European Communities', (1991) 11 YBEL 15, at 29 ff. The 'filtering system' is proposed by the President of the ECJ, above n. 23.

Commission for infringement cases, resisting the temptation of compromising the Commission's role of political mediator and transforming Article 169 into a vehicle of popular constitutional complaints.

The Court has instead opted for the preliminary reference procedure to chant the mantras of Community law. But even here it has insisted on its function of helping to resolve genuine disputes, even if it does not adhere all that strictly to its professed principles. Its recent toughening up of admissibility requirements, its growing fatigue over marginal questions, and its talk of filtering systems serve its self-interest in two ways. On the one hand, it serves to diminish the ECJ's case load and hence enables it to concentrate on frontier cases. On the other, it establishes a hierarchical relationship between the Court and national courts.

By rendering Community law the directly applicable supreme law of the land, the Court holds out a promise to Europe's citizens—a promise it expects national courts to keep. As Temple Lang has it, 'we are gradually building what has not existed for fifteen hundred years, a common law of much of Western Europe. This can be done any day in your local court.' Indeed, 'Community law is *your* law'.[123]

The scenario has some plausibility. The process of European integration inevitably increases social distance; the concomitant process of deregulation and liberalization replaces political management of the economy by the 'regulatory state'. It might even be considered attractive—an assertion of pan-European judicial power to emancipate civil society, rationalize administration, and curb raw political power. But legal cultures are thick. Spanish legal culture has been summarized with the phrase '*¡Pleitas tengas!*', 'Go to court' as the equivalent of 'May you burn in hell'.[124] Cohen-Tanugi's *droit sans l'État* remains his dream for France, not a description of reality: 'The idea that litigation could be a powerful *democratic* instrument is totally alien to French political culture.'[125] Judicial review, and the inevitable political use of the courtroom that goes with it, is not a 'tradition common to the Member States', as the phrase goes. Or at least, not yet.

---

[123] J. Temple Lang, 'The Duties of National Courts under Community Constitutional Law', (1997) 22 ELR 3, at 16–17. Emphasis in original.

[124] J. J. Toharia, *¡Pleitas tengas! Introducción a la cultura legal española* (1987).

[125] Cohen-Tanugi, above n. 7, 158.

3

Integration and Integrity in the Legal Reasoning of the European Court of Justice

JOXERRAMON BENGOETXEA, NEIL MacCORMICK,
and LEONOR MORAL SORIANO

I SOME PRELIMINARY POINTS ON JUSTIFICATION AND INTERPRETATION

The task set to the authors of this chapter was to give an account of the legal reasoning of the European Court of Justice—to look at the style and method of reasoning adopted by the Court, in the light of contemporary understandings of legal reasoning more generally. In doing so, we naturally and necessarily draw upon our own prior contributions to this study. We approach the task aware of the critique, by Rasmussen[1] and others, that the Court's reasoning is altogether too often invention in the guise of interpretation, policy enacted behind a smokescreen of alleged legal principle. In place of the modest communities created in the foundational treaties and their subsequent extensions and elaborations, a 'new legal order' has been conjured into being clothed with the doctrines of supremacy and direct effect, overriding to a substantial extent the sovereign rights, perhaps even the legal sovereignty, of the Member States.

The Court, argue those who criticize the Court as being activist, has crossed the line between the legal and the political domains by being creative and interventionist. But does such a line really exist? Rather than a line, one should talk about an area in which law and policies overlap. The question is not how to separate one from the other—by drawing lines—but rather how to manage the overlap. In the particular case of the ECJ, the overlap between law and politics has been tackled by the European integration project. The promotion first of economic integration and ultimately of political integration can also be seen as justifying and even legitimizing the active role of the Court.

---

[1] H. Rasmussen, *On Law and Policy in the European Court of Justice: A Comparative Study in Judicial Policymaking* (1986).

Judicial activism or judicial self-restraint, understood as normative or inter-pretative ideology, are concepts that should be abandoned when analysing the ECJ's judicial decision-making process. Instead, one should embrace a legal reasoning approach. By analysing the legal reasoning of the Court, one draws attention to how the Court takes account of reasons—legal norms, values, principles, policies—to justify its decisions. The question is neither whether the Court uses policy arguments nor whether it goes beyond the literal mean-ing of legal provisions. The question is rather whether and by what consider-ations its decisions are justified or, at the very least, rationally justifiable.

When analysing the legal reasoning of the Court, our starting point lies in the well-known and often noted difference between 'processes of justification' and 'processes of discovery'. Given the confidentiality of the Court's deliberations prior to judgment, it is always a matter of conjecture what led particular judges to come to one conclusion rather than another, or how the collective judgment was worked out, through what sort of debate, discussion, cajoling, masquerading, compromising, or even horse-trading. But the pub-lished judgment of the Court, and the published opinion of the Advocate-General, give us, and are meant to give us, something quite other than an account of the process of coming to a view individually or collectively. Instead, they give an account of what makes a decision the right legal decision upon the legal case or question remitted to the Court for decision or answer. That is, they state justifying reasons for what is opined or decided or answered.

We therefore seek an account of what may be deemed legally justifying rea-sons in the context of European Community law. What makes a decision count as a (or the) right decision on a point of Community law? How can the Court show its decisions to be right in law? What are we to make of the pub-lished texts of the case reports in this conceptual framework?

A. A Matter of Interpretation

At the heart of the issue lies the problem of interpretation. The 'constitutional charter' of European law and of the institutions—Commission, Council, Court, and others—of the Community (and now Union) is to be found in the Community (and Union) treaties. Whatever can be represented as legally right or legally wrong in the perspective of Community law must have some root somewhere in the treaties. So teasing out the meaning and implications of the treaties (or of instruments enacted pursuant to the treaties), and show-ing how they support one view or line of action rather than another, must be the very stuff of justification in this context.

Well, then, is 'interpretation' simply a reading of the text to see what it says, and following through the assumption that it means what it says? There is a commonly held opinion that the Court 'finds' in the EC Treaty ideas, values, concepts, norms, principles that are totally absent from the explicit words. Here arises the worry about 'invention masquerading as interpretation'. The Court's style of so-called interpretation has been, notoriously, a 'purposive' one. But whose purposes are, then, the purposes guiding such interpretation? The Court may be perceived as one of the great policy-making agencies of Community Europe, devising its own set of policy goals and gearing its interpretation of the Treaty to the pursuit of the goals in question. Where, or to the extent that, a strongly teleological approach to interpretation predominates, it is the validity or soundness of the *teloi* that justifies the interpretation and the decision rather than the wording of the text and an attempt to decipher the meaning of what it says.

There is a school of thought, however, which would respond to the doubts we have aired as based on a false antithesis. All legal interpretation is 'constructive' interpretation, as Ronald Dworkin has expressed the point.[2] Legal texts are not and could not sensibly be read as though we were parties to an ongoing person-to-person conversation between the reader of the legal text and its original author (which is probably some kind of fairly complex collective entity or agency and in the European Community, it certainly is so). Constructive interpretation has to be highly sensitive to context, and the context of any particular act of legal interpretation is the need to find a way of making sense of a text in the context of a large-scale normative scheme. This cannot be a matter of trying to read the meaning of a set of words taken in isolation. For any paragraph or article of a Treaty or of a Regulation or Directive has to be read in the setting of the whole Treaty scheme. The part makes sense in the context of the whole, and the whole gets its sense out of a dynamic interaction of the parts. It is dynamic precisely in the sense that it contains at least implicitly some answer to the question 'To what end?' What value or values in terms of lived human experience do we have to envisage being realized through the process of making the text operative as a scheme for guiding conduct if we are to be able to characterize it as socially intelligible and worthwhile? Dworkin, indeed, characterizes the task of constructive interpretation as a matter of trying to make the object interpreted the best of its kind or genre that it could possibly be. So stated, his idea may seem to blur or even breach the line between making the best of the law as it actually is and reforming the law to make it the best it could be. But there is no point in denying that interpretation is and should be teleological in the sense indicated. This is a bounded teleology, bounded by one's sense of the limits to which the Treaty or regulatory language can be pushed, and thus bounded also by the need to connect the texts to values that belong to the whole constitutional enterprise, not just to a judge's own idiosyncratic world view and personal value system.

---

[2] *Law's Empire* (1986).

Always present are arguments that work towards an acceptable understanding of a legal text seen particularly in its context as part of a legal system. Six are particularly worthy of mention in relation to EC law:

(i) The *argument from contextual harmonization* says that since any particular provision of Community law belongs within a larger scheme, whether a single Regulation or Directive, each provision ought to be interpreted in the light of the whole statute to which it belongs, which ought to be interpreted in the light of the whole Treaty scheme of things, and in particular of other norms of Community law dealing with the domain in question.

(ii) The *argument from precedent* says that if a text has previously been subjected to judicial interpretation, it ought prima facie to be interpreted in conformity with the interpretation previously given of it. Even if there is no strict doctrine of binding precedent in Community law, the ECJ and he Court of First Instance must clearly pay strong regard to the over-time coherence of the decisions they hand down in individual cases.

(iii) The *argument from analogy* says that if a legal provision is significantly analogous with similar provisions of other texts of the law, especially those dealing with closely similar subject matter, then even an interpretation of this that involves a significant extension of or departure from ordinary meaning will be justified if it brings about a like treatment of like cases.

(iv) The *Logical-conceptual argument* says that if any recognized and doctrinally elaborated general legal concept is used in the formulation of a legal provision, it ought to be interpreted so as to maintain a consistent use of the concept throughout the system as a whole, or a relevant branch or branches of it.

(v) The *argument from general principles of law* says that if any general principle or principles of law are applicable to the subject matter of a legal provision, one ought to favour that interpretation of the legal provision which is most in conformity with the general principle or principles, giving appropriate weight to the principle(s) in the light of their degree of importance both generally and in the field of law in question. In Community law, this engages an appeal both to principles that are special to the fabric of the Treaties and to the general principles commonly recognized in the laws of the Member States.

(vi) Legal systems in general recognize an *argument from history*. According to this, a statute or group of statutes may over time come to be interpreted in accordance with a historically evolved understanding of the point and purpose of the statute or group of statutes taken as a whole, or historically evolved understanding of the conception of rightness it embodies. Where that has come to be the case, any provision of the statute or group of statutes ought to be interpreted so that its application in concrete cases is compatible with this historically evolved understanding of point and purpose or of rightness.

This has spectacular relevance to the part played in Community law by the doctrines of supremacy and direct effect of Community norms, which have progressively acquired the status of general structural principles of Community law.

Such arguments are all well known to lawyers, and are easily recognizable both in general terms and quite specifically in relation to the concrete examples we discuss below. What is of importance in the present context is to reflect on the reason why such arguments carry the weight they do. Partly this has to do simply with the fact that we are dealing with communications in language—indeed, in languages, eleven or, counting the Irish official version of the constitutional text, even twelve of them currently. No linguistic communication is comprehensible save in a whole presupposed context of utterance. All legal materials are uttered in the context of the legal system in general, and in the light no doubt of a whole complex of concrete legal, political, and factual circumstances. So interpretation cannot be satisfactorily carried through even in a purely linguistic sense unless the whole context is kept in mind.

B. The Relevance of Coherence

But that is not the whole story, for it fails to say just why the legal context gives special appropriateness to arguments stressing features such as those mentioned above. As to that, it behoves us to draw attention to an ideal of overall *coherence* that governs our view of the legal system as a system and hence gives weight to the interpretive approach favoured by arguments that draw upon the systemic character of a legal system. They depend on the idea, crucial for the 'Rule of Law', that the different parts of a whole legal order should hang together and make sense as a whole. But this absolutely requires that the system be conceived as embodying a mutually compatible set of values such that detailed norms and rules can be seen as instantiations of more fundamental principles.[3]

In *Law's Empire*, Ronald Dworkin suggests that this aspect of a legal system can be attributed to a value of 'integrity' that we ascribe sometimes to whole communities of people, not only to individuals. There is an analogy between the individual value and the communal. Just as we set value on the human trait of steadiness in the upholding of a coherent set of principles, as distinct from a merely opportunistic life style, so we prefer our political communities to exhibit a steadiness of commitment to a common set of principles that apply to all cases, not capriciously to some but not others. If this is so of community in general, might it not be all the more so of 'Community', European Community?

---

[3] N. MacCormick, 'Coherence in Legal Justification', in A. Peczenik et al. (eds.), *Theory of Legal Science* (1984).

C. Integrity and Integration

Integrity in the Community context, if the idea is acceptable at all, ties closely in to integration. For the integration of Member States together in an ever closer union of peoples, and the integration of Member States' law with Community law, are omnipresent driving values ascribed by the Court, but not only the Court, to the whole Treaty scheme, and thus to the interpretation of Community law. These are themes that are implicitly explored in much of what follows, and to which we return in the concluding section of this chapter.

II RECONSTRUCTING THE JUDICIAL DECISION-MAKING PROCESS

A. Legal Reasoning at the ECJ

1. *Is There a European Legal Reasoning?*

If a provisional answer has to be put forward to this direct question we would say that there is no specific theory of judicial reasoning for the European Court of Justice, even less so any specifically European theory of legal reasoning. In other words, there is no special case of European legal reasoning, nor anything particularly European about the way the ECJ proceeds to justify its decisions. Rather, any general theory of legal reasoning, such as the comprehensive sketch suggested in Part I, could account for the ECJ's decision-making. Obviously certain rearrangements would need to be made in order to adjust the general theory to the different idiosyncratic elements of the European legal system. In this way, legal theory and the theory of legal reasoning can account for (or critically reconstruct) legal and judicial problems typical of the EC such as the lawmaking process of the European Communities and the EU; the legal order of the EC (and EU); judicial decision-making at the Court; and the interrelation between the EC legal order and the state and infra-state legal orders among others.

2. *Discovery and Justification*

The starting point of our analysis of the legal reasoning of the Court is the distinction between the context of discovery and the context of justification. This distinction refers to two different levels of analysis of judicial decision-making. The primary purpose of the distinction is to allow rational control of judicial decisions. When analysing a judicial decision from the point of view of its context of discovery one has to take account of those factors that actually lead to the 'real' process of decision-making and to the decision that has been reached. These are factors of a psychological or sociological nature, and idiosyncratic factors: context, time, resources, working conditions etc.[4]

In the particular case of the ECJ there are some factors with a great relevance in the context of discovery, such as the prior experience and legal background of the ECJ judges and advocates-general, the legal and judicial culture in which they were trained, their political and moral opinions, and their language skills. A broader notion of the context of discovery would include all aspects that influence the judicial decision but are not strictly part of a rational reconstruction of the decision in terms of justification. These formal aspects include many procedural rules or ideas deeply rooted in judicial culture and which are built into the judicial decision-making process at the Court: the role the legal community assigns to the Court, the level of consensus regarding certain sources of law, the self-understanding of the role of the Court, etc. Many of these factors are meant to guide the judicial method. Thus it is important to know at what stage the judge rapporteur is expected to dive into the case file, or whether any other agent at the Court has taken a preliminary look at the case before the rapporteur, or what happens at the Court when the case raises complex questions which require an understanding of domestic law, and so on.

It would be an unfair caricature to say that all these factors belong to the psychological realm, but all factors that can be included in the context of discovery have in common that they do not make their way into the written judgment. The written judgment is expected to give sufficient acceptable reasons to support the decision. Hence, the test of acceptability (and rationality) of judicial decisions has to be made from a different level of analysis of judicial decision-making, from the context of justification which refers to the process whereby a decision can be tested or justified. Here the focus is on the steps and the requirements that have to be met in order to consider that the decision is justified in law. The core of this process of justification is logical, that is, the jump from normative and factual premises to a conclusion (the decision) by deduction. In particular, judges will relate the established facts of a case—the minor premise—to the universal fact-descriptions of legally valid norm(s)—the major premise—and derive the conclusion by subsumption. The context of justification claims to be motivationally free, for logic and valid law are criteria to test the justification (and validity) of the decision.

The clear-cut distinction between the context of discovery and the context of justification, and the sufficiency of deductive logic in the process of justification, are true at least for clear and unproblematized cases where the formulation of the premises is straightforward. Some cases brought before the ECJ can still be characterized as clear in the sense either that the solution is not difficult to agree upon or that there is a settled case law on the point. But the

---

[4] J. Bengoetxea, *The Legal Reasoning of the European Court of Justice* (1993), 114.

majority of the cases before the Court—especially references for preliminary rulings on validity or interpretation of EC law—are hard.

The objection is then that the justification of clear cases has been adopted by the legal community and the dominant legal culture as the paradigm of judicial justification,[5] and this to such an extent that in some legal systems there is no particularly strong pressure on the judges to spell out how they have come to formulate the premises the way they have. Whereas this situation may go relatively smoothly in clear cases where the premises have not been problematized by the parties or even if they have, where the solution is not genuinely difficult, it will certainly cause difficulties when facing hard cases: deductive justification will then be necessary but it will not suffice. How then are problem cases to be justified? By providing sufficient (acceptable) reasons for the premises.

The fact that the paradigm of justification is deductive is a matter that belongs to the wider context of discovery but which influences the justification of the decision. Indeed, if the expectation is that the written judgment should present the decision as a subsumption of the facts of the case into a legal provision, then the interpretation of the legal provision may become a secondary issue. On the contrary, if the contentious issue is how the Court constructs written law, then the deductive aspect of the decision will almost go unnoticed. This dichotomy is reflected in appeal cases—*pourvoi*—before the Court, where the parties often stress each of their individual heads of claim and particular arguments so much that the structure of the reasoning leading to the judgment is out of sight. The control exercised by the ECJ also follows this scheme and enquires only whether the CFI wrongly interpreted the law, instead of also looking at the logical cogency of its ruling. Such aspects of judicial culture are crucial, but they are not normally spelt out when analysing judicial decision-making.

A nuance should therefore be introduced into the distinction between discovery and justification: there are aspects of procedure, or even of judicial culture, which are categorized neither as discovery nor as justification, but which affect both. Indeed, the requirements and the process of justification are better understood when both factors of discovery and factors of justification can be taken into account. These aspects could perhaps be contemplated as belonging to a context of explanation.

3. The Model of Judicial Decision-Making: The Subdecisions

The need for procedural rules to regulate the decision-making process is self-evident: they guide the decision-making process and ensure that any decision—justified or unjustified—is reached by a given process. The rights of litigants are thus safeguarded to an important extent, and deliberation of the

---

[5] J. Bengoetxea, *The Legal Reasoning of the European Court of Justice* (1993), 116.

Court will only take place after the Advocate General has delivered a reasoned opinion on the case, which will close the oral phase. The judges will have had a close look at the case on at least three different occasions before they start deliberating: when deciding on the administrative aspects of the case on the basis of a preliminary report prepared by the judge rapporteur; at the oral hearing, after the written arguments of the parties and interveners and their replies to possible questions put to them by the Court have been summarized by the judge rapporteur in the report for the hearing or otherwise; if there is no hearing, when examining the written report of the judge rapporteur; and finally when analysing the Advocate-General's opinion. All these steps are clearly guided by the rules of procedure and by a continued practice of the Court.

The judge rapporteur and the Advocate-General will know all the relevant details of the case, in practice, and all the judges sitting in the chamber will have heard the arguments put forward by the main parties to the case and by any intervening EU institutions and Member States (the Commission systematically intervenes and provides normally helpful orientations). There is thus an elaborate methodology for working towards the final decision. Of course, these procedural rules cannot determine what kinds of argument can be put to the Court, but they determine who can bring them forward, how, and at what stage of the procedure.

The following model does not try to describe either the context of discovery or the context of justification of the Court's decision-making process. It simply attempts to identify important moments of the judicial decision-making process, and to show how discovery and justification interrelate in the justification of preliminary rulings. To this aim several sub-decisions or steps are differentiated; in every step aspects of discovery, procedure, and justification will be pointed out in the following way: aspects of discovery are presented by *D;* aspects of procedure by *P;* and aspects of justification by *J.*

Step 0. The legal problem (*P*)

The case begins when a dispute is presented to the Court by the parties or by the referring court in one Member State. Procedural rules determine how this reference is to be lodged. In preliminary references, the dispute concerning Community law will normally be part of a wider legal issue involving the application of the internal law of the Member State. When the reference arrives, it is important to know how it will be processed by the Registrar's office. The first thing to do is to translate the full text of the reference (or the heads of claim in direct actions) into all the remaining official languages. When the case is lodged, the Member States and the EU institutions are informed about it in case they wish to make any observations and intervene. The wider public is also informed about the case because the text of the preliminary question or, in direct actions, a summary of the heads of claim of the parties is published in the Official Journal. A small, seemingly unimportant, and provincial case might turn into a fundamental law issue throughout the whole Union, and then the reference becomes a fresh opportunity to make new law.

Step 1. Categorizing the legal problem (*P, D*)

The Registrar and the Research and Documentation Division take an initial look at the reference in a technical note and pre-examine or categorize the case, looking for: (i) possible precedents that may help decide the case or that the Court may decide to send to the referring court in case it should wish to withdraw its reference and apply the doctrine of *acte clair*; (ii) other related cases pending before the Court in case the proceedings should be stayed or, if the pending cases have not proceeded very far yet, all the similar existing cases should be joined for the purposes of the written arguments, the oral pleadings, the opinion of the Advocate-General, the deliberation, or even the judgment, or at least discussed, pleaded, and deliberated in parallel; (iii) points of national law which may need clarifying; or even (iv) further factual information about the dispute before the national court. The President will assign the case to a judge rapporteur and the First Advocate General will attribute the case to one of the Advocates General. The rapporteur and the Advocate General responsible for the case will suggest to the Court any procedural or administrative decision on the case on the points highlighted above (i–iv).

Categorizing a case is not a straightforward matter, and it is rather important because it may determine how Member States and even the institutions or even the legal community will consider the case. To give only one example, *Martínez Sala* (case C-85/96, judgment of 12 May 1998) is a judgment that raises fundamental questions on citizenship of the European Union, and yet it has almost passed unnoticed largely because it has always been seen and categorized as a case concerning social security. The citizenship issue did not come up until the hearing, and even then few Member States intervened, considering it a side-issue. The judgment only discusses the citizenship issue in the final question and *obiter dictum*. Reading only the dispositif would provide no clue about the crucial issue being decided, i.e. that the status of citizenship of the Union confers in itself, once the residence rights have been acquired, a right not to be discriminated against on the basis of nationality, no other Treaty connection or Community element being necessary. This case will only attain its true significance when it starts working as a precedent, or when it is distinguished in subsequent judgments on references raising the citizenship issue.

Step 2. Identifying the applicable rules (*D*)

The Court has to identify all the legal items which might be relevant to the case. An underpinning theory of law (of sources, provisions, norms, legal systems) operates at this stage. This is an aspect of discovery which has to be incorporated into a rational reconstruction of the judgment but which is not an aspect of formal justification. It is important to discover how the legal provisions that may apply to the case are found out. The parties or interveners will plead some of them, but the Court can decide to categorize the case in a different way and choose different provisions as potentially governing the case. Again, some of the provisions alleged by the parties may have been amended, and the issue will be which is the valid provision at the time.

The background theory of law will also determine what type of provision can be chosen for application. For instance, the relevance of so-called 'soft law' should be analysed. Some of the instruments produced by the regular law-making institutions—e.g. recommendations, opinions, guidelines, communications—are not listed as official sources of EC law. The Court will research any relevant material, but it will select those materials that carry authoritative weight. In the end, only the official material which can be turned into 'authority reasons' will become the legal ground for decision (major premise), whereas the rest of the 'soft' material will only feature as an aid to interpretation or as additional reasons confirming the proposed reading of the official material. Which legal items does the Court take into consideration when defining the legal problem? These items will circumscribe the legal framework of the dispute, but will be only (the official) part of the wider concept of the legal system which will be in operation at the background. There will be other important elements which are not always made explicit but which are seen as part of the legal system. The role of principles and values is particularly important at this point.

When trying to sort out the provisions, classical problems of the legal system may appear: (i) where no provision seems to govern the case at hand one talks about gaps in the law; (ii) where more than one provision seem to govern the case one talks about redundancies; (iii) if these provisions lead to different legal solutions one talks about antinomies (intra-systemic or inter-systemic); but (iv) even where only one provision seems to govern the case it may be that the proper meaning of this provision is not clear and one will have to face problems of interpretation. The difficulties concerning the choice of the applicable provision will have to be addressed already at this stage. From a hermeneutic point of view, the choice of the applicable provisions is crucial because the rest of the reasoning process will depend on the selected provision. This operation can be complex and can take a considerable amount of time from the point of view of discovery, but none of these complications need be reflected in the justification.

In practice, the parties will have invoked several provisions as potentially applicable to the case and will have put forward their interpretive contentions from the selected provisions, but it may be that the ECJ has its own idea on which provisions should be applied. If it discovers its own idea soon enough, it will alert the parties and interveners and request new observations and contentions on those provisions. But if the change of focus occurs at a later stage the final justificatory reasoning may bear little resemblance to the contentions elaborated in the pleadings.

If one takes the view that the Court should not depart from the claims presented by the parties and interveners, then one will probably blame the Court for engaging in judicial activism. On the contrary, if one assumes that the Court is expected to know the law, then the choice of a different applicable provision will be seen as the proper exercise of judicial function.

Step 3. Introducing the major premise (J)

When the provisionally or vocationally applicable provision or set of provisions is selected, the major premise will be identified. As a matter of justification one is not really interested in the process that actually led to the choice of the applicable provisions. These will normally coincide with those provisions which the referring court, the parties to the main proceedings, and the intervening parties (especially the Commission) will have identified as applicable. But sometimes the legal issue is precisely which are the relevant provisions, in which case these can only be identified once a tentative and provisional classification of the relevant facts and interpretation of the potentially applicable provision is carried out; and then as a matter of heuristics or discovery the final presentation of the major premise will take place only after other potentially applicable provisions have been mentally discarded.

Step 4. Deciding on the validity of the chosen provision (J)

It is clear that the provision selected as applicable to the case has to be valid. The validity of the provision is not usually contested, but when the reference turns on the validity of a provision contained in a secondary source, then the issue cannot be avoided. Some questions of validity are dressed up as questions of interpretation for legal procedural reasons: the Court has no jurisdiction, under preliminary references, to rule on the compatibility of domestic law with Community law, and therefore the references enquiring about the validity of a provision of the law of a Member State will be reformulated as questions on the interpretation of Community law.

Step 5. Deciding on the need to interpret (D)

When the Court has selected one provision of Community law as applicable to the case at hand, it will have to decide whether that provision needs interpreting in a strict sense or whether it is sufficiently clear for application from the ordinary meaning of its terms. If there is doubt as to the proper meaning to be given to a provision, then a decision of interpretation in the strict sense has to be made. If there is no doubt, the provision will almost unconsciously be converted into a norm, and the process from provision to norm will be almost automatic. The test is thus whether the Court has any difficulty with the interpretation of the selected provisions. The distinction between clear cases and hard cases is pragmatic. Cases are problematized or clarified depending on different circumstances. Complex questions may have received consistent lines of precedents and become clarified (e.g. Sunday trading[6] as compared to *Keck and Mithouard*),[7] whereas apparently simple issues may become very difficult (e.g. *Swedish Monopoly on the retail of alcoholic beverages*).[8] The question thus becomes whether the interpreter has doubts regarding the law.

It is often said that there is always interpretation, and it can even be said that if there is a reference for a preliminary ruling this must be because the case is, *per se*, difficult. Yet the Court has developed an interesting doctrine on clarity in *Da Costa*[9] and *CILFIT*.[10] According to it, when a norm is clear, no interpretation is required: 'the application of Community law may be so obvious as to leave no scope for any reasonable doubt as to the manner in which the question raised is to be solved' (para. 16, *CILFIT*). However, if one accepts that clarity is impossible in theory, since a statement can be clear only after it has

---

[6] See e.g. *Torfaen Borough Council v. B&Q plc*, 145/88 [1989] ECR 3851. The question of interpretation of Article 28 EC (ex Article 30) had been solved in *Dassonville*, 8/74, [1974] ECR 837, and the problem in each of the Sunday trading cases where retail shops were not allowed to open on Sundays was only whether that ban had a restrictive effect on intra-Community trade, which was really a question of fact that could not possibly be solved by the Court's interpretation of the law.

[7] Joined Cases 267/91, and 268/91 *Keck and Mithouard*, [1993] ECR 6097. In *Keck and Mithouard* the Court pointed out that an increasing number of cases rely on the infringement of Article 28 EC (ex Article 30). To avoid such an overuse the Court considered it necessary to re-examine and clarify its case law (*Cassis de Dijon*, Case C-120/78, *Rewe-Zentral v. Bundesmonopolverwaltung für Branntwein*, [1979] ECR 649, and Case 8/74, *Dassonville*, [1974] ECR 837). It interpreted *Dassonville* by introducing a new distinction between rules relating to the product and rules relating to the marketing of the product. Whereas the first group was likely to have a restrictive effect upon intra-Community trade, the second in principle did not because they apply equally to internal products and to imports. Yet the possibility was left open to demonstrate a restrictive effect even in the second group of cases.

[8] Case 189/95, *Franzén*, [1997] ECR I-5909, concerned the compatibility of statutory monopolies with EC law and in particular with Articles 28 and 31 EC (ex Articles 30 and 37). The focus was, as in Joined Cases *Keck and Mithouard*, on the interpretation of precedents, and in particular Case 91/75, *Hauptzollamt Göttingen v. Miritz*, [1976] ECR 217, *Cassis de Dijon*, Case C-120/78, *Rewe-Zentral v. Bundesmonopolverwaltung für Branntwein*, [1979] ECR 649, and Case 91/78, *Hansen v. Hauptzollamt Flensburg*, [1979] ECR 935. However, instead of applying in a straightforward way the ruling contained in these cases, the Court decided that the aim of Article 29 EC (ex Article 31) was to reconcile the existence of monopolies of a commercial character as instruments to pursue public interest aims with the requirements of the common market. Whether or not such public interest was pursued by establishing an alcohol monopoly, and whether or not the measure was discriminatory, became the main focus of the case.

[9] Case 28-30/62, *Da Costa en Schaake NV v. Nederlandse Belanstingadministratie*, [1963] ECR 31.

[10] Case 283/81, *CILFIT Srl v. Ministero della Sanità*, [1982] ECR 3415.

being interpreted, what is the function of the *acte clair* doctrine?[11] First, a reference to a clear norm counts as a reference to a sufficient authority reason to justify the decision. In other words, to say that a norm is clear means to avoid giving more arguments to justify the validity of the norm or its meaning. Second, the doctrine of *acte clair* provides a criterion to distribute the work between courts where interpretation and application are organically and institutionally distinguished. This is the case with national courts and the ECJ regarding the interpretation of Community law. By the *acte clair* doctrine the Court guarantees its monopoly in the interpretation of Community law.[12]

The parties may try to problematize the interpretation especially as a problem of qualification as in the *Sunday trading* case. One judge may have no special difficulty but the rest of the judges may find problems. Where the judicial organ is a collegiate one, the situation of doubt is a more plausible outcome. Many cases of interpretation reach the Court precisely because there are difficulties which the referring Court is not happy to solve for itself. Again, the parties will most probably have problematized the issue by calling for contending interpretations. It can also be the case that the Advocate General detects new difficulties. For instance, a case is being discussed as a pure question of provision of services or establishment and the issue is focused by the Advocate-General as a completely different one about citizenship or fundamental rights issue. Finally, the Court may find problems that no other agent has detected before. *Keck and Mithouard* is a good example in this sense. The Advocate-General gave two opinions and the pleadings never touched the basic line of (almost esoteric) reasoning adopted by the Court.

Step 6. Interpreting the chosen provision (*J*)

When there are difficulties regarding the meaning of the selected provision, it will have to be interpreted in the strict sense. The Court will opt for one interpretation amongst the many possible ones and will be expected to justify why it has chosen the interpretation it has. Within this step there may be many heuristic aspects of the interpretative process. The judge or the Court mentally tests different proposed interpretations. The arguments that make it to the reasoning are categorized as justification. Again, from the justificatory point of view it is irrelevant how the judge arrives at certain arguments which

---

[11] Bengoetxea, *Legal Reasoning*, n. 5 above, 204.

[12] If a national court has doubt as to how to interpret Community law it may refer the question to the ECJ. However, given that a preliminary question will delay the whole procedure, the national judge may decide not to refer any question. If that occurs, national courts will capitalize the interpretation of Community law and jeopardize the role of the ECJ. To bypass this problem, the *acte clair* doctrine establishes that when the ECJ has made a ruling on exactly the same point then there is no need for national courts to request new interpretations (ibid.). Moreover, the *Foto-Frost* case is an example of how the Court monopolizes the control of validity of Community law provisions (Case 311/85, *Foto-Frost*, [1987] ECR 4199).

support a particular decision. Rather, the question is whether the selected argument is a meaningful interpretation and whether the Court provides good reasons for it.

The first question one has to raise is about the nature of the arguments of interpretation. Here we distinguish between arguments of interpretation and categories of arguments (see Table 3.1). Categories of arguments suggest what has to be looked at, e.g. the language, the context or functions. Arguments of interpretation suggest how one has to assign meaning within each category to that which is looked at. Arguments of interpretation can be (i) normative, in which case one talks about interpretive rules, principles, directives, or norms; (ii) methodological guidelines, in which case one talks about methods, reasons, criteria, or sources of interpretation; finally, (iii) axiologically normative (or second-degree arguments), in which case one talks about ideologies, theories, styles or doctrines of interpretation which try to further certain values.

Arguments of interpretation are first-order arguments which tell how to use each of the categories, e.g. functional argument: 'choose the interpretation which will serve to further the aim sought by the norm, or sought by the wider set of norms' (useful effect, *effet utile*). Second-order arguments try to rank the different arguments by establishing order of preference: 'if there is a conflict between the ordinary meaning of a provision and the useful effect of this provision, always choose the useful effect.'[13]

The underlying rationale is to be found in a certain view of the rule of law and on important systemic principles, combined with dynamic arguments. Interpretation ultimately takes us into a broader sphere of practical argumentation where the values and principles appropriate to the institutions of the societies, the states, and the supranational and international communities are taken into account: questions such as the meaning of constitutionalism or *Rechtsstaatslichkeit*, democracy and the rule of law, the separation of powers, the distribution of competences, procedural justice, the protection of individual and fundamental rights, citizenship, equality before and under the law, and the integrity of public office.[14]

The process whereby the selected provision (major premise) is properly construed from an institutional standpoint into the applicable norm (the interpreted major premise, ready for application) is not really governed by any procedural or other type of rules. From Step 3 to Step 7, the written judgment

---

[13] Take the question of direct effect of Directives. For some purposes the Court has gone beyond the strict or literal meaning of Article 249(3) EC (ex Article 189) on Directives. It has refused *a contrario* reasoning from the second paragraph on regulations. Yet it has relied on a rather strict construction as regards horizontal direct effects. Again, when interpreting the notion of State for the purposes of vertical direct effect the ECJ has adopted a very wide notion, not strictly based on linguistic arguments but rather on *effet utile*.

[14] N. MacCormick, 'Argumentation and Interpretation in Law', (1995) 9 Argumentation 479.

Table 3.1

Categories	Arguments	Values
Linguistic or semiotic	Language versions Ordinary meaning EC law meaning	Certainty Rule of law

Systemic or contextual	*Sedes materiae*
	Quasi-logical:
	    a fortiori
	    a pari
	    ad absurdum
	    analogy
	    a contrario
	    etc.
	Antinomy solution criteria
	Competence criteria
	Économie (the ratio of the system)
		System autonomy
		System integrity
		System consistency

Dynamic	Teleological[a] Functional Consequences[b]	Integrity integration Coherence

[a] It is argued that teleological arguments are used by the Court *par excellence*. The reason is to be found in the nature of the normative material the Court has to interpret, namely the EU Treaties, which are a cluster of common objectives, policies, and aims.

[b] Under the category 'arguments on consequences' both consequences as repercussions and consequences as juridical implications should be considered (Bengoetxea, *Legal Reasoning*, 256–7). Case 43/75, *Defrenne v. SABENA*, [1976] ECR 455, provides a good example of the role of both kinds of consequentialist consideration in judicial justification. Consequences as repercussions justified the interpretation of Article 141 EC (ex Article 119) on equal pay for men and women. The Court established that its judgment, which admitted that the principle had been breached in many Member States, could not be invoked to support claims for periods of retribution prior to the judgment. The reason was to avoid a flood of actions against Member States which fail to comply with Article 141 EC, since these actions would have provoked important economic losses. Consequences as juridical implications were also at stake. The widespread breach of the principle of equal pay was due to the lack of vigilance by the Commission: 'The fact that . . . the Commission did not initiate proceedings under Article 169 [new 226 EC] against the Member States concerned on grounds of failure to fulfil an obligation was likely to consolidate the incorrect impression as to the effects of Article 119 [new Article 141 EC]' (para. 73). The judgment hit the target: the Commission started to do its job properly and brought a number (an avalanche, as Mancini says) of actions against failing Member States (F. Mancini, 'From CILFIT to ERT: The Constitutional Challenge Facing the European Court', (1991) Yearbook of European Law 10). In the interpretation of Article 230(4) on individual *locus standi* the strict construction has had important juridical implications: it has limited the number of actions challenging Community acts and has enhanced the discretion of the Community institutions when adopting and applying policies.

need not be very explicit unless there is a problem of interpretation. The institutional context in which this process takes place is judicial deliberation which is not subject to scrutiny.

Step 7. Stating the law (*J*)

The major premise is finally formulated in such a manner that it covers the facts of the case. This requires the Court to have looked at the facts of the case (as settled and established or postulated by the referring court, which the ECJ cannot question), to have selected those facts that are relevant, and finally to have legally classified or qualified these facts, so that the major premise is formulated with a view to covering them, making a universal statement that does not name the particular facts but that can refer to any other particular facts materially similar to the particular facts of the case.

The ECJ might, however, choose a wider or more general formulation of the facts so that the universalizable norm it formulates as the major premise (as it will appear in the judgment as the ratio) can cover other facts as well. The risk in these occasions is that the Court makes too general a universalizable statement which may become a cumbersome precedent which it will later try to distinguish and to limit to its more original proportions. That is what happened in *Emmott*[15] on time-limits to initiate judicial proceedings within the Member States. If the ECJ sticks to the formulation which simply universalizes from the particular facts but does not try to make more general statements, then its judgments will perhaps not look so grand, but they will give clearer guidelines to the legal community. In a legal system like the EC that operates with a strong theory of precedent, it is very important to adopt a correct formulation of the major premise which could in principle operate in all the Member States and not only in the Member State of the reference.

Step 8. Establishing the facts (*P, J*)

In references for preliminary rulings on interpretation, in theory and as a matter of procedure, the facts are not at issue. But the ECJ takes extreme care in presenting the factual background of the case in order to draft a rule that will

---

[15] Case 208/90, *Emmott*, [1991] ECR 4269. In the *Emmott* case the Court established that Member States which fail to implement a Directive cannot rely on national procedural rules setting time limits for initiating proceedings to claim the rights following from the Directive. Such a general universalizable rule caused consternation because it opened the door to a flood of retrospective claims, even when Member States had acted on *bona fides* by relying on internal law. Indeed, time would not start to run until the provisions of the Directive had been correctly transposed into internal law. The Court later had to narrow down the rule, e.g. C-335/91, *Steenhorst-Neerings*, [1993] ECR I-5475. In C-312/93, *Peterbroek*, [1995] ECR I-4599, the Court said that national rules on time limits must be analysed with reference to the role of those rules in the procedure taken as a whole, its progress and special features. The basic principles of domestic legal system, such as protection of the rights of the defence, the principle of legal certainty, and the proper conduct of the procedure, can also be taken into account.

eventually work as a precedent. The facts will be distilled from the actual case situation and formulated in a universalizable formula, a ratio that can be applied in any Member State jurisdiction.

The qualification or classification of the facts into legal concepts and categories can be understood in this way. A good example is provided by Case 55/94, *Gebhard,* [1995] ECR 4165. The question was framed in terms of services but the Court requalified the circumstances of the case in terms of establishment. A lawyer qualified as a *Rechtsanwalt* in Germany can be established and exercise her profession in Italy even if she has not acquired the proper Italian title of *avvocato* and therefore cannot perform the full functions of an *avvocato.* The Court devoted its judgment to ruling under what conditions a person can be considered as established in a particular Member State. The case illustrates that the Court is bound by the facts of the case, as established by the referring organ—in this case the Italian Bar council—but it is not bound by the qualification of those facts which the referring organ has adopted and which is a matter of law, not fact.

Step 9. The syllogism (*P, J*)

This final step consists in drawing the conclusion of the syllogism. Legal reasoning is in a very important way deductive. Deduction does not solve the whole justification question but it works as a negative test: if the decision does not follow from the accepted premises, then it can be said not to be justified.

Of course, there are factors that affect the thought process of the Court but which the Court does not reflect in its judgments. These include the consequences which have to be drawn, the reasonability of the conclusion, and the efficiency of the judgment. Imagine that the Court draws a conclusion that it does not really like or approve of or which it thinks odd. From the discovery point of view, if this is the case, it may go back to the choice of a different potentially applicable provision (e.g. by attempting a different classification of the facts), or it may interpret the selected provisions in a different way and derive a different norm from them and thus formulate the major premise in a different way. But all this is in the context of discovery, and it is very likely that these processes will occur only at the Advocate General's or the judge rapporteur's chambers when suggesting a given line. Once the major premise of the reasoning is set out as a matter of justification, the consequences, efficiency, or reasonability of the proposed interpretation may feature as reasons for choosing or rejecting a given interpretation. This takes us to the important distinction between internal and external justification.

B. Internal and External Justification

We have already put forward the claim that deductive justification is a negative test of justification: if the decision does not follow from the premises it will not be justified. Deductive justification is necessary. However it is not sufficient. For a judgment to be justified, all the steps leading to the decision have to be justified as well: all the sub-decisions leading to the major premises have to be justified. These are the choice of the relevant provisions, the test of validity, the decision of interpretation, and those sub-decisions leading to the minor premise: classification of the relevant facts. Deductive reasoning will be of little help when justifying the choice of one rather than another interpretation. Other reasons will have to be provided, and these reasons have to be acceptable in the law. If the Court gives reasons for each of its decisions (premises), and if the final decision follows from the accepted premises, then the judgment is justified. At least it is internally justified. A completely different story is whether the judgment is correctly justified, but this is a problem concerning external justification.

Indeed, the distinction between internal and external justification is not always easy to grasp. The claim of internal justification is that the judgment is justified 'in law'. An external justification makes a stronger claim: not only is the judgment justified in law, but it is also a correct decision in practical philosophy; it is ethically, politically, or ideologically acceptable; it is valid. Internal justification does not go beyond system validity. External justification is not exclusively relative to the legal system. To say that the judgment is justified from an external point of view is to make a claim as to rational acceptability—the decision has respected formal reasons or discourse reasons—or even a claim as to material or substantive rightness—the decision is the right answer, not only in law but also in political morality. Of course, a decision that is not internally justified will not be externally justified either, but being internally justified does not prejudge external validity or rationality.

To assess the correctness of internal justification, two features, at least, deserve attention: the validity of the law and the criteria of validity of the justification. An essential requirement of internal legal justification is the validity of the legal provision which is applied. The major premise has to describe a valid normative proposition. In this sense, a doctrine of the sources of law (the ranking of these) is in operation. As regards gaps in the legal system, there is a certain doctrine of implied competences and subsidiarity. As regards antinomies, the doctrine of the sources and their ranking applies again.

Ultimately any connection with a Treaty provision (or more directly with a valid instrument of Community law) will constitute a sufficient internal justification basis, since they do not require any further internal justification (authority reasons need no justification). The validity of certain Community law provisions, such as Treaty provisions, cannot be challenged.[16] They are

---

[16] The only institutionally accepted form of practical argument questioning treaty provisions is in the context of an Inter-governmental Conference of the Member States, leading to a possible reform of the questioned provision.

absolute reasons of authority and become the standard against which other provisions are weighed. Interpretation will be resorted to in order to reshape the contours of a Treaty provision which is found to be dubious. However, its validity goes unquestioned. It is not true, therefore, that everything can be questioned in judicial decision-making; if one wishes to engage in practical argumentation about those reasons of authority, one has to step out of the established legal order. By contrast, the Court can strike down a provision of secondary Community law.

In theory the Court can also interpret a Community law provision in a way that in practice renders incompatible a conflicting provision of a Member State's constitution. Of course, this does mean that a practical (legal) argumentation can take place in an institutional and judicial setting where the validity of domestic constitutional norms can be questioned, something which is impossible within the Member States. The reactions of many Member States' constitutional courts are perfectly understandable: under constitutional doctrine, a constitutional norm, which lies at the hierarchy of the legal system, cannot possibly be questioned internally in a judicial setting (only in the context of constitutional reform). Yet an absolute authority reason of the domestic legal system *can be questioned* before the Court, and this does cause constitutional havoc. In the process, the constitutional norm of the Member State loses its absolute authority reason character.[17] Not only can the protectionist reaction of some Member State constitutional courts be understood, but also we would agree that the Court has itself adopted a similar protectionist attitude regarding the unquestionability of Treaty provisions. Thus in Opinion 2/94, [1996] ECR I-1759, regarding the accession to the European Convention for Human Rights, the Court opined that, at the stage of Community law at the time, in 1996 before the entry into force of the Amsterdam Treaty, the Community lacked the competence to become a party to the European Convention of Human Rights, with the consequence that the authority reasons of Community law could not be challenged before any court.[18]

Along with the validity of legal provisions, the criteria of internal validity will assess the correctness of internal justification. Which are the criteria of

---

[17] Examples where this has happened are the cases concerning Luxembourg (C-473/93, *Commission v. Luxembourg,* [1996] ECR I-3207), Belgium (C-173/94, *Commission v. Belgium,* [1996] ECR I-3265), and Greece (C-290/94, *Commission v. Greece* [1996] ECR I-3285) on the nationality condition required for certain posts in the public service, the Luxembourg case being particularly relevant.

[18] This opinion can be interpreted as follows: in order for a Treaty provision to be assessed against an external legal standard of validity—i.e. the ECHR—Member States must have given the EC explicit or at least implicit competence on human rights issues. The Court said that such a step is too fundamental from a constitutional point of view to be taken without competence. Indeed, it would amount to losing the character of absolute authority reasons.

internal validity? When can the decision be said to be justified in law? It would be interesting to detect or distil the criteria that the ECJ itself would have elaborated had it set out to address precisely that question (rational reconstruction). This reconstruction could use several sources. In some of its judgments the Court has stated which are its criteria of interpretation, or it has even set out directives of interpretation: the *acte clair* cases, the cases concerning incomplete references (inadmissible ones), or even the Court's notice to national courts as to how to draft the references, and especially the *CILFIT* doctrine.[19] Other important sources that provide criteria of internal validity are the appeal cases where the Court has controlled the quality of the justification adopted by the CFI (some of them are staff cases). These are truly useful materials. A final source are the writings of the members of the Court, or the talks they give, especially to judges visiting the Court.[20]

If it were possible rationally to reconstruct the Court's doctrine of justification, then one could say that when its own criteria are respected, the decision is justified internally, in the EC legal system. These criteria of validity are useful not only because they provide a valid internal justification in judicial decision-making; they are also instrumental in assessing the ECJ itself on its own standards.

The model of internal justification sketched above is not enough: choices concerning the (legally) valid applicable provision, the criterion of interpretation to be adopted, the meaning to be given to the law, and in general the correctness of all premises which support a particular decision need further justification. That is a matter of external justification which implies substantive reasons (values, principles, and policies) postulating the adequacy of authority reasons and the correctness of the decision. Of course, when approaching external justification one can also take into account the fact that the judgment is internally justified, a fact which in itself already carries an important prima facie institutional value of respect for the rule of law and for the rationality of judicial decision-making. The analysis of the external level of justification focuses on how the different parts of the reasoning hang together and make sense as a whole, and on how the very aims of the EC law enterprise are furthered by the actual decision. This requires taking account of all elements of the legal system, but also of normative constitutional and political theories. To undertake this task a background theory of coherence or integrity and a notion of integration are required.

---

[19] In *CILFIT* the Court reduces the abuse of *acte clair* doctrine by setting out the requirements under which a preliminary ruling should be sought by the domestic courts of last instance.

[20] Twice yearly the Court organizes a stage for the judges and higher judges of the Member States, and occasionally the Court holds separate working sessions with the constitutional courts of the Member States.

III BALANCING REASONS: THE RELEVANCE OF COHERENCE

A. Conflict of Reasons

The best example of the content of external justification is provided by conflicts of reasons. In a good number of cases—if not all—the interpretation and application of the law is a matter of making and justifying choices between colliding arguments, colliding interpretations, colliding rules, values, principles, or even policies. All these are examples of conflicts of reasons the solution of which requires a coherent justification. In this sense a notion of coherence, i.e. a notion of what is 'making sense as a whole', is needed.

The idea of universal rules, the application of which provides a clear and definitive solution for every single case, is controversial. This is especially true when reasons collide. One way of solving the conflict of reasons is by applying a universal rule which establishes a systematic priority among colliding reasons. This guarantees the unity of practical legal reasoning and the predictability of judicial decisions. However, it may lead to absurd results: the rule of formal justice, for example, justifies similar cases being decided in a similar way, however unjust the result may be. The major objection against applying such universal rules to solve conflicts of reasons is that by so doing, both the value pluralism and the importance that each reason has in a particular case are disregarded. By value pluralism it is meant that values and principles cannot be reduced to a single value or coherent set of values, nor should conflicts between reasons be interpreted as an imperfection, but rather as 'the normal state for human beings'.[21] By the importance of the particular it is meant that instead of looking for universal rules, an alternative way of solving conflicts of reasons would be by appraising the weight or importance of colliding reasons in particular cases—this would take into account the particularity of the situation.

In this way conflicts of reasons are solved by striking a balance between all values, principles, and norms involved in the particular case. The notion of balancing reasons must be clarified. Value pluralism and the relevance of the particular case are embraced as crucial features of a coherent account of legal reasoning. Consequently, the idea of 'balancing reasons' as appraising the weight of each reason according to a pre-established metric system (a universal rule, or reduced set of values) should be abandoned.[22] The practical question 'what to do?' moves from 'what to do according to the rules?' towards 'what to do according to the rules in a particular case?'

---

[21] J. Raz, 'The Relevance of Coherence', in *Ethics in the Public Domain: Essays in the Morality of Law and Politics* (1994), 301.

[22] 'Balancing reasons' means to appraise the importance, force, or weight of a reason according to the other colliding reasons in the particular case.

How does one appraise the importance of reasons? The fact that balancing does not refer to a pre-established (metric) system to appraise the importance of reasons does not mean that balancing is an arbitrary practical exercise. Criteria are provided for the weighing. Unlike universal rules, which establish a systematic priority among reasons, balancing criteria do not rely on the idea of unity. Unlike universal rules, balancing criteria do not instruct the judge as to which value or set of values should be used to solve a conflict of reasons; rather, they instruct judges on how to deal with and solve the conflict. In other words, balancing criteria do not provide the answer but they provide tools to find it. In this sense, it is argued that balancing criteria play an over-whelming function in practical legal reasoning: they organize the balancing. The notion of balancing which has been introduced does not reject, however, a theory of coherence. On the contrary, it is argued that balancing criteria play a second overwhelming function in practical legal reasoning: they promote the coherence of the legal system. Coherence is understood as *making connections* within a legal theory and between legal theory and moral and political theory, in order to appraise correctly the weight or importance of colliding reasons.[23]

The analysis of how the Court conducts the balancing exercise is particularly interesting for several reasons. First, the Court—unlike national courts such as the British House of Lords—is not reluctant to take account of policy considerations in its judgments. This guarantees the complexity of conflicts of reasons which involve not only legal norms and rights, but also community values and goals.[24] Second, the Court is engaged in constitutionalizing Community law and federalizing the European political system. This guarantees the link between interpreting the law and constitutional and political theory.

Special attention is paid to conflicts between market integration and environmental protection; since there is no hierarchical structure among these values, decisions are a matter of weighing and balancing. The Court provides three balancing criteria: the rule of reason, the test of proportionality, and the test of non-discrimination. The question we aim to answer is whether these criteria organize the balancing of reasons, and promote the coherence of the European legal system.

First, then, it is shown that the notion of coherence is linked to that of justification. This explains the importance of studying the legal reasoning of the Court. Second, four landmark judgments of the Court are discussed to analyse the criteria of rule of reason, proportionality, and non-discrimination. These show how the Court has been elaborating its notion of balancing.

---

[23] This notion of coherence is due to R. Alexy and A. Peczenik, 'The Concept of Coherence and Its Significance for Discursive Rationality', (1990) 3 Ratio Juris 130–47.

[24] In this sense, the more the features of a case are considered, the better the particular case can be described.

Third, we examine the question as to whether or not use of the above criteria promotes the coherence of European law.

B. Supporting Structure

What matters in judicial decision-making is not the kind of arguments used (authority reasons and substantive reasons) as much as whether or not the decision is justified. To justify is the activity of *supporting* by good *reasons* a particular statement. Legal justification is no different, for reasons have to be put for or against a particular judicial decision (or legal norm). Legal justification involves two kinds of reason: authority reasons—legal norms, precedents, and legal doctrine—and substantive reasons—values and principles which according to Summers include both rightness reasons and goal reasons.[25] These reasons justify, if there is a supportive structure between a set of reasons and a decision; that is, the reason *p* justifies *q* if *p* supports *q*. The supportive structure requires a connection between appealed reasons and the decision. This connection can be deductive, if *q* logically derives from *p*; the justifying connection can also be plausible if *q* cannot be logically derived from *p*, but both *q* and *p* fit together.[26] A supportive structure represents a relationship of coherence between reasons and decisions in terms of both logical consistency and fitting together.[27]

To analyse the legal reasoning of the Court means to analyse the supportive structure among premises and, therefore, their coherence. This is specially important when the supportive structure is based on plausible connections among premises, rather than deductive connections, as it happens in cases of balancing reasons (legal norms, precedents, values, rights, and goals). In these cases the Court has to create plausible connections, i.e. supportive structures, at two levels: first, between parts of the same legal system[28] and second, between legal theory and moral and political theory.[29] Coherence as making

[25] R. Summers, 'Two Types of Substantive Reasons: The Core of a Theory of Common Law Justification', (1978) 63 Cornell Law Review 716.

[26] A. Aarnio, *The Rational as Reasonable* (1987), 200. In the case of deductive connection, it is important that semantic identity should exist between the features described by the norm and the features of the particular case; in the case of plausible connection, what matters is whether or not the justification provided is relevant.

[27] The variety of metaphors to refer to substantive coherence is large: making sense as a whole (MacCormick, 'Coherence'), integrity (Dworkin, *Law's Empire*), tightly knit unit (A. Pezcenik, *The Basis of Legal Justification*) are only a few examples, see n. 3 above.

[28] For example, limits on free movement of goods are justified by Community goals such as environmental protection. Both free movement of goods and environmental protection belong to the same legal theory, even though they collide in particular cases.

[29] For example, the recognition of environmental protection as being an essential Community goal is justified by the political theory of the Court. This has allowed a move from economic integration—the original aim of the European treaties—towards political integration.

connections has at least two consequences in legal theory. First, the theory of coherence defended here is not a strong normative theory, since it does not hold that the legal system derives from a universal rule, or from a set of principles; second, it instructs judges to *make* connections rather than discover them. This requires an active role of the judiciary: it requires the Court coherently to reconstruct the legal system.

Judge David Edward, talking about the European Court of Justice's legal reasoning, says that 'the judge's role cannot be confined to that of providing a technocratic literal interpretation of texts produced by others. . . . the judge must proceed from one case to another seeking, as points come up for decision, to make the legal system consistent, coherent, workable and effective'.[30] This quotation suggests that in the attempt to reconstruct coherently the legal system judges adopt the 'insider' perspective. That is, judges (i) interpret existing legislation and precedents as forming a coherent set, and (ii) adjust the interpretation to the institutional morality of the community as it is seen by the judge. The insider perspective involves both receiving and modifying, or, in Dworkin's words, it involves being both an author and a critic of the chain novel.

C. Balancing Criteria

This understanding of the role of the judiciary excludes monistic notions of coherence. Rather than providing a universal rule which generates coherence by establishing a priority order among reasons,[31] several criteria of coherence guarantee that plausible connections among reasons can be established. This can be seen as the role to be attributed to the rule of reason, the test of proportionality, and the test of non-discrimination: three criteria used by the Court to solve conflicts of reasons in which economic freedoms are at stake.

1. The Rule of Reason

In the landmark Case 240/83, *Association de défense des brûleurs d'huiles usagés*, [1985] ECR 531 (*ADBHU* hereafter), the Court refers to the so-called 'rule of reason' to solve the conflict between economic integration and the

[30] D. Edward, 'Judicial Activism: Myth or Reality?', in A. I. L. Campbell and M. Voyatzi (eds.), *Legal Reasoning and Judicial Interpretation of European Law* (1996), 66–7.

[31] In the case of European law, economic efficiency was initially thought of as a universal rule which generates coherence in the legal system and in legal adjudication. It means that whether or not environmental protection was an objective of the Community was a matter to be appraised according to economic standards. Things have changed since European integration has been understood as something more than economic integration, when social, political, and constitutional concerns also came into play. The role of the Court changed in the sense that it was not enough to provide the most efficient economic solution. It was asked to combine all colliding interests—to generate coherence within a system of colliding interests.

protection of the environment. The case arose when a French tribunal referred a preliminary question to the Court concerning the validity of Directive 75/439/EEC on the disposal of waste oils. This Directive empowers Member States to control (and limit) the movement and disposal of waste oil for environmental purposes.[32] The French tribunal asked whether this competence was compatible with the economic rights to freedom of trade, free movement of goods, and free competition.[33]

The reasoning of the Court starts by adopting the 'rule of reason' as the major premise of the legal syllogism:[34] fundamental rights, such as freedom of trade, are not to be viewed in absolute terms, for limitations are justified by general interests pursued by the Community (para. 12). The rule of reason demands the striking of a balance between rights and goals; that is, the finding of a compromise between colliding rights and interests. The balance has to satisfy two further requirements: it must be proportional and non-discriminatory (para. 13). The Court then subsumes the facts of the *ADBHU* case into the major premise. Its reasoning is as follows: freedom of trade is not an absolute principle; environmental protection is an essential objective of the Community; the measures provided (control of the movement and disposal of waste oils) are neither disproportionate nor discriminatory; therefore, limits on freedom of trade are justified. The major contribution of the *ADBHU* judgment is that the Court establishes for the first time that environmental protection is an essential objective of the Community. This is also its main weakness.

Does the Court use the rule of reason as a criterion (i) to organize the balancing between rights and goals and (ii) to generate coherence?

The rule of reason organizes the reasoning of the Court in two ways. First, it establishes that applying fundamental rights (such as economic rights) in an absolute way may lead to irrational results. Attention has to be paid to the weight or importance of rights and other countervailing rights and interests in every particular case. Since rights are not thought of as all-or-nothing commands, in case of conflicts, legal reasoning becomes a matter of finding a compromise, that is, a matter of balancing. Second, the rule of reason determines what can be weighed against fundamental rights, namely common interests. This feature of the rule of reason is especially important in determining whether or not the Court succeeds in generating coherence.

The rule of reason instructs the Court to take account of community goals, and concludes that environmental protection is one of the Community's essential objectives (para. 13). Two objections may arise against this decision:

---

[32] For the purposes of European legislation, waste oil is considered a good.

[33] The French tribunal also referred to the Directive a second preliminary question as to whether the system of control of waste oil established by the French legislation was contrary.

[34] This rule was established in Case 120/78, *Cassis de Dijon*, [1979] ECR 649.

(i) by taking account of collective interests, rather than rights, is the Court doing wrong? (ii) by taking account of an objective—environmental protection—which was not contained in the EEC Treaty, has the Court illegitimately decided the case?

For Dworkin judges decide questions concerning rights (individual and collective).[35] In hard cases, continues Dworkin, judges do not have discretion to decide. Rather, they have to justify their decisions according to the institutional morality, that is the morality of the legal system.[36] Coherence, rather than the sort of reason, justifies a particular decision. This account of what judges legitimately do is not far from the reasoning of the Court in the *ADBHU* case. First, the Court takes account of policy considerations to apply rationally fundamental rights. Second, it recognizes that environmental protection as an essential goal of the Community is a strong policy consideration fully acceptable in legal reasoning, for it satisfies the requirement of universalizability, from the point of view of legal reasoning: it is enunciated in universal terms.[37]

The weakness of the *ADBHU* judgment is that the Court fails to justify why environmental protection is an essential objective of the Community. The absence of plausible connections between community interests and environmental protection undermines the coherence of the reasoning, for the Court fails to make connections between legal theory and moral and political theory. Such connections are crucial for the political (or constitutional) result of the judgment: the attribution of a new Community competence, and therefore the enhancement of Community powers. There is neither

---

[35] The legislature decides questions concerning policies. The differentiation is not based on a formal distinction between principles and policy reasons: it does not mean that judges have to consider arguments of rights and disregard arguments of policies, for both kinds of reason have justifying force in legal reasoning. The former is rather a differentiation concerning the kind of issue judges can legitimately decide upon (J. Bell, *Policy Arguments in Judicial Decisions* 1983: 207): matters of rights in opposition to matters of policies. The judiciary cannot undertake a political agenda, but this does not preclude it from taking account of policy considerations. Rather than the kind of argument used, attention has to be paid to whether or not the decision is coherently justified, and this is a matter far more complex than avoiding policy considerations being taken into account, or neglecting the political (yet constitutional) results of judicial decisions.

[36] Dworkin, *Law's Empire*, 225 ff.

[37] Universalizability here has to be understood in MacCormick's sense (N. MacCormick, *Legal Reasoning and Legal Theory* (1978), 75), i.e. as backward- and forward-looking. That is, a court should decide a case consistently with prior decisions; if it decides differently from its prior judgments, then it must be willing to adopt the new criterion in similar future cases. This new criterion meets the requirement of universalizability if it is enunciated according to the following model: $f1, f2, \ldots fn, \rightarrow j'$, i.e. a rule or criterion is universal if for all situations similar to fn the consequences j' ought to occur. By satisfying this requirement, policy considerations, and in particular environmental protection, get rid of the contingent value that the legislature gives to policies.

a discussion on means–effectiveness, nor on means–desirability, nor on goal–desirability[38] to justify environmental protection as a Community aim. The Court fails to build up connections between legal theory and moral and political theory.[39]

The poor justification provided by the Court in *ADBHU* does not force us to deny the importance of the rule of reason in the attempt to generate coherence, that is, in the attempt to build up plausible connections between reasons.

2. *The Criterion of Proportionality*

The weakness of the reasoning in the *ADBHU* case can be explained by the fact that the rule of reason, and the principles of proportionality and non-discrimination, were at the time of the judgment criteria too novel to be fully applied by the Court. In that case it is worth analysing further judgments.

In the *Danish bottles* case[40] the Court makes a rather wider use of the test of proportionality. The case arose when the Danish government established a deposit-and-return system of approved containers: only soft beverages and beer in approved containers could be sold in Denmark. The measure aimed at achieving a high standard of environmental protection by ensuring the reuse of empty containers. As such, the measure imposed restrictions on free movement of goods, for it compelled soft drink and beer producers to adopt those containers approved by the Danish government in order to sell their products in this Member State.[41] The Danish government tried to reduce the impact which these restrictions had upon the internal market by allowing each producer to sell imported beer and soft drinks in non-approved containers, in a quantity not higher than 3,000 hectolitres a year. This measure was challenged by the Commission, which argued that the restriction on free

---

[38] To MacCormick, arguments on policy may arise at three levels: (i) means–effectiveness arguments: 'will *x* in this context actually achieve *y*?'; (ii) means–desirability arguments: 'it is undesirable to do *x*, or undesirable to use *x* as means to do *y*'; and goal–desirability arguments: 'is it desirable to procure *y* by any means?' (ibid. 262–3).

[39] Moreover, external justification in *ADBHU* lacks the balancing exercise between environmental protection and freedom of trade. Although the criteria of proportionality and non-discrimination are thought of as instruments to rationalize and justify the balancing, these criteria scarcely affect the reasoning of the Court. At the level of internal justification there are jumps in the reasoning which have not been fully justified. For example, the Court considers it evident that the Directive has taken account of the proportionality and non-discrimination principles when establishing limits on trade. But by so doing the Court transforms an evaluation (that of proportionality and non-discrimination) into an evidence without providing further justification as to why this is so.

[40] Case 302/86, *Commission v. Denmark*, [1988] ECR 4607.

[41] The Commission argued that by imposing a system of approved containers, the Danish government limited imports of soft drinks and beer, since compliance with the measure will increase costs of production.

movement of goods was out of proportion to the aim (environmental protection).

Paragraph 6 of the judgment contains the major premise of the case:

According to an established body of case-law of the Court . . . in the absence of common rules relating to the marketing of the products in question, obstacles to free movement within the Community resulting from disparities between the national laws must be accepted in so far as such rules, applicable to domestic and imported products without distinction, may be recognized as being necessary in order to satisfy mandatory requirements recognized by Community law. Such rules must also be proportional to the aim in view. If a Member State has a choice between various measures for achieving the same aim, it should choose the means which least restrict the free movement of goods.

That is to say, in the absence of common rules, limits on free movement of goods are justified by a mandatory requirement (rule of reason) if the measure is non-discriminatory and proportional. A measure is non-discriminatory if it makes no distinction between domestic and imported products; a measure is proportional if it is the less restrictive option among all possible means.

As in the *ADBHU* case, the Court considers that there is a tension between a fundamental right, namely free movement of goods, and a Community goal, namely environmental protection. The tension is not to be solved by applying an all-or-nothing criterion, but rather by balancing the colliding reasons, that is, by finding a compromise among colliding reasons.

To this aim the rule of reason is embraced as a general framework in which the balancing exercise will take place.[42] To strike a balance the Court refers to both the principle of proportionality and the principle of non-discrimination as requirements to be met by the contested measure. It is worth noticing that proportionality and non-discrimination demand quite different kinds of supportive structure. The former principle focuses on the causal link which exists between on the one hand a particular state of affairs which is considered as valuable (internal market and environmental protection) and, on the other, an action (a recycling system based on approved containers). In addition, proportionality is a matter of degree, for a measure promotes more or less a particular value (environmental protection) by a greater or lesser intrusion into another value (free movement of goods). On the contrary, non-discrimination focuses on whether or not a measure undermines a particular value, namely equality. Moreover, non-discrimination is not a matter of degree, for a measure either does or does not undermine equality.[43]

[42] This is consistent with previous cases (e.g. *ADBHU*) and with the Single European Act 1987 (SEA hereafter), which declares environmental protection as an objective of the Community.

[43] One could object that there are degrees of discrimination, for some measures go deeper than others. However, if one looks at the degree of discrimination, the significance lies not in whether the measure is or not discriminatory but rather in whether the degree of undermining

The different content of proportionality and non-discrimination gives rise to several questions. What does the Court mean by a measure being proportional *and* non-discriminatory? On the one hand, if the principle of non-discrimination is thought of as providing a conclusive justification, does it mean that a measure which is discriminatory should be considered unlawful even if it is proportional to its aim? On the other hand, if the principle of non-discrimination provides a non-conclusive justification, does it mean that equality can be balanced against other values of the legal system? That is, can environmental protection justify a discriminatory measure? Notwithstanding the relevance of these questions, and although proportionality and non-discrimination are mentioned in the *Danish bottles* case, the Court put aside the latter, so it focused on the proportionality of the measure. What, then, is proportionality?

The answer to the above question and how the principle of proportionality organizes the balancing are interwoven issues. As has been seen, proportionality focuses on the causal relation of states of affairs (values) to acts. The main question to be answered is what is the acceptable degree of intrusion into a value to promote a different (colliding) value. To this particular question the Court gave two answers. First, it held that a restriction is proportional if it is the 'means which least restricts the free movement of goods' (para. 6). Second, it also held that a means is proportional if 'all the restrictions on free movement of goods are necessary to achieve the objectives pursued' (para. 12). The first notion of proportionality refers to the less restrictive measure, and in this sense is a command of minimum intervention. The second demands a more complex judgement, which involves not only ascertaining the causal relation of means to aims but also a decision concerning the desirability of these aims: to maintain that M is a necessary means to achieve the aim Z presupposes that Z is desirable.[44]

of this value is justifiable. This later justifiable notion of non-discrimination has recently been embraced by the Court. One can find a three-tier system: (1) direct or outright discrimination on the ground of nationality or origin (can only be justified by an explicit exception found in the Treaty; (2) indirect discrimination or imposing a condition that can more easily be satisfied by national or by domestic products (can be justified by objective reasons that have nothing to do with nationality or origin); (3) restrictions that equally affect nationals and non-nationals, domestic goods or imports, but which do restrict intra-Community trade or free movement (like (2), these can be justified by other reasons, but they have to be proportionate). The Court has struck down national measures on all these grounds.

[44] It is interesting that the Court refers to the necessity of the measure, and to the less restrictive measure as two independent tests of proportionality. To Alexy, proportionality involves a three-level judgment: suitability, necessity, and proportionality in a narrower sense (R. Alexy, 'Rights, Legal Reasoning and Rational Discourse', (1992) 5 Ratio Juris 149 ff.). The first and second concern the relationship between a particular state of affairs and a particular action. The third refers to how one principle can be realized at the expense of the other: 'the more intensive the interference in one principle is, the more important must be the realization of the other principle' (ibid. 150).

The Court used both notions of proportionality (as minimum intervention and as the necessity of the means), and arrived at two different results. As far as the prohibition on selling more than 3,000 hectolitres of beverages in non-approved containers per year and per producer, the Court held that the measure is not proportional. Why? Because environmental protection is also promoted by a *less restrictive* recycling system. As far as the system for returning approved containers is concerned, the Danish measure is proportional. Why? Because it is *necessary* to achieve its aim, namely a very considerable degree of protection of the environment (para. 20). The judgment is Solomonic: the Danish recycling system is proportional and non-proportional. Perhaps it is better to say that the judgment is wrong: it becomes unclear whether or not the Danish measure is proportional. Moreover, it becomes uncertain what makes a measure proportional, and therefore how a balance is to be struck between free movement of goods and environmental protection.

But does the Court fail to generate coherence? One way of explaining the twofold notion of proportionality which the Court embraces in the *Danish bottles* case is by affirming that by so doing it has promoted the coherence of European law. How? Although they are somewhat hidden, the Court does take into account values other than free movement of goods and environmental protection. Indeed, the level of discretion of Member States under European law and the enhancement of Community legislation are crucial values that the Court considers in striking a balance. The clash could have been solved by fixing a particular level of environmental protection the Community is willing to support.[45] However, such a decision will pre-empt the competence which Member States have under Community law (i) to establish stricter measures than those issued by Community institutions, and (ii) to establish measures in those areas which are not regulated by Community law. What alternative remains possible without jeopardizing the strength and efficiency of Community law? The Court considered that it is up to Member States to determine the level of environmental protection; in a case-by-case basis the Court should determine whether or not the chosen level is compatible with European law (and in particular to Article 28 EC (ex Article 30)). This explains the twofold decision of the Court: it supports the recycling system issued by the Danish government by declaring its proportionality, and at the same time declares the Danish measure not to be proportional as far as restrictions on free movement of goods are concerned.

This ruling of the Court has two immediate consequences. As far as the juridical implications of the ruling are concerned, the Court strengthens the

---

[45] In the *Danish bottles* case several levels of protections are likely: (1) obligation to use reusable approved containers; (2) obligation to use reusable containers; (3) obligation to use recyclable containers; (4) voluntary return system (L. Krämer, *European Environmental Law Casebook* (1993), 102). The Court says nothing about what level Member States should choose.

federal feature of the constitutionalization of European law by finding an equilibrium between the competence of the Community and that of Member States. Moreover, it also strengthens Community law, for the Court can control the compatibility of domestic measures. As far as the repercussions of the ruling are concerned, the ruling of the Court causes the breakdown of the Danish recycling system.

3. The Criterion of Non-discrimination

As mentioned above, the criteria of proportionality and non-discrimination demand the evaluation of a measure at different levels and according to different supportive structures: while the test of proportionality focuses on the efficient promotion of colliding values (it is a 'more or less' criterion), the test of non-discrimination focuses on whether or not the principle of equality is undermined (it is an all or nothing criterion). To combine both criteria is a difficult task, especially since they may lead to contradictory results. A measure can be proportional and yet it may impose discriminatory treatment among Member States; it also can be non-proportional although non-discriminatory. What, then, is the relevant criterion for deciding?

We shall argue that the Court has been changing the notion of non-discrimination to meet the requirements of balancing reasons. Initially a measure was considered discriminatory if it made a distinction between domestic and imported products.[46] However, since the SEA, a measure is *arbitrarily* discriminatory[47] if the different treatment has not been sufficiently justified. According to this new notion, the discrimination test becomes part of the test of proportionality. Rather than establishing a priority value (that of equality), the test of non-discrimination demands an appropriate justification of the violation of equality. In this sense, the principle of non-discrimination organizes the balance of reasons by focusing on the supportive structure among reasons.

A balanceable notion of non-discrimination

The *Walloon waste* case[48] provides a good example of how to balance colliding reasons when the principle of non-discrimination is involved. The case

---

[46] This notion excludes any balancing exercise, for either a measure is discriminatory or it is not, regardless of the more or less successful promotion of other values.

[47] Article 100a(4) EC (new Article 95(4)) establishes that Member States can adopt stricter measures than those laid down by a Community provision if 'they are not a means of arbitrary discrimination or a disguised restriction on trade between Member States'. A similar provision is established by the consolidated version of the EC Treaty. In particular Article 95 EC lays down that stricter measures which Member States deem it necessary to *maintain* or to *introduce* after a Community measure has been adopted should be neither a means of arbitrary discrimination nor a disguised restriction on trade between Member States, nor shall they constitute an obstacle to the functioning of the internal market.

[48] Case 2/90, *Commission of the European Communities v. Kingdom of Belgium*, [1992] I-4431.

arose when the Walloon Regional Council established the prohibition of the storage, tipping, or dumping of waste from a foreign state. The measure aimed to protect the environment of the region due to the massive import of waste into Wallonia. The Commission found this general prohibition of trade of waste to be contrary to Community law, and in particular, contrary to Articles 28 and 30 EC (ex Articles 30 and 36), since the measure was discriminatory in imposing restrictions on free movement of imported goods.

The Belgian government argued that the prohibition on imports of waste was justified by a mandatory requirement, namely environmental protection. The Commission counter-argued that this mandatory requirement could not be relied upon, for the measure discriminated against waste coming from other Member States.[49]

The Court started its reasoning by subsuming the 'facts' into the major premise.[50] First, it established that waste is to be considered a 'good' for the purpose of Article 28 EC (ex Article 30), regardless of whether or not it is recyclable (able to generate benefits).[51] Second, the prohibition on import of waste (import of a good) is justified by a mandatory requirement: environmental protection (para. 32). Third, mandatory requirements can be taken into account only if the measure is indistinctly applicable, i.e. applied without differentiating domestic from imported products (para. 34). Finally, although the Belgian measure does discriminate between domestic and imported goods, the Court did not conclude that it was discriminatory. (Who expects the Court to be predictable?) Instead of the 'therefore' which seemed to follow from the above reasoning of the Court, it concludes by a 'however'. Here the Court took account of principles which have to be added to the initial clash between free movement of goods and environmental protection. These principles, which were introduced at a rather late stage of the judgment, are the principle that damage should as a matter of *priority* be remedied at source (Article 174(2) EC, ex Article 130r (2)), and the principles of self-sufficiency and proximity set out in the Basel Convention on control of disposal and shipments of hazardous wastes to which the Community is a signatory (para. 35).

This more comprehensive test of non-arbitrary discrimination has immediate consequences for the legal reasoning of the Court. First, reasons other than free movement of goods and environmental protection are taken into

---

[49] If the danger to the environment is caused by the storage, tipping, or dumping of waste, it is irrelevant whether the waste is 'domestic' or 'imported': either the measure imposes restrictions on both domestic and imported products or it is discriminatory.

[50] The major premise in cases of conflict between economic rights and environmental protection is that established in *ADBHU*: limits on economic freedoms are justified by mandatory requirements provided that restrictions are proportional and non-discriminatory.

[51] The Court's position is justified by technical progress that allows in the course of time the reutilization of waste that previously was not recyclable (para. 27).

account in order to justify an eventual discrimination. In this sense, the Court is compelled to gather as many elements of the same legal theory as possible to deal with the particular case. The complexity of the case increases at the same time as the solution of the case increases the coherence of the legal theory.

Second, this more complex conflict of reasons is thought of as a conflict of principles. What is important is not the systematic order among principles but rather the promotion of all of them (demand of proportionality). A measure such as that established by Wallonia restricts free movement of goods but promotes a high level of environmental protection, the principle that damage should be remedied at its source, and the principle that the polluter pays (which is mentioned in the EC Treaty although the Court does not refer to it). The Court understands proportionality in Alexy's sense: as a command to optimize, that is, as a command to find an equilibrium among all colliding principles and values. The criterion to be followed is 'the more intensive the interference in one principle is, the more important must be the realization of the other principle'.[52] So, an interference into the principles of non-discrimination and free movement of goods is justified by the greater realization of other (equally important) principles, namely a high level of environmental protection, the principle that damages have to be remedied at source, and the principle 'the polluter pays'.

Finally, the test of non-arbitrary discrimination promotes coherence within the legal system, because it requires that plausible connections have to be made among colliding reasons, all of them belonging to the same legal theory.

Following the track?

The Court, we claim, sticks to the former test of proportionality and non-arbitrary discrimination, despite decisions such as *Outokumpu Oy*.[53] Here the Court looked at the protection of the environment and the principle of non-discrimination. The case arose when *Outokumpu Oy* (a Finnish electricity producer) brought an action before the national judge against the Finnish law that established the levying of excise duties determined on the basis of the method of production for electricity produced in Finland, whilst the duty chargeable on imported electricity was determined according to a flat rate. This flat rate on imported electricity 'is higher than the lowest excise duty chargeable on electricity produced in Finland, but lower than the highest excise duty chargeable on electricity produced in Finland' (para. 17). The aim of the Finnish measure was to promote the use of 'clean' energy by imposing a lower duty on electricity which is produced in an environmentally friendly manner, or by using environmentally friendly raw materials. This distinction could not be applied to imported electricity, the Finnish

---

[52] Alexy, 'Rights', n. 44 above, 150.   [53] Case C-213/96 [1998] ECR I-1777.

government claimed, because of a technical problem: once the imported electricity entered the distribution network it was impossible to determine its method of production or the raw materials which were used.

One of the questions that the Finnish national judge referred to the Court was whether an excise duty which is levied on domestic electricity by the method of production, while at a flat rate on imported electricity, is in compliance with Article 90 EC (ex Article 95) (non-discrimination in taxation). The answer to this question is very interesting, for the Court gave three answers as the result of striking three balances.

First, the Court examined whether a system which differentiates between products is compatible with Community law. In this sense, it established that Article 90 EC (ex Article 95) does not preclude an internal tax which varies according to the manner in which the electricity is produced and the raw materials which are used. Why? The Court gave several reasons: Member States have the freedom to establish a tax system which differentiates between products; the differentiation is based on environmental considerations which are an essential objective of the Community; finally, environmental considerations such as energy policy have to be integrated into other policies. The real tension, in this first balance, is between the discretion of Member States under Community law and the level of legal (and political) integration pursued by Community law. It is argued that the Court strikes a balance, i.e. a sort of equilibrium, by recognizing the freedom of Member States to impose different duties on domestic products, depending on objective criteria.[54] Hence, discrimination in relation to domestic products is compatible with Community law (para. 30).

Second, the Court discusses whether the tax system is compatible with the principle of non-discrimination of Article 90 EC (ex Article 95). The Court concluded that the Finnish measure is discriminatory because imported electricity is subject to a flat-rate duty whatever its method of production and the raw materials used. The Finnish government argued that the decision to impose a flat rate on imported electricity is justified by a practical reason: once the electricity enters the distribution network, it is impossible to determine its method of production. The Court rejected this argument: practical difficulties cannot justify the application of a taxation system which is discriminatory. The tension, in this second balance, is between the principles of non-discrimination between domestic and imported products, the banning of reliance on practical difficulties to avoid compliance with Community law, and the integration of environmental considerations into other Community policies—such as energy policy and the 'polluter pays' principle. However, rather than finding a compromise, the Court considers that non-discrimination and non-reliance on practical

---

[54] This judgment and that contained in the *Danish bottles* case coincide: it is up to Member States to establish measures which aim at a stricter protection of the environment.

difficulties are principles which tilt the balance against the 'polluter pays' and the integration principles. Indeed, the strong notion of non-discrimination, and the fear that Member States might rely on practical difficulties to avoid compliance with Community law, leave little space for a compromise, i.e. to establish a tax system which is compatible with environmental considerations.

As such, the judgment of the Court has a clear implication for the environment: the failure of an environmentally friendly taxation system. If imported electricity must be subject to a flat rate which is equal to the lowest rate imposed on domestic electricity, the consumption of 'dirty' imported electricity would increase. There would be no such thing as promotion of the use of 'clean' electricity. It also has a juridical implication: it reinforces the strength of European law, for Member States cannot rely upon practical difficulties to avoid compliance with European law.

However, at the end of its judgment the Court does strike a third balance. In paragraph 39 it says that 'the Finnish legislation at issue does not even give the importer the opportunity of demonstrating that the electricity imported by him has been produced by a particular method in order to qualify for the rate applicable to electricity of domestic origin produced by the same method'. It seems that if the Finnish government established a burden of proof on importers of electricity, the Court would deem the tax system to be in compliance with EC law. Indeed, such a taxation system would contain a balance between colliding principles: (i) it would be non-discriminatory, for there is no distinction between domestic and imported electricity, both being subject to the same excise duty;[55] (ii) environmental protection will justify the different treatment; (iii) practical difficulties will not be mentioned; (iv) the polluter pays; and (v) environmental policy will be incorporated into the energy policy.

The balance which the Court struck in its main judgment is based on a strong notion of the principle of non-discrimination. This does exclude an equilibrium among colliding principles or interests. Rather, it transforms the balancing exercise into an all-or-nothing matter. Surprisingly, in paragraph 39 the Court strikes a balance which reflects an equilibrium among all principles involved. The equilibrium is inspired by a sort of efficiency criterion according to which the rational agent (the Court) tries to satisfy as far as possible all colliding interests. What allows the Court to strike a balance is the different notion of non-discrimination embraced: a certain degree of discrimination is acceptable if justified by other reasons (environmental protection), rather than the all-or-nothing character of non-discrimination.

---

[55] There is, though, an implicit discrimination, for only importers are required to prove the method of production of electricity and the raw materials used. This sort of discrimination, however, seems not to outweigh other principles involved.

D. Towards Coherence?

The Court solves conflicts in which economic freedoms are involved by applying the rule of reason, and the principles of proportionality and non-arbitrary discrimination. These criteria have an overwhelming function in legal reasoning, for they organize the weighing and balancing of economic freedoms against other principles or policies. The rule of reason determines that mandatory requirements can be balanced against economic freedoms. The test of proportionality determines the causal relationship that should exist between a particular state of affairs (environmental protection or free movement of goods) and an action (restrictions on free movement of goods). This causal relationship will determine the level of intrusion into a right which can be accepted and justified. Finally, the test of non-arbitrary discrimination establishes a requirement of justification. All three stages of the balancing demand connections to constitutional and political theory. What amounts to a mandatory requirement? What are the interests and goals of the community? If a means is necessary to promote certain aims, are these aims desirable? Is an eventual discriminatory means sufficiently justified? What are the plausible connections between reasons that justify discriminatory actions? These are questions that have to be answered from the point of view of the institutional morality, i.e. from the perspective of the morality of the law. This requires the Court to interpret the law, and to adapt the interpretation to the constitutional and political theory.

The use of the criteria as analysed in the cases discussed above shows that balancing in the Court has evolved from finding the less (economic) restrictive measure towards finding a compromise between colliding principles and policies. This way of understanding and dealing with conflicts of principles and policies promotes coherence at several stages.

First, as far as the rule of reason is concerned, the Court refuses an all-or-nothing application of rights (such as free movement of goods). This means that rights have to be balanced against other rights and goals involved in a particular case in order to determine their weight or importance. This way of applying rights does not promote coherence if it is thought of as a systematic order among values and principles, for the notion of coherence on which the balancing relies does not impose a systemic or hierarchical order among principles. However, it does promote coherence if it is thought of as establishing supportive structures among reasons. To exemplify the connection of supportive structure and coherence, we must recall the *ADBHU* case. Here the Court missed a great opportunity to justify environmental protection as being an essential Community goal. At the time of the judgment, environmental protection was not recognized by Community law as a mandatory requirement able to restrict economic freedoms. Since no deductive connections were possible to justify the importance of environmental protection,[56] the Court should have looked for plausible connections. This involves connecting not only parts of the same legal theory but also different theories: legal, constitutional, and political theories. For example, the constitutionalization of European law which transforms the European project into something far more complex than an economic community could have justified taking into account rights and goals other than economic ones. Alternatively, the Court could have argued that protecting and improving the environment is a precondition[57] of improving the living conditions of European citizens. Relatedly, this improvement in the quality of life paves the way toward an effective equal-opportunities situation which utilizes civil rights.[58] This justification would have strengthened the role of the Court as a tribunal of European citizens rather than as a tribunal of European institutions. A less complex justification would have been that obstacles caused by different environmental standards among Member States should be removed in order effectively to achieve a single market.

Either enhancing Community law, promoting the quality of the environment in which to implement individual rights, or removing obstacles to market integration are possible justifications which connect different features of legal theory and constitutional and political theory. The failure of the Court to elaborate a sound justification in *ADBHU* has serious drawbacks for the coherence of European law because related issues which have come up recently cannot be decided in a coherent manner. For example, whether or not to recognize the right of environmental organizations such as Greenpeace to bring judicial actions is an issue the solution of which depends on what was the justification provided by the Court when it recognized environmental protection as a mandatory requirement.[59]

Second, the Court enhances the description of cases, i.e. it recognizes a larger number of policies and principles involved in a particular case. That becomes clear if *Danish bottles* is compared to *Outokumpu Oy*. In the former the Court refers almost exclusively to the principle of free movement of goods

---

[56] The SEA eventually recognized environmental protection as a Community goal.

[57] In this sense, market integration and environmental protection are both considered means to achieve a major goal: improvement in the quality of life and standards of living. This was the content of the declaration of heads of state and government of Oct. 1972: 'Economic expansion is not an end in itself. Its first aim should be to enable disparities in living conditions to be reduced. . . . particular attention will be given to intangible values and to protect the environment, so that progress may really be put at the service of mankind' (Commission, *6th General Report* (1972), 8).

[58] J. Habermas, *Between Facts and Norms* (1996), 123.

[59] As a matter of course, the case law of the Court is consistent with the *ADBHU* judgment, for environmental protection is taken into account as an essential Community goal. However, the absence of an explanation as to *why* this was the case prevents the Court from achieving coherence at other levels.

and the mandatory requirement of environmental protection. Other principles introduced by the SEA such as rational use of resources, the precautionary principle, and the integration of environmental protection in other Community policies are not mentioned by the Court, even though they were in force when the judgment was issued. In *Outokumpu Oy*, however, the Court refers to a greater number of colliding principles: the level of discretion of Member States under Community law, European integration, non-discrimination, the impossibility of reliance on practical impossibility to avoid non-compliance with European law (principle of efficiency of European Law), integration of environmental protection into other Community policies, and the principle that the polluter should pay. This far more complex picture of the case leads toward a more complex balancing exercise. It involves not only finding an equilibrium between Member States and Community powers, but also integrating a number of features belonging to the same constitutional and political theory: European integration, effectiveness of EC law, high level of environmental protection, energy policy etc.

Third, a sign of the evolution toward a more complex notion of balancing is provided by the principle of non-discrimination. This has evolved from an 'all-or-nothing' question towards a 'more-or-less' question. Whereas in the *Danish bottles* case the Court defined the principle of non-discrimination in an absolute way (either a domestic measure is or it is not discriminatory), in later judgments this principle is balanced against other colliding features. Indeed, in the *Walloon waste* judgment the Court considered that a discriminatory domestic measure can be justified by the principles of self-sufficiency and remedy of environmental damages at source. The Court embraced the notion of principles, including equality, as commands to optimize.[60] Legal reasoning is, therefore, a matter of fitting together all (colliding) features, i.e. legal reasoning becomes a matter of finding coherence.

The rule of reason, the test of proportionality, and finally the test of non-arbitrary discrimination are thought of as directions to perform an optimal weighing and balancing of colliding principles and policies, rather than criteria which provide a clear and ultimate solution. In this sense balancing colliding values and/or principles promotes coherence, not only because common values and/or principles are fulfilled,[61] but also because in fulfilling them supportive connections are created. In this sense, coherence as making connections represents a dynamic process of reconstructing the legal system with no guarantee that an end will be reached.

---

[60] Alexy, 'Rights', n. 44 above, 149.
[61] MacCormick, 'Coherence', n. 3 above, 238.

IV INTEGRITY AND INTEGRATION

The former analysis of the legal reasoning of the Court has dealt with a number of issues: the critical reconstruction of the decision-making process by distinguishing several sub-decisions; legal syllogism and the requirement of deductability as the core of legal justification; several types and categories of argument; the distinction between internal and external justification; conflicts of reasons; the use of balancing criteria; the creation of a supportive structure between arguments, etc. Moreover, consistency,[62] comprehensive account of reasons,[63] and coherent justification have been identified as requirements compliance with which guarantees the rationality of the justification. However, what are the standards by which to determine that a consistent, comprehensive, and coherent justification is acceptable? As to the ECJ, this question has to be answered from the point of view of the role of the Court in the project of European integration which is the *raison d'être* of the very Treaty establishing the European Community.

This remark returns us to reviewing the concepts of integrity (coherence) and integration. As follows from earlier comments, the issue of 'integrity' in the sense intended by its original author, Ronald Dworkin, might be framed as follows: can the European Community, as one pillar of the European Union, be considered a community of principle? Does this give us any insight into, or further help in clarifying, the reasoning of the Court? Or would it be nearer the truth to depict the Court as acting in an opportunistic and policy-responsive way concerned more with the momentarily advantageous handling of a particular problem than with interpretation of the Treaties and the subordinate norms of Community law as a body of law animated by some coherent body of governing principles? To questions posed in such terms, integrity rather than opportunism seems on the whole to constitute the better account of the Court's whole record. It does not follow, of course, that there have not been momentous choices to be made, nor that one can or should elide the enormous impact of the decisions the Court has made in relation to the big questions. Nor is the Court immune from criticism either in respect of its general line of decision-making or in respect of particular decisions. As for the

---

[62] Consistency refers both to the principle of formal justice (similar cases have to be treated equally) and to the formal or logical correctness (premises cannot be contradictory).

[63] Reasons or arguments are to be found not only in the legal system. Moral, constitutional, and political theory also provide arguments supporting legal decisions. General principles are in this sense handy tools to introduce into the legal system values elaborated outside the system. The very enterprise of Community law is loaded with teleology: creating a single market, achieving ever greater integration, eliminating restrictions, realizing free movement and harmonizing essential standards to make free movement possible, even improving basic living standards, etc.

general line, even those who are most inclined to criticize that whole line of decision-making, as perhaps Rasmussen[64] and Phelan[65] have tended to do, are surely of the view that the wrong principles have prevailed rather than contending that no principles have prevailed. What both might object to is the risk of a false antithesis here between 'principle' and 'policy', for the very hallmark of judicial policies is that they are expressed in terms of principles, and the 'policy choices' that Courts make are choices between alternative principles. For example, at the very beginning there was room to argue, and some argued, that an internationalist treaty-oriented reading of Community law was perfectly possible and was in principle desirable. This, however, was the reading of the position that the Court rejected in *Van Gend en Loos*,[66] and in *Da Costa*[67] and the other decisions on the *sui generis* character of the Community and its law and on the supremacy and direct effect of that law. Either view was open to argument on the basis of principle, and either view implied a body of principles that later decisions would have to explicate and concretize. It is trite learning that one of the rival sets of principles did prevail in the judgment (and judgments) of the Court. But one cannot seriously argue other than that the chosen line of decision was one that formed the basis of a whole run of confirming cases that in various ways gave body to the doctrines of which the principles were the cornerstones.

The Court's reading of the inner meaning of the Treaties settled the most fundamental question of policy opened by the creation of an Economic Community (and the other Communities). But this is not a case of 'policy as opposed to principle'; it is a case of policy expressed in principles, and particularly in a choice between rival principles. There is no point in saying that judges should not make policy choices of that kind, for when two avenues of principle are opened up by the problem posed in a case for decision, one or other line simply has to be chosen, and justified on what seems the best line of argument. The arguments are interpretive in that they try to make the best available sense of the documents and decisions laid down by the authoritative decision-makers, in this case the states which are party to the Treaties. They are not absolute and final, for the process of treaty revision left (and in a rather etiolated sense still leaves) it open to the States through a later Inter-governmental Conference to abandon the Court's view and explicitly favour a different one. Probably there would now be chaos if the *acquis communautaire* were to be discarded by an IGC, but at least one aspect of the Maastricht Treaty was its effort to define other 'pillars' of the Union that were not to be sucked into that particular orbit.

[64] *On Law and Policy*, n. 1 above.
[65] D. R. Phelan, *Revolt or Revolution: The Constitutional Boundaries of the European Community* (1997).
[66] Case 26/62, *Van Gend en Loos*, [1963] ECR 1.
[67] Joined Cases 28, 29 and 30/62, *Da Costa v. Netherlandse Belastingadministratie*, [1963] ECR 31.

Decisions that have pushed further down the line of direct effect, such as the *Defrenne* case about the vertical direct effect of Directives, do not detract from this argument. It very firmly called on the Member States to live up to an idea of integrity in upholding principles to which the Treaties and Treaty-derived norms paid lip-service. The Court perhaps rightly took the view that only a decision to extend the doctrine of direct effect could preserve the over-all integrity of the system. Again, of course, a policy decision—but a decision of principle, a decision about principles, and an interpretive decision, all at the same time.

Following the notion of integration as integrity, and European community as community of principles, the Court has elaborated the constitutional aspect of the doctrine of direct effect, namely the fact that courts enforce rights against Member States. Individuals can exercise the rights which Community law generates in order to eliminate obstacles or restrictions even if these are not strictly discriminatory, and very few implementing instruments have been issued. Direct effect is about courts protecting individual rights drawn directly from instruments which bind the Member States, with no further need for legislation detailing those rights. It is, indeed, a federal instrument: the obligations assumed by the Member States can be directly invoked and enforced by individuals. The direct effect of Community norms, together with the direct applicability of many Community law instruments in a purely monistic vein, and together with the principles of primacy, sub-sidiarity, and the doctrine of parallel competences, make up a set of integrity principles typical of EC law which also reinforce its federal make-up.[68]

More particular decisions may be objected to on the ground of failure to walk the line between interpretive exploration of principles and mere invention. Arguably the first lurch into environmentalism as a principle of European law was open to this objection (though not for too long, since the States in due course confirmed the line taken), and some of the environmental decisions do perhaps have an opportunistic whiff. But they have this not when they adhere to the principles of environmental protection, but when they appear to compromise them without an explicit basis in other principles requiring proportional attention.

[68] This concern for individual rights and remedies is developed to the utmost when what is at stake is ensuring the fulfilment of Treaty obligations by Member States (primacy and direct effect, direct applicability and the internal monist theory, Member States' liability for damages caused to the individual when in breach of EC law). However, the ECJ has not been so keen on developing those rights and remedies when they can be used against the legal order of the EC itself—Article 230(4) EC (ex Article 173), or even the *Foto-Frost* doctrine, which tries to centralize all questions of validity of derived EC law in spite of the text of Article 234 EC: a question on validity has to be referred even if the court is not of last resort. *TWD* has also limited the possibility of raising the validity of a decision in an Article 234 (ex Article 177) action when the plaintiff could have had recourse to a direct individual action), see Case C-188/92 *TWD Textilwerte Deggendorf GmbH v. Bundesrepublik Deutschland* [1994] ECR I-833.

Finally, it seems no mere pun to link this with the idea of integration. The early decisions on the *sui generis* character of the Community were decisions that favoured the aspiration to integration, to an ever closer union of peoples, spoken of in the Treaties' preambular sections against the more austere and internationalist view that might have been taken. The guiding value is integration of the states and their peoples into a community or union that succeeds in being more than an international association of treaty-observing states, while not yet leaping to the other pole of becoming a sovereign union state (like the UK or Spain) or a sovereign federal union (like the USA or Australia or India). Just what is the character of this third thing, this new entity of its own kind, is what scholars and citizens figure out as they live through its evolution. If the law of the Community has integrity, it has it on the basis of evaluation by the Courts, the statespersons, and the citizens of this new-style integration of countries and peoples, this diversity-cherishing unity.

4

Gender and the Court of Justice

JO SHAW

I INTRODUCTION

This chapter seeks to uncover and explain the relevance of the concept of 'gender' in the context of the role of the Court of Justice within the legal and political order of the European Union. The Court remains an important subject of analysis within the discipline of European Union legal studies, both because of its institutional position within the system of the EU as political and legal order reaching deep into each of the domestic systems directly implicated in the EU,[1] and because the normative effects of its pronouncements on questions of gender have a unique geographical spread. They are not only binding within the legal systems of the fifteen current Member States, but also influence in strong ways both the legal systems of the states belonging to the European Economic Area and those of the candidate countries in the current Enlargement rounds which are tied to the EU by association agreements mandating the pre-emptive introduction into the domestic legal order of much of the *acquis communautaire*.

Central to much of the argument developed here is a dual vision of the Court as both 'political' and 'legal' institution within the EU system. It accepts the simultaneous validity of *legalist visions* of the Court as operating within normatively constraining systems of legal reasoning, argument, and interpretation and subject to conceptions of the proper judicial role within a constitutional system and *political visions* of the Court as developing as well as responding to the changing agendas inherent in the politics of the EU.[2] This dual conception, based on neatly fitting the Court of Justice into a system of integration/disintegration and polity formation, nicely explains in the EU context the puzzle that 'the power of the judges as elaborators of law seems to exceed what their occasional responsibilities as custodians of constitutionally

---

[1] See further D. Chalmers, 'European Union Law', in A. El-Agraa (ed.), *The European Union*, 5th edn. (London: Prentice-Hall, 2000).

[2] For a similar argument see G. de Búrca, 'The Principle of Subsidiarity and the Court of Justice as an Institutional Actor', (1998) 36 Journal of Common Market Studies 217.

entrenched individual rights can explain'.[3] In other words, the legal and political roles are irrevocably linked in a holistic conception of adjudication within the wider context of a constitutional framework, a political order, and an economic market order. In a further step, the argument then seeks to place 'gender' into this system. Gender can have a disruptive power, challenging the conceptual bases driving the two parallel agendas of a legal *and* a political Court, such as 'reason', 'constitution', and 'integration'.

Underpinning the argument are the concepts of 'gender' and 'gender analysis'. It is important, in the first place, to distinguish 'gender' and 'feminism', especially in the context of legal scholarship. It is widely agreed amongst scholars that feminist legal analysis necessarily implies a broad commitment to progressive social change as the basis for the analysis of law and socio-economic relations.[4] For example, as a political project, feminism is aware of the asymmetrical nature of the notions of 'equality' and 'discrimination', so far as these notions are capable—as legal concepts—of remaining blind to structurally based disadvantage and injustice especially for women rooted in patriarchal capitalist societies. However, whilst the analysis which follows in this chapter is broadly feminist in this sense, it does not take the step of equating 'gender' with 'woman' alone, and engages instead with a broader critical project of analysis around the production of identities and subjectivities within and through law. Thus issues of difference based on race, class, sexual orientation, or other identity criteria can enter wherever relevant into the analysis. There is no 'essential woman'.[5] Furthermore, it is vital to note that in the strategic context of the European Union, its legal order, and, specifically, its Court of Justice, concepts of gender themselves operate in a dynamic relationship with the shifting social, political, legal, and economic relations mediated through the integration process and the ongoing multi-levelled process of EU polity formation. In other words, they interact with both the *legal* and *political* visions of the role of the Court of Justice.

Although definitions of the term 'gender' can vary dramatically, two main usages of the term at the present time can be identified.[6] The first usage sees gender as a broadly social category standing in some form of dichotomous relationship with sex. The sex/gender distinction in early 'second wave feminist' work involved viewing gender as a 'complex of socially constructed characteristics, which are held to relate to the two sexes'.[7] More recent work has become increasingly uncomfortable with a crude nature/social distinction

---

[3] R. Unger, *What Should Legal Analysis Become?* (London: Verso, 1996), 108.

[4] S. Millns and N. Whitty, 'Public Law and Feminism', in Millns and Whitty (eds.), *Feminist Perspectives on Public Law* (London: Cavendish, 1999), 1.

[5] E. V. Spelman, *Inessential Woman: Problems of Exclusion in Feminist Thought* (London: Women's Press, 1988).

[6] J. Squires, *Gender in Political Theory* (Cambridge: Polity Press, 1999), ch. 2.

[7] Ibid. 54.

implicit in the sex/gender distinction, and has challenged the suggestion that sex itself is a pre-social essentialist category of nature. Quoting and summarizing the work of Judith Butler, Judith Squires shows how Butler argues that

gender ought not to be conceived merely as the cultural inscription of meaning on a pregiven sex; gender must also designate the very apparatus of production whereby the sexes themselves are established. As a result, gender is not to culture as sex is to nature; gender is also the discursive/cultural means by which 'sexed nature' or a 'a natural sex' is produced and established as 'prediscursive', 'prior to culture' . . .[8]

The second definition of gender suggests a more instrumentalist use of the term as an intellectual conduit assisting and facilitating certain types of analysis and theorizing. Thus Squires suggests that gender is 'a category that was developed to explore what counts as "woman" and as "man"' in feminist theory.[9] Drawing in this chapter upon the more pragmatic approach to the question which this suggests, I focus less upon the identification and theorization of a specific notion of gender, and the consequent problematization of the very possibility of a feminist politics through the undermining of the common-sense category 'woman', and more upon a limited and strategic 'gender analysis' and the use of gender as an interpretive principle.

This chapter addresses the task of 'importing gender' into EU law.[10] This involves the endeavour to uncover the (often hidden) 'gendered character' of aspects of the legal order, legal actors, and legal processes of the European Union. It is easy to consign the 'gendered approach' to being 'just' another 'strand' of thinking, for example, about laws, institutions, processes, or concepts. Two essential points need to be made here: 'gendered' approaches must not be ghettoized as merely providing, for instance, useful insights in relation to a limited range of social or political institutions (such as the family or the household); on the contrary, they offer potentially useful perspectives upon a whole range of varieties of institutional behaviour, based upon a set of assumptions which envision relationships between institutional settings and individual actors which are structured by connection, associability, and trust, rather than by choice, preference formation and maximization, and the conceptual separation, even cleavage, between actor and institution.

Second, there is no single universal approach to 'importing gender'. In legal scholarship as so often elsewhere, feminist analyses of any kind generally remain a form of transgressive if not downright deviant scholarship, in that in any form they challenge 'the neutrality which has a central place in the

---

[8] J. Butler, *Gender Trouble: Feminism and the Subversion of Identity* (New York: Routledge, 1990), 1–25; Squires, above n. 6 at 65.

[9] Ibid. 54.

[10] See J. Shaw, 'Importing Gender: The Challenge of Feminism and the Analysis of the EU Legal Order', (2000) 7 Journal of European Public Policy 406, where I develop this argument in more detail.

framework of modern thought and in the modern ideal of the rule of law'.[11]
Indeed, feminist analyses tend to undermine 'the idea of law as an
autonomous structure generating claims to truth which are insulated from
political critique. Feminism in common with other critical approaches in
social theory, will always be concerned to undermine, to expose as false, law's
pretended autonomy, objectivity and neutrality.'[12] In that sense, a feminist
approach necessarily imports a 'politics' of law.

This scepticism about grand theory pairs neatly, of course, with a general
scepticism about 'grand theories' which pervades EU studies.[13] Without
abandoning altogether the endeavour to theorize, many EU scholars suggest
that there need to be a variety of different explanations for both the existence
and operation of the EU, working at different levels.[14] Within feminist work,
moreover, ever-growing scepticism about a single feminist (legal or political)
theory having any effective explanatory or predictive force has extended to the
methodological field as well. Consequently, it is perhaps wise to limit the
claims of feminism in relation to the process of intellectual enquiry: in relation to the nature of social scientific enquiry, it can effectively challenge the
objects of that enquiry; in relation to methods of enquiry, it questions the
underlying assumptions upon which methodologies proceed. Often this has
been revealed by the simple device of 'asking the woman question'. Thus the
impact of much feminist work on law can be to expose the ways in which a
body of knowledge—i.e. legal doctrines and legal practices—is constructed in
a manner which tends to exclude the interests of the less powerful, in particular women. On the other hand, only to ask 'the woman question' 'is to make
men and masculinity the unnamed norm and silence gender (in its fullest
sense) as an analytic category'.[15] Asking 'the woman question' has the vital
outcome of challenging the implicit primacy of 'the man question' masquerading as 'the person question'. On the other hand,

this demand is itself now challenged by the proposal that the more important task is
to consider the complexities of gender questions beyond the confines of the dichotomous construction of masculinity and femininity.[16]

So, to illustrate the possibilities of gender analysis in relation to EU law, the
importation of gender might include (amongst other approaches) something

---

[11] N. Lacey, *Unspeakable Subjects: Feminist Essays in Legal and Social Theory* (Oxford: Hart,
1998), 188.

[12] Ibid. 186.

[13] See generally B. Rosamund, *Theories of European Integration* (London: Macmillan,
2000).

[14] Examples include A. Warleigh, 'History Repeating? Framework Theory and Europe's
Multi-level Confederation', (2000) 22 Journal of European Integration 173; J. Peterson,
'Decision-making in the European Union: Towards a Framework for Analysis', (1995) 2
Journal of European Public Policy 69.

[15] Squires, above n. 6 at 2.   [16] Ibid.

as simple as the critique of doctrinal concepts such as equality and non-discrimination and their instrumentalization by courts which operate within the paradigm of a society, an economy, and a polity in which women suffer structural disadvantage as well as, from time to time, personal prejudice. Such an approach would involve the attempt to show why 'equality', as it has been deployed by the various institutions of the EU, and especially the Court of Justice, should be construed in substantive rather than in formal terms.[17] Similarly, it might involve the deconstruction of sexual stereotypes and the critique of sexism in law;[18] or the challenging of dominant ideologies about women, motherhood, family life, and the sexual division of labour;[19] or indeed the transgression of women's marginality in law, under law and as legal subjects, or assessments of the impact of laws upon women's (real) lives, including the attempt to 'predict the impact of policy'.[20] Moreover, as many have observed, in so far as the object of most policy-making in relation to equal opportunities for the sexes (and consequently much of the scholarly analysis commenting upon those policies) has been women within the labour market or women potentially within or seeking to be within the labour market (e.g. those receiving or wanting training), EU law reinforces the disciplinary divides between work and market on the one hand and social exclusion on the other hand.[21]

[17] For examples see C. Barnard, 'Gender Equality and the EU: A Balance Sheet', in P. Alston (ed.), *The EU and Human Rights* (Oxford: Oxford University Press, 1999); S. Fredman, 'European Community Discrimination Law: A Critique', (1992) 21 Industrial Law Journal 119–34; T. Hervey and J. Shaw, 'Women, Work and Care: Women's Dual Role and Double Burden in EC Sex Equality Law', (1998) 8 Journal of European Social Policy 43–63; H. Fenwick and T. Hervey, 'Sex Equality in the Single Market: New Directions for the European Court of Justice', (1995) 32 Common Market Law Review 443–70; G. More, 'Equal Treatment of the Sexes in European Community Law: What Does "Equal" Mean?', (1993) 1 Feminist Legal Studies 45; G. More, 'Equality of Treatment in European Community Law: The Limits of Market Equality', in A. Bottomley (ed.), *Feminist Perspectives on the Foundational Subjects of Law* (London: Cavendish Press, 1996).

[18] e.g. L. Flynn, 'The Body Politic(s) of EC Law', in T. Hervey and D. O'Keeffe (eds.), *Sex Equality Law in the European Union* (Chichester: Wiley, 1996).

[19] e.g. C. McGlynn, 'Ideologies of Motherhood in European Community Sex Equality Law', (2000) 6 European Law Journal 29; I. Moebius and E. Szyszczak, 'Of Raising Pigs and Children', (1998) 18 Yearbook of European Law 125.

[20] On the principle of gender auditing see F. Beveridge and S. Nott, 'Gender Auditing: Making the Community Work for Women', in Hervey and O'Keeffe, above n. 18. See further the TSER-funded project on *Predicting the Impact of Policy: A Gender Impact Assesment Mechanism for Assessing the Probable Impact of Policy Initiatives on Women*, University of Liverpool, Feminist Legal Research Unit, reported in F. Beveridge, S. Nott, and K. Stephen, 'Addressing Gender in Community and National Law and Policy-Making', in J. Shaw (ed.), *Social Law and Policy in an Evolving European Union* (Oxford: Hart, 2000); F. Beveridge, S. Nott, and K. Stephen (eds.), *Making Women Count* (Aldershot: Ashgate, 2000).

[21] e.g. I. Ward, 'Beyond Sex Equality: The Limits of Sex Equality Law in the New Europe', in Hervey and O'Keeffe, above n. 18.

In order to bring the Court of Justice more closely into focus as the subject of the analysis, the following sections outline the contexts in which the analysis must be developed. The next section comprises a summary of important feminist work on EU law. Sections III and IV set out the legal/policy and institutional contexts. The policy context concentrates for the most part upon the legal framework of equal opportunities law, and the primacy given to court-centred analyses deploying and critiquing various concepts of equality, equal treatment, and discrimination.[22] It also profiles the gradual shift in policy terms towards discourses and practices of positive action and mainstreaming. In relation to the institutional context, it is important to describe the nature of the institutional framework within which arguments about equality have been developed. Put simply: what are the prospects for a principle of substantive equality within institutions which are 'masculinist' in terms of personnel and orientation?

Returning to the Court of Justice, Section V attempts to explain how the Court's work and its role within the system of EU law have been conventionally understood. It highlights various interpretations of the Court's role in terms of its legal reasoning, and its self-understanding as an instrument of 'integration' within the EU legal order. In other words, it addresses the duality of the Court as 'legal' and the Court as 'political' within the orthodox frames given to both interpretations. As I will show, much analysis examines the work of the Court in terms of its contribution to integration as a self-conscious project of the European Union and/or in terms of its legitimacy as a judical organ within a legal order which is not rooted within a nation-state but which is distinctively supranational in character. Gender is 'imported' into this analysis as a principle of interpretation, with a focus upon the pressure points to be found within the system in relation to the Court's legal and political roles. Without wishing to dismiss the importance of such work, Section VI envisions two alternative approaches to the process of legal reasoning which are not specifically constrained by this way of framing the judicial legitimacy debate. In similar terms it addresses both alternative approaches to the Court as judicial institution with normative constraints and the Court as political actor. In other words, it imports gender into justice and integration as a centrepoint rather than a principle of interpretation. Section VII brings the chapter to a conclusion.

---

[22] Sex equality law does make numerous appearances in this chapter; however, it is not subjected to detailed and systematic description and analysis, taking into account the complex framework of Treaty measures, legislative instruments, and case law developments which have evolved over more than 25 years. Those unfamiliar with the field may find it useful to consult a textbook account of the subject such as that in P. Craig and G. de Búrca, *EU Law: Text, Cases and Materials*, 2nd edn. (Oxford: Oxford University Press, 1998), ch. 19, or the detailed account by Barnard, above n. 17.

Sections V and VI are, therefore, the key sections expanding upon the broad idea of 'importing gender' in the context of the dual vision of the 'legal' and 'political' institutional status and role of the Court of Justice. In keeping with the view that theoretical and methodological pluralism is more helpful to the analysis than an attempt to elaborate a single grand theory and dominant method explaining every dimension of the relevance of gender within law, politics, society, culture, and economy, in its reconstructive endeavour Section VI adopts a broadly interrogatory approach. It is also somewhat speculative in nature. It seeks to widen the debate about the role of the Court within the EU system both in terms of its overall legitimacy and in terms of the evaluation of the concrete outputs from this judicial system by suggesting different ways of conceiving of the 'legal questions' that come before the Court. In other words, one key question which it asks is the following: what would happen if the fact situations in some of the key cases which the Court has already decided were constructed not in terms of the disciplinary categories of EC law as it stands at the present time where symetrical concepts of equal treatment and non-discrimination are dominant, but in terms, for example, of the policy approaches of 'mainstreaming' or 'positive action'? Building on the attempt to assess the institutional context in Section IV, Section VI also addresses the 'gender of justice' asking questions about the relevance of the identity of the judges to processes of judicial reasoning.

II GENDER, FEMINISM, AND EU LAW

This section outlines some of the most important feminist approaches to EU law within existing scholarship, highlighting areas where analyses have focused specifically upon the Court of Justice as well as those analyses which have concentrated upon the framework of the legal order without paying specific attention to the constructive role of the Court of Justice. A distinction is drawn between sectional, or subject-based, approaches and analyses which attempt a more general approach. Feminist critique has remained, however, largely peripheral or 'bolt-on'[23] in the discipline of European Union legal studies, although in that situation it hardly differs from other fields of law.[24]

A. Feminist Critiques of Sex Equality Law

As is well known, much feminist work on the EU has both begun and ended with the most obvious engagement of EU law with the legal status of women

---

[23] A. Morris and T. O'Donnell, 'Employment Law and Feminism', in Morris and O'Donnell (eds.), *Feminist Perspectives on Employment Law* (London: Cavendish, 1999), 1.
[24] Shaw, above n. 10.

(and men) as actors within the marketplace for labour: equal treatment law and policy and the slightly broader field of equal opportunities policy. That is, feminist analyses have tended to concentrate in areas where the primary legal instrument is that of discrimination, and the general principle most often under consideration is that of equality.

There has certainly been no shortage of analyses of EU sex equality law of a predominantly liberal feminist character, implicitly accepting the conventions and discourses of liberal legal institutions as capable of delivering upon a promise of equality under or before the law, although perhaps opening up some questions about the nature of the concepts of equality deployed by the Court of Justice.[25] The task of much scholarship here has been to track the case law of the Court of Justice, as it has followed a winding path between applying models of formal and substantive equality to the resolution of concrete disputes about the scope of the equal treatment rules.[26] Such analyses often draw upon a wider argument about sex equality law as a fundamental right, drawing strength from the gradual (but yet incomplete) concretization of the EU's human rights policies.[27] Likewise, they may be linked to a more general analysis of the use of the equal treatment principle elsewhere in EC law, and the growing range of functions which that principle can play within the EU legal order.[28] They often conclude with calls for reforms of the existing law or improvements in effectiveness of enforcement.[29] There is also a strand of 'pragmatically liberal' work. This involves the analysis of rights and institutions under law in terms of the possibility of limited gains through litigation strategies which accept the liberal legal status quo, but this pragmatic liberalism is often twinned with a more critical analysis of the weaknesses and limitations of equality and, especially, discrimination as legal instruments in terms of a wider socio-economic debate.[30] This leads to an approach which combines some criticism of the Court for certain inconsistencies in its

[25] e.g. G. F. Mancini and S. O'Leary, 'The New Frontiers of Sex Equality Law in the European Union', (1999) 24 European Law Review 331–53; E. Ellis, *EC Sex Equality Law*, 2nd edn. (Oxford: Oxford University Press, 1998); C. Barnard, 'The Principle of Equality in the Community Context: *P, Grant, Kalanke* and *Marschall*: Four Uneasy Bedfellows?', (1998) 57 Cambridge Law Journal 352.

[26] Mancini and O'Leary, above n. 25.

[27] Alston, above n. 17; T. Loenen, 'Rethinking Sex Equality as a Human Right', (1994) Netherlands Quarterly of Human Rights 253; C. Docksey, 'The Principle of Equality Between Women and Men as a Fundamental Right under Community Law', (1991) 20 Industrial Law Journal 258.

[28] From 'market-unifier', through 'regulatory' concept, to a 'constitutional' principle: G. More, 'The Principle of Equal Treatment: From Market Unifier to Fundamental Right', in Craig and de Búrca, *The Evolution of EU Law*.

[29] Ellis, above n. 25; B. Fitzpatrick, 'Towards Strategic Litigation? Innovations in Sex Equality Litigation Procedures in the Member States of the European Community', (1992) 8 International Journal of Comparative Labour Law and Industrial Relations 208.

[30] Barnard, above n. 25; Ellis, above n. 25.

approach and some failures of the legal and institutional imagination, with a strong awareness of the ultimate limitations of a single-track *legal* strategy in relation to the goal of equality between the sexes in societies marked by difference in relation to race, ethnic origin, class and economic power, and so on as well as sex.

As we shall see in more detail in the next section, in fact, scholarly critiques of sex discrimination law in its current form have received high-level recognition through significant changes to the EC Treaty basis of gender equality rules through the medium of the Treaty of Amsterdam.[31] One of the strengths of the women's lobby—noted for its relative success in capturing influence within the policy process[32]—is that it has drawn upon a powerful crescendo of arguments grounded in feminist analyses of the equal treatment provisions to the effect that 'simple' equal treatment based upon a formal equality model is not enough to bring about hoped for socio-economic transformations, and that there are profound problems with EU law's deployment of the work/family divide, its location within a system of 'market law', and the inevitable resistance in such a system to all attempts to orient the argument towards the relevance of 'care' for the analysis of 'equality'.[33] Thus stepping beyond the limits of a liberal feminist analysis, scholars have pointed to the weakness of all types of equality-based analysis when it comes to confronting structural disadvantage resulting from labour market or family/household structures. Here the line between what is 'discrimination' and what is 'personal lifestyle choice' (e.g. in relation to childbearing and child-raising) tends to collapse in an equal treatment analysis, making it difficult to translate public policy choices about the regulation of pregnancy, childbirth, and parenting into justiciable concepts of 'equality'.[34]

This leads to a more radical critique of the Court's case law, which goes beyond the task of highlighting any inconsistencies in its use of concepts of

[31] See Article 2 EC on the 'task' of the European Community as including 'equality'; Article 3(2) EC on gender mainstreaming into the EC's activities; and changes to Article 141 EC especially in relation to positive action policies.

[32] C. Hoskyns, *Integrating Gender* (London: Verso, 1996); U. Liebert, 'Gender Politics in the European Union: The Return of the Public', (1999) 1 European Societies 197; S. Mazey, 'The European Union and Women's Rights: From the Europeanization of National Agendas to the Nationalization of a European Agenda', (1998) 5 Journal of European Public Policy 131.

[33] e.g. Fenwick and Hervey, above n. 17; T. Hervey, 'The Future for Sex Equality Law in the European Union', in Hervey and O'Keeffe, above n. 18, D. Schieck, 'Sex Equality Law after Kalanke and Marschall', (1998) 4 European Law Journal 148; Fredman, above n. 17; Barnard, above n. 17; More, above n. 17, L. Luckhaus and S. Ward, 'Equal Pension Rights for Men and Women: A Realistic Perspective', (1997) 7 Journal of European Social Policy 237; Moebius and Szyszczak, above n. 19; H. Cullen, 'The Subsidiary Woman', (1994) 16 Journal of Social Welfare and Family Law 407, and the work of many others.

[34] J. Conaghan, 'Pregnancy, Equality and the European Court of Justice: Interrogating *Gillespie*', (1998) 3 International Journal of Discrimination and the Law 115.

equality. One important task is challenging the *ideologies* upon which both sex equality law[35] itself and, specifically, the approach of the Court of Justice[36] are based. McGlynn finds, for example, that the Court's approach betrays a strongly and perhaps disturbingly 'maternalist' orientation towards issues of child care. Stychin, meanwhile, shows how the claim of Lisa Grant,[37] who sought a spousal benefit for her lesbian partner, was consistent with the family orientation of the Court's case law towards exclusive partnerships of couples, even if the claim was disruptive to a classification of equality in terms of sex rather than sexual orientation.[38] Equally important is the problematization of the use of rights and rights discourse as the basis for the making of political claims within the legal system.[39] Finally, numerous analyses have highlighted the subject-based limitations of the EU's principle of equality: it fails to address many significant fields within which women face systematic subordination within society, such as the domestic sphere including issues of violence and care.[40]

Moreover, while the feminist basis of much of the work described here certainly demands as a pragmatic minimum a more substantive principle of equality wherever this concept is in fact used,[41] the logical conclusion of the argument often appears to suggest that equality as such is not the issue. For if we argue that substantive equality is context-specific, sensitive to difference as well as sameness, and inimical to systems of gender stereotyping, then it becomes clear that the classic legal tools of equal treatment law will be insufficient to solve the issues of interpretation which arise. Increasingly, it becomes clear that 'equality' is here operating merely as an inadequate surrogate for other values such as justice, fairness, and individual autonomy, and it may be better to shift the focus specifically onto those values themselves and to abandon the attempt to ground the analysis on equality altogether. These are arguments which are common to critiques of all systems of discrimination law, and which carry little specificity in relation to the EU legal order's *sui generis* supranationality. The demands upon the Court, therefore, are similar to those placed on any court adjudicating such questions.

[35] e.g. I. Ward, 'Beyond Sex Equality: the Limits of Sex Equality in the New Europe', in Hervey and O'Keeffe, above n. 17.

[36] McGlynn, above n. 19.

[37] Case C-249/96, *Grant v. South West Trains*, [1998] ECR I-621.

[38] C. Stychin, 'Consumption, Capitalism and the Citizen: Sexuality and Equality Rights Discourse in the European Union', in Shaw, above n. 20.

[39] C. Stychin, '*Grant*-ing Rights: The Politics of Rights, Sexuality and European Union', (2000) 51 Northern Ireland Legal Quarterly 281.

[40] e.g. the work of Amy Elman: A. Elman (ed.), *Sexual Politics and the European Union: The New Feminist Challenge* (Oxford: Berghahn Books, 1996); A. Elman, 'The EU and Women: Virtual Equality', in P.-H. Laurent and M. Maresceau (eds.), *The State of the European Union*, iv (Boston: Lynne Rienner, 1997).

[41] e.g. Hervey and Shaw, above n. 17.

B. Beyond Sex Equality Law

Outside the field of equal opportunities law, there have been a number of important analyses of EU free movement law, citizenship, migration, and the principle of non-discrimination on the grounds of nationality.[42] Here the analysis must, of necessity, engage directly with the EU as the legal basis for a single market for goods, services, capital, and especially persons, an Economic and Monetary Union, and—increasingly—a putative Area of Freedom, Security, and Justice. In other words, the analysis of the gendered effects of free movement law on women, for example, where there is a mistaken tendency to assume that they are more often the objects of migration than its active subjects,[43] directly engages with the interrelationship between migration and the legal transgression of national boundaries, along with the interaction of national (e.g. welfare) and supranational (e.g. non-discrimination rights) systems of law.

Where feminist analysis of EU law has, thus far, been least well developed has been in relation to the examination of EU law as system or 'quasi-system' of law, or in relation to the institutional analysis of EU law. A comparison could be drawn with the analysis of international law. Thus EU law has not so far been subjected to the type of analysis which led Charlesworth, Chinkin, and Wright to conclude in 1991 that international law is 'thoroughly gendered'.[44] This would necessitate an analysis which addresses both the foundation stones of the legal order and specific building blocks in terms of the fields and sub-fields of EU law. One possible reason for this lack, and a weakness in feminist work hitherto (shared with other 'critical' work on EU law), is that it has accepted rather too easily the given categories of EU law as the basis for analysis, which has made the transgression of boundaries between social and economic law or between the free movement of persons and provisions on equality and non-discrimination more difficult to achieve. Yet more lateral thinking seems urgently needed, not only because the horizontal spread of EU activities and competence into ever more fields of policy brings

---

[42] H. L. Ackers, *Shifting Spaces* (Bristol: Policy Press, 1998); K. Scheiwe, 'EC Law's Unequal Treatment of the Family: The Case Law of the European Court of Justice on Rules Prohibiting Discrimination on Grounds of Sex and Nationality', (1994) 3 Social and Legal Studies 243; T. Hervey, 'Migrant Workers and their Families in the European Union: The Pervasive Market Ideology of Community Law', in J. Shaw and G. More (eds.), *New Legal Dynamics of European Union* (Oxford: Oxford University Press, 1995); M. Everson, 'Women and Citizenship of the European Union', in Hervey and O'Keeffe, above n. 18.

[43] Ackers, above n. 42.

[44] H. Charlesworth, C. Chinkin, and S. Wright, 'Feminist Approaches to International Law', (1991) 85 American Journal of International Law 85—although this chapter is based on a specific and rather controversial reading of 'women's nature' drawn primarily from the work of Carol Gilligan, *In A Different Voice: Psychological Theory and Women's Development* (Cambridge, Mass.: Harvard University Press, 1982). See generally Lacey, above n. 11 at 5–6.

to the fore ever-increasing numbers of possible interrelationships between different fields of law, but also because of the shift to policies of mainstreaming and positive action which is discussed in the following section. Yet in one area of clear interrelationship—between an emerging 'constitutive'[45] policy field of non-discrimination law based on the legal basis of Article 13 EC, where new directives are under discussion, and the existing body of equal treatment law related to sex equality, which has been thus far limited to issues related to the labour market and some aspects of the welfare state—there has been some evidence of uncertainty. Should the existing framework of sex equality law (including the associated case law of the Court of Justice) be treated as a pioneer and ideal to which new discrimination laws should seek to live up, or will the generalization of a non-discrimination policy lead to the 'dumbing down' of the existing framework?[46] Will there be, for example, a decisive shift from the use of hard law measures to soft law measures, thus moving away from the tradition—evidenced hitherto—of according justiciable rights to the immediate beneficiaries of EC sex equality law?

Hitherto most general work has concentrated upon the market basis of the system. Examples include analyses of gender and the internal market[47] and of the 'body politic(s)' of EC law,[48] the latter attempting to view EC law using the prism of various established feminist perspectives on law, specifically 'law as sexist', 'law as masculine', and 'law as gendering'. The interaction between emerging international markets for reproductive technology, gene technology, and biotechnology, on the one hand, and EC law's tendency to commodify and assimilate more or less any object to the market systems established under the Treaty freedoms, on the other, offers some interesting insights into a new regulatory field for the body and bodily identities. An equally fruitful line of analysis is suggested if the lens is switched from the EU's market properties to its complex interrelationship with the state.[49] For attempts to theorize the EU, the concept of state can be problematic. The EU is both 'near-state' in its operation as a governance system and antithetical to stateness, in so far as it has a disruptive effect on binary divisions between national law and international law, and between national (domestic) politics and international (inter-state) politics.[50] Equally, feminist theory and feminism as practice have

---

[45] i.e. a policy field which contributes directly to the incremental construction of the constitutional framework of the EU polity.

[46] L. Flynn, 'The Implications of Article 13 EC: After Amsterdam, Will Some Forms of Discrimination Be More Equal Than Others?', (1999) Common Market Law Review 1127.

[47] Shaw, in O'Keeffe and Hervey, above n. 18; L. Flynn, 'The Internal Market and the European Union: Some Feminist Notes', in A. Bottomley (ed.), *Feminist Perspectives on the Foundational Subjects of Law* (London: Cavendish, 1996).

[48] Flynn, above n. 18.   [49] On this point in more detail see Shaw, above n. 10.

[50] See further J. Shaw and A. Wiener, 'The Paradox of the "European Polity"', in M. Green Cowles and M. Smith (eds.), *State of the Union*, v: *Risks, Reforms, Resistance or Revival* (Oxford: Oxford University Press, 2000).

a complex and ambiguous relationship with the state. For the state can be both patriarch and protector. The state confers rights, and establishes systems of protection through law upon which claims can be based. The state's legal and institutional processes offer the prospect of reform, and incremental changes to a system which has historically disadvantaged both women as a group and, especially, groups of women who suffer multiple disadvantage based, for example, upon ethnic origin or race. The EU as near-state and non-state, therefore, adds another layer of complexity both to the attempt to dis-aggregate the gendered effects of constitutionalism and constitutive policies and to any attempt to use EC law as a strategy for reform or resistance.

To conclude, it would appear that feminist work hitherto on the EU—whether or not explicitly deploying an analytical category of gender as sub-stance or method—has not offered a full understanding of the significance of gender for the analysis of the work of the Court of Justice, or the role of the Court of Justice as institution within the EU system. Much work has been solely reactive, systematizing and footnoting the work of the judges using a variety of feminist approaches in which the concept of equality in its formal and substantive versions has been the dominant force. Traditional subject bases have placed limitations upon the cross-cutting insights of much femi-nist scholarship. Technical legal analysis structured around disciplines and subjects hides, of course, a vast array of choices about alternative futures for society.[51] We should not be constrained by the disciplining force of defining legal categories such as 'equality law' or 'free movement law' in assessing both the impact of case law and possible alternative futures. It is to that end that I develop both the interpretive tools of Section V and the variety of methodo-logical approaches suggested in Section VI. To reach that point, however, it is vital to set in place a number of critical contexts.

III THE LEGAL FRAMEWORK OF EQUAL OPPORTUNITIES POLICY—AND BEYOND

A. Introduction

The premise lying behind this section of the chapter concerns the continuing centrality of what has often been termed 'the women's policy',[52] especially in terms of its capacity to set a broader 'agenda for gender' in the EU. While the previous section has already outlined the importance of more general approaches to deploying 'gender' as a category of analysis in relation to EU law, and the broad potential of feminist analyses of EU law, it remains true that as a distinctive field of analysis, equal treatment or sex discrimination law

---

[51] Unger, above n. 3.   [52] e.g. by Catherine Hoskyns, above n. 32.

has an important cornerstone function. This is not simply because, as many commentators have argued, equality—whatever its weaknesses as a tool of analysis and whatever its limitations as defined in EC law—can and does make a difference when enshrined in law.[53] It certainly has a flagship function, and, as has frequently been shown, problems arise in relation to the balance of EU law between sex equality law as a *presence*, and race equality law as *absence*.[54] Hence the existence of sex equality law cannot be ignored. It also brings 'the new European woman'[55] into focus, establishing the basis for arguments about whether, for example, the internal market is good or bad for women. For all these reasons, the law on sex equality needs to be viewed as the opening of the debate about gender and EU law, rather than as a closure.

Most importantly, however, without the pre-existing sex equality law and policy, it is doubtful to what extent the EU institutions would have taken up the wider international agenda[56] of gender mainstreaming at the European level. It seems unlikely that gender-mainstreaming would have achieved the status it has (although this status may continue to be more rhetorical than real) without the existence of the women's policy.[57] It is more, therefore, than a mere backdrop to policy, but an important causal factor. Indeed, Pollack and Hafner-Burton[58] identify an important interaction between the European Parliament and the Commission, where Commission President Santer resisted a push from the Parliament's Women's Rights Committee in 1995 to have the equal opportunities portfolio removed from Social Affairs Commissioner Padraig Flynn and given to someone with a better record in that policy field, but repaid the Parliament by promising that greater attention would be paid to this question. Without the background legal framework for sex equality that particular committee might very well never have been established, or at least certainly would not have had the influence which it has in fact acquired within the system. Accordingly, there has been since 1995 a

---

[53] This point is argued strongly in Hoskyns, above n. 3, esp. in chs. 9 and 10.

[54] e.g. E. Szyszczak, 'Racism: The Limits of Market Equality', in B. Hepple and E. Szyszczak (eds.), *Discrimination: The Limits of Law* (London: Mansell, 1992); J. Gregory, 'Racial Discrimination and the EC', (1993) 22 ILJ 59; B. Hepple, 'Equality and Discrimination', in P. Davies et al. (eds.), *European Community Labour Law: Principles and Perspectives* (Oxford: Clarendon Press, 1996). See more recently C. Gearty, 'The Internal and External "Other" in the Union Legal Order: Racism, Religious Intolerance and Xenophobia in Europe', in Alston, *The EU and Human Rights*; T. Hervey, 'Putting Europe's House in Order: Racism, Race Discrimination and Xenophobia after the Treaty of Amsterdam', in D. O'Keeffe and P. Twomey (eds.), *Legal Issues of the Amsterdam Treaty* (Oxford: Hart, 1999).

[55] See Ward, above n. 21 at 375.

[56] L. Reanda, 'Engendering the United Nations: The Changing International Agenda', (1999) 6 European Journal of Women's Studies 49.

[57] For a full survey of the current policy see M. Pollack and E. Hafner-Burton, 'Mainstreaming Gender in the European Union', (2000) 7 Journal of European Public Policy 432; see also Mazey, above n. 32.

[58] Above n. 57.

special 'Commissioners' Group' on Equal Opportunities. As we shall see, in the pursuit of mainstreaming some concrete steps have been taken to ensure that gender issues are taken into account in all policy made or proposed by the Commission. Yet despite the shift in practical emphasis to mainstreaming and positive action, it is interesting to note how often policy measures continue to use the 'equality before the law' argument as the foundation stone for future developments. This is as evident in the most recently proposed equal opportunities action plan for 2001–5 as it has been in the past.[59]

B. Equal Opportunities: The Legal Framework

The basic framework of EU equality law is well known, and long established. It has been recently amended in significant ways, both through the medium of Treaty amendments and because of the addition of some important complementary legislative provisons. It does not provide a complete system of equality law consisting of justiciable rights, procedures, *and* remedies. It provides a set of basic guarantees, enshrined in what began life as Article 119 EEC and is now Article 141 EC, along with a group of Directives requiring implementation in national law. In particular, it is national law which supplies the detailed procedures through which equality claims can be brought before national courts by aggrieved individuals (or sometimes organizations) and, by means of a reference for a preliminary ruling under Article 234 EC, before the Court of Justice. Moreover, the Court of Justice has recently confirmed that stricter national guarantees of sex equality—although they might have acquired a new interpretation as a consequence of the influence of EC law as is the case with certain German constitutional provisions—continue to coexist and can be relied upon in circumstances where EC law does not provide a remedy.[60] Article 141 provides *inter alia* for equal pay for men and women, and it has been supplemented by the following Directives, adopted on the basis of what were Articles 100 and 235 EEC (renumbered as Articles 94 and 308 EC):

Directive 75/117 (equal pay and especially equal value);[61]
Directive 76/207 (equal treatment in employment);[62]
Directive 79/7 (equal treatment in social security);[63]
Directive 86/378 (equal treatment in occupational pensions);[64] this

---

[59] 'Gender Equality: A Joint Approach for a New Programme' (2001–5): (europa.eu.int/comm/dg05/equ_opp/news/gender_equ_en.htm: visited 13 Mar. 2000).

[60] Case C-50/96, *Deutsche Telekom v. Schröder,* [2000] ECR I-743; Cases C-234 and 235/96, *Deutsche Telekom v. Vick and Conze,* [2000] ECR I-799; Cases C-270/97 and C-271/97, *Deutsche Post v. Sievers and Schrage,* [2000] ECR I-929.

[61] OJ 1975 L45/19.   [62] OJ 1976 L39/40.   [63] OJ 1979 L6/24.

[64] OJ 1986 L225/40.

Directive was amended by Directive 96/97[65] in the light of the judgment of the Court of Justice in *Barber*;[66]
Directive 86/613 (equal treatment for self-employed women).[67]

The legal framework has been further developed in more recent years, through a number of additional measures based on a variety of legal bases, away from the direct question of sex equality. Directive 92/85, improving the health and safety of workers who are pregnant or who have recently given birth (the Pregnancy Directive),[68] was adopted on the basis of what was then Article 118a EEC, according a legislative competence in relation to health and safety of workers (now Article 137 EC), and two further measures were originally adopted during the course of the UK's opt-out from the Maastricht social policy provisions. In other words, they were adopted on the basis of the then Social Policy Agreement, and involved not a 'normal' legislative process (involving the Commission/Council/Parliament and sometimes the ECOSOC and the Committee of the Regions) but a dialogue between employer and employee representatives which produced an agreement then enacted by the Council into EU law on the basis of a proposal from the Commission. These were Directive 96/34 on reconciling family and working life (the Parental Leave Directive)[69] and Directive 97/80 on the burden of proof in cases of discrimination based on sex.[70] They were later extended by separate Directives to cover the UK. Both measures—were they now to be adopted—would fall under the legislative competence in Article 137 EC, which brings the social-partner-based legislative procedures of the Social Policy Agreement into the Treaty mainstream following the Treaty of Amsterdam, combining them with qualified majority voting in the Council. However, the burden of proof Directive could also be adopted using the new legal basis in Article 141(3) EC, allowing the Council to adopt—by a qualified majority and in co-decision with the European Parliament—measures 'to ensure the application of the principle of equal opportunities and equal treatment of men and women in matters of employment and occupation, *including* the principle of equal pay' (emphasis added). This excludes the social partners, but gives the European Parliament—with its formidable Women's Rights Committee—more say.[71]

Furthermore, after a long gestation period and numerous earlier proposals from the Commission, measures on various aspects of atypical work are now

---

[65] OJ 1997 L56/20.
[66] Case 262/88, *Barber v. Guardian Royal Exchange*, [1990] ECR I-1889.
[67] OJ 1986 L359/56.   [68] Directive 92/85, OJ 1992 L348/1.
[69] OJ 1996 L145/4.   [70] OJ 1998 L14/6.
[71] On the legitimacy of the 'social partner process' see N. Bernard, 'Legitimising EU Law: Is the Social Dialogue the Way Forward? Some Reflections around the *UEAPME* case', in Shaw, above n. 20.

being adopted by the EU. The legislative processes of the social dialogue have again been the key to progress. The Part-Time Work Directive,[72] based on a Framework Agreement between the social partners, was adopted in 1997 and later extended to the UK, and is now covered by the Article 137 competence. A Framework Agreement on Fixed-Term Work was agreed in March 1999, leading to a Commission proposal[73] and the adoption of a Council Directive later the same year.[74] The factual relevance of such measures to women's situation in the labour market is hard to contest. Greater controversy surrounds the effects of equalizing the status of part-time work and flexible working more generally in terms of women's future participation in the marketplace.

The 'hard' secondary legal framework of directives is complemented and supplemented by some soft law measures of variable effect and visibility. Notably, there are measures in relation to child care, largely regarded as disappointing by commentators.[75] The European Parliament has turned to this area of its own initiative, adopting a report and resolution on the situation of single mothers and one-parent families calling for EU measures to be adopted.[76] A Code of Practice on the equal pay principle[77] has received little publicity. In contrast, the Recommendation and Code of Practice on sexual harassment[78] have been regarded as more significant because of the link— through the Equal Treatment Directive—to the construction of sexual harassment as a (problematic) form of sex discrimination.[79] Controversy has continued, however, about the need for a binding legal instrument and about the possible role of the social partners in negotiating a framework agreement. The recently proposed fifth framework programme on equal opportunities would, according to the Commission,[80] include a commitment to bring forward a new proposal for a Directive addressing *inter alia* the sexual harassment point directly.[81]

In terms of developments in the primary legal framework for sex equality, the Treaty of Amsterdam—which was agreed in 1997 and entered into force

---

[72] Directive 97/81, OJ 1998 L14/9. [73] COM(1999) 203.

[74] Council Directive 1999/70/EC of 28 June 1999 concerning the framework agreement on fixed-term work concluded by ETUC, UNICE, and CEEP, OJ 1999 L 175.

[75] Recommendation on Childcare, OJ 1991 C129. See S. Fredman, *Women and the Law* (Oxford: Oxford University Press, 1997), 211; V. Randall, 'Childcare Policy in the European States: Limits to Convergence', (2000) 7 Journal of European Public Policy 346.

[76] Report A4-0273/98; OJ 1998 C313/298.

[77] Code of Practice on the Implementation of Equal Pay for Work of Equal Value for Women and Men, COM(96) 336.

[78] Commission Recommendation 92/131 on the protection and dignity of men and women at work, OJ 1992 L49/1; Code of Practice on meures to combat sexual harassment, *Equal Opportunities Review* 41 (1992), 39.

[79] J. Dine and B. Watt, 'Sexual Harassment: Moving Away from Discrimination', (1995) 58 Modern Law Review 343.

[80] See above n. 59. [81] For support for this point see Barnard, above n. 17 at 253–5.

following ratification in 1999—was undoubtedly a watershed. It contained the most significant amendments to the framework of rights, principles, and legislative competences since the original Treaty of Rome of 1957. Article 3 EC enshrines the principle of gender mainstreaming into the Treaty and into all policies and activities of the European Community. Article 136 brings into the formal treaty framework the (declaratory) rights, including equality, contained in the Community's 1989 Charter of Fundamental Social Rights for Workers and, as noted above, Article 137 establishes a broad basis for qualified majority voting in the social policy arena. Amendments to Article 141 EC have strengthened the case, in terms of legal principle, for positive action measures to benefit the disadvantaged sex in fields of employment (most often women, of course) without conflicting with the equal treatment principle itself. Declaration 28, appended to Article 141 EC, provides that 'when adopting [positive action measures], Member States should, in the first instance, aim at improving the situation of women in working life', offsetting the gender neutrality with which the relevant provision of Article 141(4) EC is now drafted. This followed the controversy generated by the Court's judgment in the case of *Kalanke*, where it appeared to cast doubt upon the possibility of any national or subnational positive action measures pursued by public authorities not coming into conflict with the formal principle of equality enshrined in the equal treatment directive.[82] Also generated by changes introduced in the Treaty of Amsterdam is a body of proposals from the Commission based on the Article 13 non-discrimination legislative competence.[83] However, sex discrimination is excluded from both proposed measures (although it is specifically included in Article 13): a Directive establishing a general framework for equal treatment in employment and occupation and a Directive specifically concerned with race discrimination in a wider range of areas. Finally, a treaty basis has been established for the EU's evolving employment policy (Articles 125–30 EC) and, as we shall see, employment policy is at the forefront of the mainstreaming debate.

In addition to fostering the creation of an EU level framework through legislative proposals and its animation of the social dialogue, the Commission's preoccupations have lain with the tasks of implementation and enforcement.

---

[82] Case C-450/93, *Kalanke v. Land Bremen*, [1995] ECR I-3051.

[83] The Commission has made a whole raft of proposals: Communication from the Commission to the Council, the European Parliament, the Economic and Social Committee, and the Committee of the Regions on certain Community measures to combat discrimination, COM(1999) 564; Commission Proposal for a Council Directive establishing a General Framework for equal treatment in employment and occupation, COM(1999) 565; Commission Proposal for a Council Directive implementing the principle of equal treatment between persons irrespective of racial or ethnic origin, COM(1999) 566; Commission Proposal for a Council Decision establishing a Community Action Programme to combat discrimination 2001–6, COM(1999) 567.

To this end, it has been assisted in the gathering and dissemination of information not only by the national governments (which are subject to legal obligations under the Treaty: Article 5 EEC, now Article 10 EC) but by its own independent networks, such as the Expert Legal Group on the application of European law on equal treatment between men and women, which has published the *Equality Quarterly News*.[84] In addition to seeking the implementation by the Member States of additional *international* instruments on gender equality, such as the ILO Convention 177 on homeworking,[85] the Commission has monitored the implementation of the key equality directives, and has been prepared to embark upon legal action before the Court of Justice to ensure enforcement. A good example would be the actions brought against the UK under Article 169 EEC (now Article 226 EC) in relation to both equal pay and equal treatment rules.[86] The very limited residual competence left to the Member States in many areas of the equality field is well illustrated by the action brought against France in relation to its prohibitions on women doing night work.[87] Enforcement actions are now concentrated on ensuring the effective implementation of the parental leave Directive and the pregnancy and maternity Directive.[88] The Commission's Third Annual Report on Equal Opportunities[89] communicates the somewhat unnerving information that the Commission was obliged to commence infringement proceedings against *every* Member State to force them, as a minimum in terms of compliance, to communicate to the Commission as watchdog their implementing measures in respect of the 1996 Directive amending the occupational pensions directive.[90]

Article 141 is fully enforceable in national courts. It has direct effect.[91] Moreover, as is well known, the impact of the EU legislation in the form of directives is not confined simply to requiring national legislatures to introduce measures which conform to these provisions, or indeed to making national courts seek to interpret national law in conformity with these provisions.[92] Rather, directives can also give separate and justiciable rights to individuals which they can enforce in national courts, in accordance with the principles of national procedural law, but which take precedence over any

[84] Available, latterly, on the DG Employment and Social Affairs website.
[85] Commission Recommendation OJ 1998 L165/32.
[86] Case 61/81, *Commission v. UK*, [1982] ECR 2601; Case 165/82, *Commission v. UK*, [1983] ECR 3431.
[87] Case 312/86, *Commission v. France*, [1988] ECR 6315.
[88] See the Fourth Annual Report on Equal Opportunities, COM(2000) 123 at 22–3. The Commission adopted a report on the implementation of the pregnancy directive in 1999: COM(1999) 100.
[89] COM(1999) 106 at 24.   [90] See above n. 65.
[91] Case 43/75, *Defrenne v. SABENA (No. 2)*, [1976] ECR 455.
[92] This is the so-called principle of 'indirect effect' or 'sympathetic interpretation': Case 14/83, *Von Colson and Kamann v. Land Nordrhein-Westfalen*, [1984] ECR 1891.

contradictory national provisions (the principles of direct effect and supremacy).[93] The question of justiciable rights depends upon the interpretation—in each case—of the provisions of the directive in question. However, directives can only be enforced against the state, and not directly against other individuals.[94] The rights of individuals before national courts are buttressed by a very important system of procedural guarantees. Remedies for breach of EC law must be no less effective or extensive than national remedies in equivalent cases, and must not operate such as to make it practically impossible for individuals to obtain legal redress. These principles have been extensively interpreted by the Court of Justice, in order, for example, to force the removal of the upper limit on compensation in UK sex discrimination cases.[95] These rights are sometimes called 'third generation rights',[96] and their interpretation and scope remains a matter of some controversy in EC law at present, precisely because they involve a considerable interference in national legal orders and the administration of justice at national level.

Given the significance of national courts in the enforcement of EC sex equality law, it is important to emphasize the limitations of the Court's role in the context of individual actions brought before national courts, and referred to the Court of Justice under the Article 234 EC preliminary ruling procedure. The Court does not actually decide the case. It simply answers a set of questions posed by the national court, which the latter deems to be necessary for the purposes of resolving an issue of EC law which arises before it. The preliminary reference procedure does not guarantee 'perfect' interpretation or enforcement of EC law at national level. It does not ensure that the Court of Justice will be asked the right questions. It does not bring about by 'force' legislative changes at the national level. However, the fact that the use of litigation strategies at national level by interested parties such as trades unions or equality agencies seems set to continue is evidenced by the readiness of the UK Trades Union Congress to take legal advice immediately after the date for UK implementation as to whether or not UK law is in line with the requirements of the Parental Leave Directive, and to make clear its intention to consider litigation.[97]

It is perhaps misleading to try to summarize the formidable and dense case law of the Court of Justice in the area of sex equality law in the domain of

---

[93] S. Moore, 'Enforcement of Private Law Claims of Sex Discrimination in the Field of Employment', in Hervey and O'Keeffe, above n. 18; D. O'Keeffe, 'Third Generation Remedies and Sex Equality Law', in Hervey and O'Keeffe, above n. 18.

[94] Case 152/84, *Marshall v. Southampton and South West Hampshire AHA*, [1986] ECR 723.

[95] Case C-271/91, *Marshall v. Southampton and South West Hampshire AHA*, [1993] ECR I-4367.

[96] O'Keeffe, above n. 93.

[97] R. Bennett, 'TUC Warns Ministers on Work Time Rules', *Financial Times*, 11 Feb. 2000.

employment since the groundbreaking case of *Defrenne II* established the direct effect of Article 119 EEC prospectively from the date of that judgment (6 April 1976).[98] Some comments will be of assistance, however, in constructing the arguments which follow below. These will concentrate upon Article 234 references, as it is in the context of these judgments that the Court of Justice has made its most significant findings of principle about the scope and effect of the relevant provisions of EU law. It is worth noting that the patterns of preliminary references from national courts have been extremely uneven. The early years saw the Court of Justice being reasonably well supplied by references from the UK courts, a pattern which has always bucked the trend of a generally low level of reference-making by the UK courts.[99] On the other hand, in figures up to date by July 1999, Tesoka reports *in total* 31 preliminary references from the UK courts, 37 from the German courts, and just 3 from the French courts.[100] After a rather slow beginning, which has been attributed to an uncertain relationship between the (decentralized) lower German labour courts and (centralized) Federal labour court,[101] the German courts have now clearly made a considerable impact in terms of numbers upon the case law of the Court of Justice. Equally, there is no doubt that EU sex equality law has had a profound effect upon the interpretation of equality guarantees within the German domestic system. In addition, the Dutch, Belgian, Danish, Irish, and—more recently—Swedish and Austrian courts have supplied a small core of references.

The point can be made somewhat 'anecdotally' (and somewhat arbitrarily) by means of a brief analysis of some key case law in 1999 and 2000, which also has the advantage of highlighting some of the continuing pressure points in this field. The first point to note is an absence: after a rash of cases seeking interpretations of the Social Security Directive as women have contested what they believed to be the discriminatory (patriarchal?) effects of many aspects of the various national benefits and welfare systems,[102] there is very little activity in this domain at present. Crucially, as we shall note again below,[103] the

---

[98] Above n. 91.

[99] See D. Chalmers, 'The Positioning of EU Judicial Politics within the United Kingdom', (2000) 23 Western European Politics 169; A. Stone Sweet and T. L. Brunell, 'The European Court and National Courts: A Statisticial Analysis of Preliminary References, 1961–95', (1998) 5 Journal of European Public Policy 66.

[100] S. Tesoka, 'Judicial Politics in the European Union: Its Impact on National Opportunity Structures for Gender Equality', MPIfG Discussion Paper 99/2. Some of the issues raised by these variations are considered further below in the text accompanying n. 217.

[101] J. Shaw, 'Recent Developments in the Field of Labour Market Equality: Sex Discrimination Law in the Federal Republic of Germany', (1991) 13 Comparative Labour Law Journal 18.

[102] On this see J. Sohrab, *Sexing the Benefit* (Aldershot: Dartmouth, 1996); Ellis, above n. 25, ch. 4; Hervey and Shaw, above n. 17.

[103] See below, text accompanying n. 196.

key policy decision has already been made by the Court of Justice to allow a relatively wide discretion to the Member States as they modernize their welfare systems (both in view of the sex equality principle and also because of the increasing demographic pressures which they are experiencing), by allowing them to demonstrate a legitimate social policy aim as justification for schemes which are indirectly discriminatory in terms of effect upon women. Member States are also allowed to level down when eradicating inequality. There were only two cases in 1999 on the Social Security Directive. The first was a successful enforcement action under Article 226 EC brought by the Commission against Greece, seeking a declaration from the Court that Greece was infringing Article 141 EC and a number of provisions of the Equal Pay and Social Security Directives by maintaining in force a measure which laid down special substantive conditions for married women employees which were not laid down for married men employees.[104] This illustrates the work that still needs to be done by the Commission in policing the national systems. The second case was the well-publicized UK case of *Taylor* referred by the High Court, which concerned the so-called 'winter fuel' Regulations. A man who retired early aged 62, having paid social security contributions throughout his working life, was denied a winter fuel payment which would have been paid to a woman of the same age.[105] The 'discrimination' was conceded by the government. So *Taylor* was a case about the scope of the Social Security Directive, allowing the Court to remind us that the scope is limited to benefits which are part of a statutory scheme providing protection against one of the risks listed in Article 3(1), but that in this case it was correct to construe this as a measuring protecting against the risk of old age (rather than protection against lack of financial means, as contended by the UK government). Hence, it was covered by the Directive. In addition, the Court found that the situation was not covered by the derogation in Article 7(1)(a), which excludes the setting of the pensionable age from the scope of the Directive. Consequently, the UK government took immediate remedial action during the winter of 1999/2000 to ensure compliance with the judgment.[106]

In view of the continuing profound earnings gap between men and women, with the latest figures released by Eurostat continuing to show women earning an EU average of 76.3 per cent of the pay of men,[107] with variations between Greece (68 per cent) and Denmark (88.1 per cent), it is not surprising to find that issues of equal pay remain a constant preoccupation in case

---

[104] Case C-187/98, *Commission v. Greece*, [1999] ECR I-7713.

[105] Case C-382/98, *R v. Secretary of State for Social Security, ex parte Taylor*, [1999] ECR I-8955.

[106] H. Carter, 'Euro Ruling Brings Fuel Payment U-Turn', *Guardian*, 17 Dec. 1999.

[107] Eurostat news release, 8 June 1999, No. 48/99. The figures actually date from the mid-1990s, but the earnings gap has proved sufficiently enduring for these figures to have strong currency in the early 21st century.

law before the Court of Justice. Two references from Austria raised interesting questions. The *Wiener* case[108] concerned the issue of whether two groups of workers (psychologists and doctors employed as psychotherapists) performing what appeared to be identical tasks, but with different training and/or professional qualifications, were called upon to perform the 'same work'. The Court concluded that they are not, because they draw upon different knowledge and skills even though they perform seemingly identical activities, and thus they cannot be regarded as in a comparable situation for the purposes of the application of Article 141 EC. Those who are not doing the 'same work' will, therefore, need to rely upon the more complex construction of a claim for equal pay for work of *equal value*. More controversial was the ruling in the case of *Gruber* that a woman who gave up work because she was experiencing difficulties in obtaining child care for her children was not entitled to a higher rate of termination payment available under Austrian legislation.[109] These payments are made when employees leave for so-called 'important reasons', including unfitness for work or risk from the employment to the employee's health or moral welfare, or other matters relating to working conditions in the place of employment or to the conduct of the employer, all of which make continued work impossible. According to the Court, they were reasons such that 'no worker could be expected to maintain his employment relationship, even during the period of notice normally provided for in the event of resignation'.[110] Child care difficulties obviously did not fall into this category by analogy, as far as the Court was concerned.[111]

On the other hand, the limits of 'pay' continue to creep outwards. In *Krüger*, the Court held that an end-of-year bonus paid under a collective agreement is 'pay', and Article 141 applies even though the collective agreement in question excluded those in 'minor employment' under a minimum weekly threshold of hours.[112] A 'Christmas bonus' is also pay, even if paid voluntarily by the employer and as an incentive for future work and loyalty, and was payable, the Court held in *Lewen*, even to a woman who had been on maternity leave for part of the year.[113] An employer can, however, require that the employee is in active employment when the bonus is actually paid. Moreover, in *Seymour-Smith* the Court held that a judicial award of compensation for breach of the right not to be unfairly dismissed falls within Article

---

[108] Case C-309/97, *Angestelltenbetriebsrat der Wiener Gebietskrankenkasse v. Wiener Gebietskrankenkasse*, [1999] ECR I-2865.

[109] Case C-249/97, *Gruber v. Silhouette International Schmied GmbH & Co. KG*, [1999] ECR I-5295.

[110] Para. 32 of the judgment.   [111] See further below at n. 212.

[112] Case C-281/97, *Krüger v. Kreiskrankenhaus Ebersberg*, [1999] ECR I-5127.

[113] Case C-333/97, *Lewen v. Denda*, [1999] ECR I-7243.

141, as do the conditions under which such awards are made.[114] The case arose because the UK Conservative government in 1985 increased the qualifying period for compensation for unfair dismissal from one to two years. The applicants contended that this discriminated indirectly against women, and brought a direct challenge to the relevant regulations by means of an action for judicial review in the High Court. They were able to adduce statistical evidence to demonstrate that on average over a period of years from 1985, for every ten men who would be able to satisfy the qualifying period if dismissed, only nine women would be able to do so. The issue was, therefore, one of whether there was disparate impact. Interestingly, although the Court's (not unequivocal) judgment seems to indicate that the difference in the impact on men and women might not mean that a 'considerably smaller percentage of women than men' will qualify, in fact the House of Lords, on re-hearing the case, concluded by a majority of three to two that it *did*.[115] This question was not the only one which the Court of Justice left it to the national court to decide, since it found that it was for the national court to determine at what point in time any objective justification is to be measured (the date when the measure was adopted, perhaps, or the date when the claim arose), and offered the prospect that the measure could be objectively justified provided the Member State could show that the means chosen were suitable for promoting the policy asserted (promoting employment). The question of objective justification was the 'escape route'[116] which the majority of the House of Lords eventually took, finding the Secretary of State to have satisfied the burden placed upon him, thus avoiding the potentially highly disruptive finding that the measure was unlawful, as many similar claims were also pending before the UK courts.

Continuing the theme of 'pay', the Court concluded—in a case brought by male workers at a Renault factory aggrieved at the award of a one-off payment to women workers who took maternity leave—that such an award, although covered by Article 141, was not precluded by this provision as it was designed to offset the occupational disadvantages associated with pregnancy, such as exclusion from promotion or performance-related pay.[117] Finally, in a group of cases on issues of pay decided in early 2000,[118] the Court confirmed that

[114] Case C-167/97, *R v. Secretary of State for Employment, ex parte Seymour-Smith and Perez*, [1999] ECR I-623.

[115] *R. v. Secretary of State for Employment, ex parte Seymour-Smith and Perez*, judgment of 17 Feb. 2000 (HL). However, even those who found there was disparate impact also allowed the Secretary of State's appeal against the Court of Appeal's earlier judgment ([1995] ICR 919) on the grounds that he had successfully demonstrated an objective justification related to the attempt to make the labour market more flexible.

[116] C. Barnard and T. Hervey, 'European Union Employment and Social Policy Survey 1998', (1998) 18 Yearbook of European Law 613 at 636.

[117] Case C-218/98, *Abdoulaye v. Renault*, [1999] ECR I-5723.

[118] *Schröder*, above n. 60.

the exclusion of part-timers from an occupational pension scheme infringed Article 141 EC and was not a 'pensions scenario' covered by the temporal limitation in the case of *Barber*, where there was reasonable ground for uncertainty about the scope of Member State discretion to fix discriminatory retirement ages having regard to the network of provisions and derogations surrounding this question.[119]

Turning now in conclusion to equal treatment, the Court continues to receive references on the vexed issues raised by pregnancy discrimination. In *Mahlburg* the applicant was refused appointment to a post with a contract of indefinite duration (having previously been carrying out such duties on a fixed-term basis) because a provision of the relevant protective German legislation prohibited employment in the area covered by the post (as an operating theatre nurse) because of the risk of infection. The pregnant applicant, meanwhile, was assigned to other duties, still on a fixed-term contract. The protective German legislation is justified by Article 2(3) of the Equal Treatment Directive, as a derogation from the equal treatment principle covering the protection of pregnant women and issues related to maternity. The Court had already considered the scenario of a woman dismissed whilst pregnant, because of the effects of a statutory prohibition on night work by pregnant women.[120] The Court was happy to extend this principle to the refusal to appoint, arguing that it is not permissible for an employer to refuse to take on a pregnant woman on the ground that a prohibition on employment arising on account of the pregnancy would prevent her being employed from the outset and for the duration of the pregnancy in the post of unlimited duration to be filled. Implicitly, there will be plenty of time afterwards. The Court refused to countenance financial arguments on behalf of the employer.

The equal treatment provisions have also led to a review of British and German restrictions on women in the armed forces. The applicant in *Sirdar* had been a chef with the British Army for a number of years when she was informed that she would be made redundant.[121] She was initially offered the possibility of a transfer to the Royal Marines, subject to passing an initial selection board and following a commando training course, but the offer was withdrawn when the authorities in the Royal Marines became aware of the fact that she was a woman. There is a policy of excluding women from that regiment. Sirdar was duly made redundant and brought an industrial tribunal action claiming sex discrimination. As a matter of principle, the Court found decisions taken by Member States regarding access to employment, vocational training, and working conditions in the armed forces for the purpose of

---

[119] Case C-262/88, *Barber v. Guardian Royal Exchange Assurance Group*, [1990] ECR I-1889.

[120] Case C-421/92, *Habermann-Beltermann*, [1994] ECR I-1657.

[121] Case C-273/97, *Sirdar v. The Army Board*, [1999] ECR I-7403.

ensuring combat effectiveness do not fall outside the scope of EC law altogether. On the other hand, the UK was able to invoke the derogation in Article 2(2) of the Equal Treatment Directive, under which the sex of the worker may be a determining factor for a particular occupational activity, on the grounds of the specific organization of the Royal Marines as the first line of attack, in which chefs as well as other troops are required to serve as frontline commandos. In *Kreil* the blanket ban under German law on women from all military posts involving the use of arms was held to be contrary to the Equal Treatment Directive, and so the refusal to employ Kreil in the army's electronic maintenance service was illegal.[122]

This review has necessarily been very selective in its coverage of the breadth and depth of the Court's case law on the sex equality provisions. Some issues will be picked up again in Section V, which attempts to interpret the role of the Court as *legal* and as *political* institution. Suffice it to say, in the mean time, that the richness of the case law for 1999 and early 2000 demonstrates the continuing vitality of this field in terms of legal practice and legal evolution. As a body of case law, sex equality law has dominated the gender issue.

C. Beyond Sex Equality: An 'Agenda for Gender'

Returning now to the broader 'agenda for gender' which—it was argued at the outset of this section—is in fact derived from the foundational fields of 'women's policy' and sex equality law, it can be seen that a wider range of concerns has been visible for many years in the Commission's programmes and reports, and in its sponsoring and fostering of research and information and publicity activities such as conferences and workshops. Since 1996, the Commission has been publishing Annual Reports on Equal Opportunities by the Commission.[123] Looking further backwards, three action programmes on equal opportunities for women and men have now been completed, a fourth is in its concluding stages, and a fifth is in the process of being set up.[124] There is often a tendency to decry the importance and constructive effects of the programmatic endeavours so beloved of the Commission, but there seems little doubt that the programmes have been a contributory factor in the diffusion of equal opportunities policies into the wider framework of Commission and Community activities more generally. Historically, policymaking away from the equal opportunities in employment field has been largely limited to soft law, of which the 1996 Council Recommendation on

---

[122] Case C-285/98, *Kreil v. Bundesrepublik Deutschland*, [2000] ECR I-69.

[123] See, for the most recent reports, the 1998 Annual Report COM(1999) 106 and the 1999 Report COM(2000) 123.

[124] 1982–5, OJ 1982 C186/3; 1986–90, Supp. Bull. EC 3/86; 1991–5, COM(90) 449; 1996–2000, Council Decision 95/593, OJ 1995 L335/37; 2001–5 (above n. 59). For a review of earlier programmes see Elman, 'Virtual Equality', above n. 40 at 231–3.

the balanced participation of women and men in the decision-making process[125] or the 1999 Council Resolution on women and science[126] are good examples. Exceptions are the measures taken to combat violence against women and trafficking in women. In December 1999, a Council and Parliament Decision[127] adopted the DAPHNE Programme on measures, including financial support for initiatives, to combat violence against women, building on the earlier, soft DAPHNE initiative.[128] These are in the nature of 'positive action' measures, which can be seen as an interim step towards mainstreaming in which 'the emphasis shifts from equality of access[129] to creating conditions more likely to result in equality of outcome'.[130] They complement well-established funding programmes in the field of education and training and in relation to the use of the structural funds to support women's employment and training. However, with the move to 'mainstreaming' there has been a shift from specific programmes for women to mainstreaming equal opportunities into general programmes,[131] complete with targeted 'initiatives' for women and other disadvantaged minorities.

'Mainstreaming' has now superseded notions of 'equal opportunities' as the organizing concept for policy in the gender field. It dominates the structure and content of recent Equal Opportunities Annual Reports from the Commission.[132] For some, this change is viewed optimistically as evidence of a broader agenda, linked to the success of social movements lobbying around this question at national and EU level.[133] For others, the change is no more than a rhetorical shift within a consistent pattern of equality policy which is 'virtual', not 'real'.[134] According to the Commission, mainstreaming is now both a policy goal in itself and 'a strategy for achieving change in all other targeted policy'.[135] That strategy proceeds, according to the Commission, through

the systematic integration of the respective situations, priorities and needs of women in all policies and with a view to promoting equality between women and men and mobilising all general policies and measures specifically for the purpose of achieving equality by actively and openly taking into account, at the planning stage, their effects

---

[125] Council Recommendation 96/694, OJ 1996 L319/11.
[126] Council Resolution of 20 May 1999 on women and science, OJ 1999 C 201/1.
[127] European Parliament and Council Decision No. 293/2000, OJ 2000 L 34.
[128] COM(1999) 82, OJ C 89 of 30 Mar. 1999.   [129] i.e. equal treatment.
[130] T. Rees, *Mainstreaming Equality in the European Union: Education, Training, and Labor Market Policies* (New York: Routledge, 1998), 34.
[131] Council Resolution on mainstreaming equal opportunities for men and women into the European Structural Funds, OJ 1996 C386/1. See now the General Regulation on the Structural Funds (2000–6), EC Regulation No. 1260/1999 of 21 June 1999, OJ 1999 L161.
[132] Mazey, above n. 32.   [133] e.g. Pollack and Hafner-Burton, above n. 57.
[134] e.g. Elman, above n. 40.
[135] Interim Report of the Commission on the implementation of the 1996–2000 Action Programme on equal opportunities for men and women, COM(98) 770, Executive Summary.

on the respective situation of women and men in implementation, monitoring and evaluation.[136]

The attempt to make gender mainstreaming something close to comprehensive within the Commission itself has resulted in patchy outcomes. Commission President Romano Prodi continued the Commissioner's Group on Equal Opportunities chaired by Employment and Social Affairs Commissioner Anna Diamantopoulou. The Commission has produced guidelines and checklists for officials, and in every Directorate-General there is at least one official with responsibility for gender mainstreaming. The most obvious progress has been in two areas: employment policy and development aid policy. The example of employment policy demonstrates a positive conjunction of a new opportunity structure for policy-making opened as a result of the new Employment Policy title in the EC Treaty after Amsterdam, and in particular its pre-emptive implementation by the Member States and the institutions after the Luxembourg Summit, along with the opening of the gender mainstreaming debate. The result sees equal opportunities as one pillar of the employment policy and gender mainstreaming as a Guideline adopted by the Council on national employment policies.[137] The (strongly worded) gender Guideline was inserted in the 1999 versions of the Guidelines because of strong support from the British and Austrian Presidencies of the Council in 1998, and then retained for 2000. The framework for employment policy is now much more than the so-called 'ritualistic denunciations' of the evils of unemployment at periodic summits and European Council meetings highlighted by Dinan.[138] Member States must prepare national action plans (NAPs) and the Commission can scrutinize and even issue specific recommendations or criticisms directed at individual Member States or the Member States as a whole.[139] Pollack and Hafner-Burton highlight changes in NAPs which can directly be attributed to Commission pressure.[140] The acid test would then concern whether the NAPs result in real policy changes at national level. This is particularly important since the relevance of

[136] Commission Communication, *Incorporating Equal Opportunities for Women and Men into All Community Policies and Activities*, COM(96) 67. See also Progress Report from the Commission on the follow-up of the Communication, 'Incorporating Equal Opportunities for Women and Men into All Community Policies and Activities', COM(1998) 122; 'A Guide to Gender Impact Assessment', DG Employment and Social Affairs Website, 1998.

[137] See Council Recommendation 00/164 on the implementation of Member States' employment policies, OJ 2000 L 052/32.

[138] D. Dinan, *Ever Closer Union*, 2nd edn. (London: Macmillan, 1999), 402.

[139] The legal ambiguity of the employment provisions and the measures which they give rise to are considered by E. Szyszczak, 'The Evolving Employment Strategy', in Shaw, above n. 20, and S. Sciarra, 'The Employment Title in the Amsterdam Treaty: A Multi-Language Legal Discourse', in O'Keeffe and Twomey, above n. 54.

[140] Pollack and Hafner-Burton, above n. 57.

the gender issue here is established by hard factual evidence regarding the higher rates of unemployment amongst women, especially younger women, and the training and skills deficits suffered by women.[141] In the area of development policy, the legislative process has given rise initially to discursive measures[142] and latterly to a Regulation specifically on the question of integrating gender.[143] These measures have been viewed as an interesting example of 'norm spread' within the EU based on norm negotiations within Council committees, amongst other fora.[144]

The shift towards gender mainstreaming and its possible relevance in terms of feminist approaches to the EU and its legal order has yet to be investigated in full. If legal frameworks are, on average, 'softer' and more generalist, what does that mean? Will it imply, in the long term, a watering down of already relatively weak equality concepts enshrined in the equality directives? Or might it imply a strengthening of these concepts at least in terms of substantive meaning, but a consequential weakening of enforcement and structures of enforceability? Alternatively, should the institutional adoption of an agenda of mainstreaming be seen as the 'framing out' of the disruptive and radical aspects of feminism?[145] These questions, as yet unanswered, provide an important context as we move towards linking the issue of gender and the Court of Justice.

IV THE INSTITUTIONAL CONTEXT

Charlesworth, Chinkin, and Wright argue that the organizational structure of international law—by excluding women in large measure from access to decision-making—contributes to the gendered nature of international law.[146]

---

[141] For recent unemployment figures see *CREW News* 11, 13 Mar. 2000, on the basis of Eurostat figures: although falling, women's unemployment in Dec. 1999 was 10.5% in the EU15 (11.9% in Euroland), while men's unemployment is 7.5% (EU15) and 7.9% (Euroland). 18.4% of young women are unemployed in EU15 and 20.2% in Euroland, against 15.7% and 16.4% for young men.

[142] Commission Communication on integrating gender issues in development cooperation, COM(95) 423.

[143] Council Regulation 2836/98 on integrating gender issues in development cooperation, OJ 1998 L354/5. This is supplemented also by Regulations 975/99 and 976/99 on human rights in external policies, OJ L 120 of 8 May 1999.

[144] O. Elgström, 'Norm Negotiations: The Construction of New Norms regarding Gender and Development in EU Foreign Aid Policy', (2000) 6 Journal of European Public Policy 457.

[145] A. S. Runyan, 'Women in the Neoliberal "Frame"', in M. Meyer and E. Prügl (eds.), *Gender Politics in Global Governance* (Lanham, Md.: Rowman & Littlefield, 1999).

[146] Above n. 44 at 621. For detailed information see the chapter on 'International Institutions' in H. Charlesworth and C. Chinkin, *The Boundaries of International Law* (Manchester: Manchester University Press, 2000).

Right up to the present time, most of the institutions of the European Union have had a very poor record in relation to the participation and employment of women. Since the 1996 Council Recommendation on balanced participation of women and men in the decision-making process,[147] however, consistent efforts have been made to scrutinize gender balance not only in the EU institutions themselves, but also within the political and legal institutions of the Member States. A recent Report from the Commission on the implementation of the Council Recommendation,[148] which can usefully be coupled with evidence from the Annual Reports of the Commission on Equal Opportunities, frames the EU and national initiatives within the wider international context of the Beijing Platform for action and addresses 'progress' in relation to nine indicators, including representation in different levels of the legislature at EU, national, subnational, and local level, representation in governments and executives, and representation amongst the senior judiciary.

In relation to the Court of Justice there have recently been some small but significant changes. The Commission's Equal Opportunities Annual Reports shift between 1998 and 1999; in 1998 it is reported that there is 'no progress' in the Court of Justice, but in 1999 the Commission notes with obvious pleasure that for the first time in history a woman judge was appointed to the Court. The Irish judge, Fidelma O'Kelly Macken, appointed in October 1999, joins the only woman ever previously appointed to the Court—Advocate-General Simone Rozès (1981–5)—as a 'first'.[149] In 2000, came the appointment of a woman judge by Germany and of a woman Advocate General by Austria. There are also two women judges at the Court of First Instance, perhaps predictably the Finnish and Swedish judges appointed on the accession of those states to the EU in 1995. This pattern of very limited female participation in the Union's judicature reflects the vertical segregation of women within the judiciaries of most of the Member States (especially where entry to the judiciary is by competition): although women, as a percentage of the judiciary as a whole, are frequently better represented than in other professions, they are very poorly represented in the highest positions.[150] This implies difficulties with national promotion procedures. An appointment to the Court of Justice represents a very senior appointment which by definition excludes most women judges at national level. However, of course, appointments to the Court of

---

[147] Above n. 125.

[148] Report from the Commission to the Council, the European Parliament, and the ECOSOC on the implementation of Council Recommendation 96/694 of 2 Dec. 1996 on the balanced participation of women and men in the decision-making process, COM(2000) 120.

[149] On the Court of Justice and its judges see further S. Kenney, 'The Members of the Court of Justice of the European Communities', (1998/9) 5 Columbia Journal of European Law 101.

[150] See generally M. Anasagasti and N. Wuiame, *Women and Decision-making in the Judiciary in the European Union* (Brussels: OOPEC (DG for Employment, Industrial Relations and Social Affairs, Unit V/D.5), 1999).

Justice do not have to be judges at national level, but can be qualified by virtue of their work in other ways (as academics, as national officials, or as practising lawyers). The further point about the national judiciaries concerns the role of national courts as 'Community courts' so far as they can and do apply EC law in the context of national proceedings. Here horizontal segregation and the ghettoization of many women judges in 'soft' issues such as family law has an impact upon their interaction with EC law. Only 9 per cent of the judges in German tax courts—whence many German cases referred to the Court of Justice in practice come—are women.[151]

Turning the spotlight to the *internal* workings of the Court of Justice, what little work has been done on the *référendaires* or legal secretaries at the Court of Justice has not addressed the gender issue in any depth, in terms either of numbers or of attitudes towards the Court of Justice and its work.[152] Figures are confined to an overall percentage up to 1994: 14.6 per cent over the years had been women, and at the time when the research was completed in 1994, ten out of the fifty-six *référendaires* were women (18 per cent), with seven out of twenty-four at the Court of First Instance (29 per cent). This was prior to the accession of Sweden and Finland, which might well have increased the percentages. Interestingly, in terms of *perception* and visibility of women's presence, the interviewee respondents commented that *one-third* of the legal secretaries at the Court were women, thus in their own minds doubling their actual representation.

Elsewhere[153] amongst the EU institutions, five of the members of the present and previous Commission are women. Commissioner Diamantopoulou is a Vice-President of the Commission. The Commission is committed to ensuring a more balanced representation throughout committees, expert groups, working groups, etc. A 1998 Regulation integrates equality clauses into the recruitment procedures and status of officials.[154] The numbers of female members of the Council is, of course, constantly shifting and therefore difficult to track, but within the national governments the Commission's report notes a significant increase in female representation which is higher than in relation to national parliaments. In the European Parliament, the 1999 elections brought the percentage of women members to 30.2 per cent, although representation is spread unevenly across the Member States, with highs in Denmark and Finland (both 43.8 per cent) and lows in Greece (16 per cent and steady) and Italy (11.5 per cent and dropping). Thirty per cent

---

[151] Anasagasti and Wuiame, above n. 150.

[152] See S. Kenney, 'Beyond Principals and Agents: Seeing Courts as Organizations by Comparing *Référendaires* at the European Court of Justice and Law Clerks at the U.S. Supreme Court', MS, May 1999.

[153] Figures taken from the Commission's 1999 and 1998 Equal Opportunities Annual Reports, above n. 123.

[154] Council Regulation 781/98, OJ 1998 L113/4.

is, in any event, much higher than the average female representation in the national parliaments, which stood at just 18.6 per cent on average in 1999. In the European Parliament elections in 1999 the use of the list system and proportional representation made a difference in the UK (an increase from 18.4 per cent to 24.1 per cent). In 1998 the ECOSOC had 22 per cent women members holding a mandate from 1998 to 2000, and for the second term of the Committee of the Regions female participation rose from 9.9 per cent (1994–8) to 14.9 per cent (1998–2002). There are two female members of the fifteen-person Court of Auditors.

These figures do not give a full enough picture to allow comprehensive conclusions to be drawn about the 'gendered' nature of the EU in institutional terms. They demonstrate a trend of change, at least, but not a definitive shift to feminized institutions. Significant differences amongst the Member States are charted, notably between the southern and northern European Member States, the latter of which have pursued longer-term equal opportunities initiatives and some of which now operate quota systems in some areas of political life. Certainly, these trends assist—as with the previous sections—in setting the stage for the attempt, through this chapter, to interpret and interrogate the work of the Court of Justice as an institution of the European Union.

V INTERPRETING THE COURT OF JUSTICE

A. Introduction

To enquire into the Court of Justice's work in relation to issues of gender would appear, at first sight, to be a rather banal question. Surely the Court will simply apply its general mandate under Article 220 EC 'to ensure that in the interpretation and application of [the] Treaty, the law is observed'?[155] Moreover, as the review of the policy framework in Section III has shown, this seems likely to be limited in terms of scope to interpreting and applying the law on equal treatment of the sexes, as and when required to do under its Article 226 enforcement jurisdiction and its Article 234 preliminary ruling jurisdiction. It is in that context, one must begin by assuming, that the constitutional limits of the jurisdiction of the Court will operate. Bearing in mind the limited nature of the scope of EU law and of Community competence under the EC Treaty, it is not immediately apparent how else *gender*—as a facet of social organization and as the basis for a critique of social order—could possibly be relevant *in a legal sense* to what the Court actually does. For adjudication only occurs if there is litigation, and presupposes that there must

---

[155] This is a link also made by Mancini and O'Leary, above n. 25 at 352; it is an unsurprising deduction to find in a paper co-authored by a judge of the Court of Justice, writing in a non-judicial capacity, and one of his legal secretaries.

be some legal issue which *implicates gender* before there can be any manner of justiciable dispute.

Section VI examines the latter issue, juxtaposing directly the broader challenge of gender with the Court's work under the Treaties. It attempts a (speculative) gender-centred analysis in order to reflect upon aspects of the Court's work inside and outside the field of sex equality law, adopting an interrogative approach. This section, however, works outwards from the first assumption of a limited role for the Court of Justice, examining and reinterpreting the interpretative work of the Court of Justice in relation to the sex equality provisions, placing it, in turn, in its legal and political contexts.

What has been said thus far would seem to implicate what Weiler calls the 'classical' approach to understanding and evaluating the role of the Court of Justice and of the judicial process in the evolution of the EU and the European integration process.[156] It involves the laying down of doctrine, that is, a normative framework purporting to govern certain fundamental constitutional issues and certain material socio-economic relationships, in the language of binding rules. Arnull's work on the Court of Justice, which includes an exposition of the points of pressure in relation to equal treatment case law, seems to sit comfortably within the classical paradigm. At least, that is the self-portrait offered by the author in his preface to his recent book on the Court.[157] In fact, it would be better to describe it as a 'classical-plus' or 'doctrine-plus' approach. For in a more wide-ranging final chapter to his book, Arnull seeks to examine 'the extent to which the approach of the Court to its task has evolved over time and to speculate about the causes of such variation',[158] although he does not develop a single hypothesis which can be used to explain *why* the Court might be sensitive to its political environment.[159] Rather, he characterizes the Court, in conclusion, as neither activist nor passive but as 'radically conservative' in its interaction with its environment. In other words, he implicitly accepts the thesis of the dual legal and political role of the Court of Justice, and links the argument to contentions about the *legitimacy* of the Court of Justice. What the approach begins to bring out, however, is the structuring force of the Court's position within the EU system. To

[156] J. H. H. Weiler, *The Constitution of Europe* (Cambridge: Cambridge University Press, 1999), 189.

[157] A. Arnull, *The European Union and Its Court of Justice* (Oxford: Oxford University Press, 1999), p. ix.

[158] Ibid. ch. 16, 'Judging Europe's Judges'.

[159] Compare the work of Jo Hunt and the use of the concepts of 'framing' and 'governance regimes' to examine interactions between the Court and its environment: J. Hunt, 'Interdisciplinary Approaches to EU Decision Making: Law, Politics and the Multi-level Governance Regime', (2000) Current Politics and Economics in Europe 165; J. Hunt, 'The Development of the Law and Policy Relating to the Acquired Rights Directive: A New Institutionalist Perspective' (Ph.D. dissertation, University of Leeds, 2000).

reveal this point more clearly, the analysis in this section will chart the boundaries of a Court positioned between legal and political understandings of integration in its fullest sense (including 'disintegration' in certain circumstances),[160] while at the same time highlighting the limits of such an approach, thus opening the conceptual space for a critical focus through the analysis of 'gender'. The cornerstone of this section must be, therefore, understandings of the role of the Court within the paradigm established by the legal and political boundaries of the process of integration. In other words, it deals with a currency in which the primary functionality of legal order of the EU emerges in relation to its contribution to the many and varied processes of integration (and sometimes disintegration).

B. The Court as Legal Institution

The first task is thus to excavate some understandings of the role of the Court as a *legal institution*, dealing specifically with its quality of *judgment* as well as the choices of the *judge*. The main currency of such an expedition within a liberal legal order must necessarily be the belief that the judge can and does in some sense embody 'reason in law'.[161] Dominant traditions of positivist legal analysis adhere to the notion that there is a specific and autonomous quality to legal reasoning and legal discourse which separates it from, for example, ethical reasoning or discourse. Breaking down the process and content of legal reasoning into its composite elements, we find in turn some more specific questions about the permissible scope of the interpretation of legal texts, the role of 'rule following' and precedent as opposed to reasoning from first principle according to a notion of justice or analogical reasoning, the extent to which *judgment* also necessitates justification, persuasion, or advocacy in the form of extended reasoned argument, and the role of political, economic, social, and cultural context in supplying the 'purposes' for which laws exist or have been made.[162] Closely linked questions are the extent to which the judge herself is ascribed authority within the wider political and constitutional system (and in the EU context the extent to which the rulings of the Court of Justice are in fact followed at national level or are complied with by the Member States who remain the formal 'Masters of the Treaty'), the relationship between the different 'powers' of the state, and the extent to which judges are subservient to democratic legitimacy in the form of legislative texts or constitutional legitimacy in the form of a higher law. In the EU context, this latter point raises some special questions, as the EU does not have a conven-

---

[160] J. Shaw, 'European Union Legal Studies in Crisis? Towards a New Dynamic', (1996) 16 Oxford Journal of Legal Studies 231.

[161] See e.g. the critique by Unger, above n. 3, 110.

[162] For general guidance, see J. W. Harris, *Legal Philosophies*, 2nd edn. (London: Butterworths, 1997), esp. chs. 12–15.

tionally elected legislature or a conventional executive or government produced by party politics which dominates that legislature. Although Unger rejects the specificity of legal reasoning as such, he nonetheless supplies a definition of the *legal* role of a court which can function as a useful template to examine the role of the Court of Justice:

the heart of most legal analysis in an adjudicative setting should and must be the context-oriented practice of analogical reasoning in the interpretation of statutes and past judicial decisions. This analogical reasoning must be guided by the attribution of purpose to the interpreted materials, an attribution that can often remain implicit in situations of settled usage but that must be brought out into the open whenever meanings and goals are contested.[163]

This statement reminds us that while it is useful to deploy a distinction between the Court as legal and as political institution, the two roles are fundamentally linked wherever there is societal contestation. This occurs quite frequently in relation to the interpretation of EU law, and it is clear that this could place special responsibilities upon the Court of Justice.

Arnull defends the view that the Court's approach to legal interpretation is not especially unorthodox, having regarding to the rules of international law, including the Vienna Convention on the Law of Treaties, which allows interpretations in the light of 'object and purpose'.[164] This is a defence against a charge of undue activism, and against the suggestion that the Court goes *outside* the boundaries of permissible interpretation by ignoring the plain words of relevant provisions.[165] Equally, in relation to its interpretations of the sex equality provisions, Arnull defends the actions of the Court of Justice against a charge that it has been too passive and accepting of unduly limited interpretations of the scope of those provisions. He would deny the claim by Ellis that the Court of Justice in the 1990s 'often appears to have lost sight of the objectives of the legislation and to be operating as a drag on the system'.[166]

What, briefly, is the basis for such divergent views of the *legal* role of the Court of Justice in relation to the sex equality provisions which were described in Section III? Is it right to suggest that the Court of Justice fails fully to exploit the available interpretive space?[167] Do all the commentators still agree that the Court of Justice remains a key actor within the framework of EC sex equality law, as was always the traditional view despite scepticism on some parts?[168] Is it the use of gender as an interpretive principle which pushes

---

[163] Unger, above n. 3, 114.   [164] Arnull, above n. 157, 525.

[165] See e.g. the work of Hjalte Rasmussen (*On Law and Policy in the European Court of Justice*, Dordrecht: Martinus Nijhoff, 1986) and, more recently, Trevor Hartley (*Constitutional Problems of the European Union*, Oxford: Hart, 1999).

[166] E. Ellis, 'Recent Developments in EC Sex Equality Law', (1998) 35 CMLRev. 379 at 379.

[167] As I have contended with Tamara Hervey in an earlier piece, above n. 17 at 45.

[168] e.g. most notably Fredman, above n. 17.

commentators towards a critical stance on the work of the Court, and indeed leads in turn to the uncovering of gendered frameworks and structures?

Arnull asserts that the Court has been just as activist and 'purposive' as it could reasonably have been in the development of sex equality law, pointing to the decision in *Defrenne II* establishing the crucial principle of direct effect,[169] the wide definition which the Court has given to concepts such as 'pay',[170] and most—if not all—aspects of the principle of indirect discrimination which it has developed.[171] But if, in essence, the complaint of those who criticize the Court comes down to disappointment that changes in the law have not been matched by societal change and 'real equality' for women, then this can hardly be laid at the door of the Court, which is only responsible for giving effect 'to the policy choices made by the authors of the applicable Community rules'.[172] The suggestion is there that disappointment arises because the expectations which were placed upon the Court were too high and completely unrealistic.[173] Gender is deeply embedded in societal structures, and law is viewed as incapable of addressing these questions, with judicial institutions lacking most, if not all, agency in this regard. On this view, the only 'judicial politics' which really matter in this field are those surrounding the temporal limitations which it laid down in its decisions in *Defrenne II* and the leading pensions case of *Barber*,[174] thus restricting access to equal pay, and not in fact the vagaries of the Court's demarcation of the concept of equality. Those actions have received considerable criticism from those who believe the Court has been too activist in favour of promoting the integration of the EU and usurping the role of the legislature.[175] The crux of the issue will, on that view, be debating whether the Court is (a) correct to invoke the principle of legal certainty to allow it to impose temporal limitations upon its rulings in exceptional circumstances, and (b) correct to do so in the particular cases of *Defrenne* and *Barber*.[176]

If the *Defrenne* and *Barber* temporal limitations were attempts to accommodate or even appease the interests of Member States,[177] moves on the part of the Court of Justice which Arnull is somewhat reluctant to concede on the

---

[169] Above n. 98.

[170] Including, most dramatically, pensions: Case C-262/88, *Barber v. Guardian Royal Exchange Assurance Group*, [1990] ECR I-1889.

[171] Case 170/84, *Bilka Kaufhaus GmbH v. Weber von Hartz*, [1986] ECR 1607.

[172] Arnull, above n. 157 at 509.   [173] Mancini and O'Leary, above n. 25 at 353.

[174] See above n. 170.   [175] e.g. Hartley, above n. 165 at 41–2.

[176] Arnull, above n. 157 at 193 and 464.

[177] In the latter case, a move buttressed by the decision of the Member States to attach a protocol specifically addressing the same issue to the Treaty of Maastricht. On the effects of the '*Barber* Protocol' see T. Hervey, 'Legal Issues concerning the *Barber* Protocol', in D. O'Keeffe and P. Twomey (eds.), *Legal Issues of the Maastricht Treaty* (Chichester: Wiley, 1994).

facts[178] while remaining enthusiastic about the principle,[179] it is interesting to speculate as to how he might react to the most recent group of cases on this question, where the Court of Justice has deliberately 'limited the limitation', having regard to the specific sensitivities of German constitutional law. In *Schröder* and the related cases on access to occupational pension schemes for part-time workers,[180] one of the questions before the Court of Justice concerned the effects in national law of temporal limitations which it has imposed upon equality rights under EU law and of other limitations of scope, such as its conclusion that the right of (primarily female) part-time workers not to be excluded from occupational pension schemes does not in itself automatically imply the right to a pension. On the Court's construction, all that is required of national law under EU law is that part-time workers may join pension schemes, but they cannot claim the right to a pension unless they have paid the relevant contributions. This would mean, for example, buying back the lost years. This operates as a form of effective temporal limitation, since such rights are only in truth likely to assist part-time workers now embarking upon the process of buying their pension.

Schröder and its sister cases challenged the much-criticized parsimony of the Court's rulings, by reference to the legal situation *now* applicable in Germany (partly as a result of the influence of EU law as well as internal political developments in which sex equality issues have been brought to the fore) which allows all part-time workers retroactive membership of occupational pension schemes and access to a pension. Avoiding directly addressing the question of priority between provisions of EU law and the German Constitution, Article 3 of which guarantees equality and is the present basis for the rights of part-time workers in *national* law, the Court concluded that there was nothing either in the temporal limitations which the Court has established or in the scope of Article 141 as it has been interpreted which precludes such generosity on the part of national law. In its reasoning the Court invoked the fundamental rights status of Article 141, a technique which it uses in some, but not all, of its cases to add a deeper seam of moral force to its argument.[181] Yet the impression remains on reading the cases that however powerfully worded the Court's invocation of human rights, it is in truth a rendering of the politics of gender into a politics of subsidiarity or sovereignty, once again to appease national sensitivities. On this occasion, the hidden subtext of the Court's judgment is not a deep-rooted concern for particular constructions of the status of equality as a right but rather the long-standing tensions between the

---

[178] Arnull, above n. 157 at 464 and 473.

[179] He describes the development of the Court's capacity to limit the temporal effect of its rulings as a 'stroke of genius': ibid. 464.

[180] Above n. 118.

[181] e.g. in Case C-13/94, *P v. S and Cornwall County Council,* [1996] ECR I-2143, and Case 149/77, *Defrenne III,* [1978] ECR 1365.

Court of Justice and the German courts on the question of fundamental rights. In effect, the German courts have 'forced' this interpretation by invoking the national fundamental rights guarantees in the Constitution and by standing in the formidable shadow of the German Federal Constitutional Court, with its famed doubts about the capacity of the Court of Justice to determine the scope of Community competence and the effects of EC law.[182]

A more imaginative blending of a defence of the Court's limitations as a 'judge of equality' with an awareness of the need for new policy solutions comes from Mancini and O'Leary, who paint a picture of the Court 'struggling to deal with the constraints imposed by Article 119 and the Equality Directives while attempting to live up to the standards of rights protection which it has set itself'.[183] As they point out and as we have just seen, the Court has, from time to time, resorted to 'alternative means to vindicate the rights of complainants, most notably with reference to the general principles of law and fundamental rights which it is bound to protect', and 'the results have sometimes been spectacular'.[184] The implication of Mancini and O'Leary's argument is that this is for reasons of the politics of gender, not the politics of sovereignty. Perhaps the *cause célèbre* for the invocation of fundamental rights arguments is the case of *P v. S and Cornwall County Council*, in which 'sex' equality was extended to cover discrimination against a transsexual dismissed after gender reassignment as a form of discrimination based 'essentially if not exclusively' on sex, using a fundamental rights argument.[185] Yet two years later, the Court took a markedly different approach in *Grant*.[186] In dismissing a claim for a spousal benefit for a lesbian partner, the Court used a strict comparison basis for determining whether there had been equal treatment, determining that the relevant comparator was a man with a male partner, who would have been likewise denied the spousal benefit, not the man with a female partner who preceded Lisa Grant in her employment.[187]

---

[182] From the early conflicts over the existence and status of fundamental rights in what was then the 'Community legal order' and the effects vis-à-vis constitutionally entrenched rights in the Basic Law (Case 11/70, *Internationale Handelsgesellschaft*, [1970] ECR 1125, and *Internationale Handelsgesellschaft*, [1974] 2 CMLR 549 (*Solange I*)) to more profound systemic doubts about what has become the EU legal order in the context of the ratification of the Treaty of Maastricht (*Brunner*, [1994] 1 CMLR 57).

[183] Above n. 25 at 353.   [184] Ibid. 334.   [185] Above n. 181.

[186] Above n. 37. The Court of First Instance also held in Case T-264/97, *D v. Council of the European Union*, [1999] ECR Staff I-A-1 and II-1, that a gay Swedish employee of the Council whose partnership was registered under Swedish law was not entitled to the spousal benefits in respect of his partner given to heterosexual married couples under the Council staff regulations. AG Mischo, Opinion of 28 Feb. 2001 in Cases C-122/99 P and C-125/99 P, *D and Sweden v. Council*, also found that only the Community legislature could have brought about the assimilation sought by the claimant by changing the law.

[187] On this see further J. Shaw, 'The Problem of Membership in European Union Citizenship', in Z. Bankowski and A. Scott (eds.), *The European Union and Its Order: The Legal Theory of the European Union* (Oxford: Blackwell, 2000).

Mancini and O'Leary comment on this disappointment: 'Expecting the Court always to rule with reference to this technique and in a fashion which could be regarded as an expansion of the frontiers of Community law is, however, unrealistic.'[188] Rather than consigning the issues raised by material disadvantage to an arena outwith the range of 'law' as such, Mancini and O'Leary call for the use of 'other means to protect disadvantaged groups, while avoiding the marginalisation which those opposed to special protection most fear.'[189] Some evidence of this can be seen from recent changes in the policy context charted in Section III such as the shift towards 'mainstreaming', and recent legal developments in the protection of atypical workers and reconciliation of family life and work such as the Parental Leave Directive, limited as some of these initiatives might so far be.

For critics of the Court, meanwhile, at the heart of the question remains the concept of equality, and all that flows from this in terms of functions, principles, standards, and indeed remedies.[190] Some lines of the feminist argument have already been sketched out in Section II. It is right to distinguish criticisms of the Court and criticisms of the functions and possibilities of a legal framework based upon concepts of discrimination and equal treatment within a liberal legal system and a capitalist mixed market economy.[191] Criticisms which have been directed at the Court come from a variety of different positions, and concern its failure fully to develop the 'human rights' dimension of equality highlighted in the previous paragraphs,[192] the accusation that its approach to family relationships reflects less an unwillingness to interfere in the private sphere (its ostensible public position[193]) and more a certain type of (outdated) 'maternalist' ideology in relation to the care of children,[194] its importation of too many market-based criteria into the concept of justification for indirect discrimination,[195] and its deference to Member State interests and the policy aims of welfare states in circumstances where Member States are called upon to justify indirectly discriminatory

---

[188] Above n. 25 at 334.   [189] Ibid.

[190] See Case C-185/97, *Coote v. Granada Hospitality Ltd.*, [1998] ECR I-5199, para. 23, on the link between remedies and the 'fundamental objective of equal treatment'.

[191] On this see esp. Fredman, above n. 75; see also N. Lacey, 'From Individual to Group? A Feminist Analysis of the Limits of Anti-Discrimination Legislation', in Lacey, above n. 11; Conaghan, above n. 34; J. Conaghan, 'Feminism and Labour Law: Contesting the Terrain', in Morris and O'Donnell, above n. 23; D. Ashiagbor, 'The Intersection between Gender and "Race" in the Labour Market: Lessons for Anti-Discrimination Law', in Morris and O'Donnell, above n. 23.

[192] Barnard, above n. 25, and C. Barnard, 'Some Are More Equal Than Others: the Decision of the Court of Justice in *Grant v. South West Trains*', (1998) 1 Cambridge Yearbook of European Law 145.

[193] See most famously Case 184/83, *Hofmann v. Barmer Ersatzkasse*, [1984] ECR 3047.

[194] McGlynn, above n. 19.

[195] Case C-127/92, *Enderby v. Frenchay Health Authority*, [1993] ECR I-5535.

social security schemes.[196] But above all, there has been a sense of impatience amongst critics that the Court has flirted with a more 'substantive' concept of equality as underlying its interpretations of the legal instrument of discrimination, but has failed to be consistent.[197] These seem to be arguments about *quality* of judgment as much as about judicial *choice* when faced with the 'contested meanings and goals' highlighted by Unger.[198] Here the Court has a special responsibility to articulate clearly the grounding of its judgment in precedent, analogy, or principle.

Many of these issues were thrown up by the controversy surrounding the Court's case law on positive actions schemes at national level supporting the employment or promotion of 'the underrepresented sex' (i.e. typically women who have faced greater historical and long-term disadvantage than men in the labour market) at the expense inevitably of the 'overrepresented sex'.[199] This has already been briefly referred to above.[200]

Until the agreement upon the Treaty of Amsterdam, the relevant legal framework for positive action was limited to Article 2(4) of the Equal Treatment Directive, which provides that the Directive shall be 'without prejudice to measures which promote equal opportunity for men and women, in particular by removing existing inequalities which affect women's opportunities'. An essentially exhortatory Council Recommendation was agreed in 1984 calling on the Member States to adopt positive action policies designed to eliminate existing inequalities affecting women in working life and to promote a better balance between the sexes in employment.[201] What should be the relationship between the EU-level guarantee of equality contained in the directive (Article 2(1)), read in the light of the saving clause in Article 2(4), on the one hand, and on the other the national and regional legislative frameworks which seek to establish, for example, quota systems to promote women's employment in areas where they have been underrepresented, which have been developed in accordance with the encouragement provided in the Council Recommendation? These are particularly common in Germany, where each of the *Länder* has some form of legislative framework for using the *Land* public service as a laboratory for equal opportunities.[202] The scope was

---

[196] e.g. Case C-280/94, *Posthuma-van Damme*, [1996] ECR I-179.

[197] e.g. Hervey and Shaw, above n. 17; Fenwick and Hervey, above n. 17.

[198] See above at n. 163.

[199] See C. Barnard and T. Hervey, 'Softening the Approach to Quotas: Positive Action after *Marschall*', (1998) 20 Journal of Social Welfare and Family Law 333; S. Fredman, 'After *Kalanke* and *Marschall*: Affirming Affirmative Action', (1998) 1 Cambridge Yearbook of European Law 199; L. Charpentier, 'The European Court of Justice and the Rhetoric of Affirmative Action', (1998) 4 European Law Journal 167.

[200] See n. 82 above.

[201] Council Recommendation 84/635 on the promotion of positive action for women, OJ 1984 L331/34.

[202] Barnard and Hervey, above n. 199.

clear for conflict between programmes for substantive equality agreed on a majoritarian basis at national or regional level, and whatever construction the Court chooses to place upon the EU level equality guarantee.

From the perspective of those campaigning for affirmative action programmes, the worst-case scenario appeared to be happening when the Court of Justice was faced with its first challenge by a disappointed man to the refusal of appointment under the Bremen *Land* positive action law. The applicant in *Kalanke* argued that his (EC) right to equality was infringed when he and a female co-worker applied for a promotion to the post of section manager within the public service of the City of Bremen.[203] A tie-break situation emerged, because it was decided that the two applicants were equally qualified for the post, and accordingly the female applicant was given preference in accordance with the Bremen law. This provided that 'in the case of an assignment to a position in a higher pay, remuneration and salary bracket, women who have the same qualifications as men applying for the same post are to be given priority if they are under-represented'. This was a radical variant of the tie-break and preference rule, because under-representation was defined at 50 per cent, and because it did not contain an *explicit* hardship clause allowing the balance to be tipped back in favour of men where circumstances required this.

In answer to questions posed by the national court about the relationship between this rule and the EC equal treatment guarantee, the Court found that applying the strict quota rule would be unlawful discrimination against the man because it was incompatible with the EC guarantee of equal treatment. It reached this conclusion notwithstanding the strong majoritarian and (national) constitutional legitimacy of the measure (agreed within regional and national legislatures, accepted as lawful under the German constitution). The Court was unable—or unwilling—to bring the Bremen clause within the scope of the limited Article 2(4) exception for equal opportunity measures.

Showing powerfully the interaction between the Court's role as *legal* institution and its wider environment, there followed a strong negative reaction to the Court's judgment in Germany (and indeed elsewhere[204])—where affirmative action measures have become very much an accepted part of equal opportunity policies, and many public and private interests and groups, including local and regional women's bureaux, trades unions, and other groups, have

---

[203] Above n. 82.

[204] The academic comment was predominantly negative: see e.g. E. Szyszczak, 'Positive Action after *Kalanke*', (1996) 59 Modern Law Review 876; S. Prechal, 'Case Note on Case C-450/93 *Kalanke v. Freie Hansestadt Bremen*', (1996) 33 Common Market Law Review 1245; S. Moore, 'Nothing Positive from the Court of Justice', (1996) 21 European Law Review 156; H. Fenwick, 'Perpetuating Inequality in the Name of Equal Treatment', (1996) 18 Journal of Social Welfare and Family Law 263. In an interesting example of academic-judicial interaction, Advocate-General Jacobs' Opinion in *Marschall* is heavily laced with negative reactions to those criticisms by academic feminists.

invested considerable energy in attempts to enshrine positive action in national and regional laws. The Court's ruling was felt to be insufficiently respecting of national and regional policy choices, and difficult to reconcile with the principle of subsidiarity (Article 5 EC, after renumbering) which should precisely protect the autonomy in such matters of sub-units of the European Union. Measures were proposed to change the Equal Treatment Directive to ensure that at least the softer variants of national affirmative action programmes were safe from the scrutiny of the Court of Justice (perceived now to be a negative influence, after so many years of being held up as the great hope of liberal rights-based feminism).[205] More dramatically, agreement was reached in the Amsterdam Inter-governmental Conference to amend the Treaties themselves to protect equal opportunities measures in terms highlighted above.[206] A new paragraph 4 was added to Article 141, extending its reach into equal treatment generally, and elevating the status of equality of result or outcome, at the expense of 'mere' equality of opportunity:

With a view to ensuring full equality in practice between men and women in working life, the principle of equal treatment shall not prevent any Member State from maintaining or adopting measures providing for specific advantages in order to make it easier for the underrepresented sex to pursue a vocational activity or to prevent or compensate for disadvantages in professional careers.[207]

In a Declaration attached to the EC Treaty, the Conference directed the Member States in taking such positive action measures to 'aim at improving the situation of women in working life'. These developments should be seen in the light of the inclusion of the Article 3(2) EC mainstreaming provision.

It is worth recalling that the 'women's lobby' is noticeably more organized and more closely keyed into the decision-making centres at national and supranational levels than almost any other social movement within the EU. Certainly, it demonstrated an enviable capacity to translate its objections to the *Kalanke* judgment (and one should note, of course, the extent to which the debate on affirmative action has divided rather than unified feminist and anti-racist movements in the United States) into concrete proposals then adopted at the highest level in the EU.[208] Perhaps it was in response to these

---

[205] Proposal for a Council Directive amending Directive 76/207 COM(96) 93; OJ 1996 C179/8.

[206] See above at n. 82.

[207] The provision had a direct progenitor in Article 6(4) of the Social Policy Agreement, in force between 1993 and 1999. This referred specifically to 'women', and Szyszczak comments negatively upon the 'neutering' of this earlier provision: E. Szyszczak, 'The New Parameters of European Labour Law', in O'Keeffe and Twomey, above n. 54.

[208] U. Liebert, above n. 32, identifies lobby politics as one of a number of linked answers to the puzzle of why gender policies should have been advanced in the Treaty of Amsterdam. She cites also the influence of small Nordic states who placed this issue on their IGC agenda, the responsiveness of the Commission as a strategic actor to changes in public opinion which

types of reaction that when the Court was faced shortly after the Amsterdam agreement with another affirmative action case—but this time involving the more common variant of affirmative action legislation, which included a hardship clause to protect the interests of men finding themselves in specific problematic circumstances—it concluded that such a measure *did not* conflict with the EC guarantee of equal treatment. Thus, in contrast to the negatively worded Opinion of Advocate-General Jacobs in the *Marschall* case, the Court's rhetoric in its judgment was markedly changed from the formalism of *Kalanke*. It reminded its readers that:

even where male and female candidates are equally qualified, male candidates tend to be promoted in preference to female candidates particularly because of prejudices and stereotypes concerning the role and capacities of women in working life and the fear, for example, that women will interrupt their careers more frequently, that owing to household and family duties they will be less flexible in their working hours, or that they will be absent from work more frequently because of pregnancy, childbirth and breastfeeding.

For these reasons, the mere fact that a male candidate and a female candidate are equally qualified does not mean that they have the same chance.[209]

This is an example of a statement of principle contained in a judgment of the Court which is not strictly necessary to support the logic of the reasoning, but is clearly included as a 'political signal'. Perhaps in deference to a sense of the exclusion of female citizens from the full enjoyment of membership within the polity, the Court concluded in favour of a *restriction* in the scope and reach of EC law and the EC constitutional guarantee of formal equality. It did not transmute that guarantee at EU level into a guarantee of substantive equality. Rather, it pulled back the *reach* of EC law, in order to allow *German* women (or, better, women employed in Germany) to enjoy the benefit of their struggles for equality at national and regional level and therefore their enjoyment of the benefits of membership at that level. The *Marschall* case, therefore, provides nothing positive in the sense of delivering the promise of equality through EU citizenship for those arguing in favour of affirmative action in other Member States, although together with *Kalanke* the saga of positive action in the Court of Justice must be seen as indirectly contributing to the strengthening of a concept of substantive equality in the EC Treaty through the Treaty of Amsterdam itself. However, yet again the politics of gender have become the politics of subsidiarity and sovereignty, as the Court resiled from the severity of the *Kalanke* judgment and softened its overall stance by

---

include approval of equal opportunities policies alongside a growing gender gap in approval ratings for the EU, the role of the European Parliament, and more general cultural changes in values and attitudes towards gender and equality issues. See also Mazey, above n. 32.

[209] Case C-409/95, *Marschall v. Land Nordrhein-Westfalen*, [1997] ECR I-6363 at paras. 29–30.

reference to a statement of general principle about the disadvantages which even well-qualified women face in the labour market, and by opening the degree of discretion enjoyed by national and sub-national legislatures. The Court confirmed the opening for sub-national legislatures to develop positive action policies in accordance with these principles in its third foray into this area, the case of *Badeck*.[210] It examined the compatibility of the positive action laws of the German *Land* of Hesse, in a case referred by the State Constitutional Court of Hesse after a direct constitutional challenge to the legality of the relevant law was mounted by a group of members of the Hesse legislature. In other words, the case arose as a general issue, not because of a claim of a specific aggrieved individual who had been passed over for promotion. In relation to every aspect of the challenge, which concerned such matters as quota systems for the appointment of women in posts or grades where they were under-represented (where under-representation is prima facie defined as < 50%) or guaranteed training places or interviews for qualified women, the Court concluded that the relevant provisions were drafted with sufficient suppleness not to fall foul of Article 2(4). It did not need, therefore, to interpret the effects of Article 141(4), which remains an open question. In particular, in relation to the quota system the Court found that the rules as drafted guaranteed that candidatures are subject to an objective assessment which takes account of the specific personal situations of all candidates. The result could, therefore, be seen as a triumph for drafting.

The pressure of further pending cases,[211] however, demands that the issue should be dealt with as a matter of (equality) principle within the EU institutional system, rather than as a byproduct of the politics of a multi-level governance system with a dispersed pattern of sovereign powers and weak legitimacy at the supranational level. *Badeck* appears to come closer to such a resolution than the case of *Marschall*, perhaps because of the more general nature of the review which the Court was able to undertake in the context of the reference made by the national court.

There is a similar example of the invocation of general principle by the Court in the case of *Hill and Stapleton*.[212] The case concerned the entitlements of part-time workers who convert to full-time to pay increments on a yearly basis. Should they be put onto the same point on the full-time pay scale which they would have been on if they had worked full-time continuously? Or are they only given recognition on the full-time pay scale for the full-time

---

[210] Case C-158/97, *Badeck v. Land Hessen*, [2000] ECR I-1875.

[211] The positive action controversy is still with the Court of Justice. See the highly problematic Swedish case of *Abrahamsson* (Case C-407/98, *Abrahamsson and Anderson v. Fogelqvist*, judgment of 6 July 2000) concerning special professorships created to promote the employment of women in senior positions in Swedish universities (which was 'equality-proofed' by the Swedish Ombudsman for Equality).

[212] Case C-243/95, *Hill and Stapleton v. Revenue Commissioners*, [1998] ECR I-3739.

equivalent of their part-time work, e.g. two yearly increments in respect of four years' half-time working? The Irish public service scheme in question placed part-time workers at a disadvantage by placing a previously job-sharing employee who converted to full-time work at a lower level on the scale than she had previously occupied on the job-sharing scale, and below the equivalent level for a worker who had worked full-time for the same number of years. The Court reasoned that this was a form of indirect discrimination, as it overwhelmingly affected women rather than men, and thus placed the onus on the Irish Revenue Service to demonstrate that the criterion of service which it was using which related to actual hours worked in fact was justified by objective factors unrelated to any discrimination based on sex. Significantly, the Court also invoked a higher level of 'principle':

Community policy in this area is to encourage and, if possible, adapt working conditions to family responsibilities. Protection of women within family life and in the course of their professional activities is, in the same way as for men, a principle which is widely regarded in the legal systems of the Member States as being the natural corollary of the equality between men and women, and which is recognised by Community law.[213]

The principle of adaptability (*of* the working environment *to* the family) thus invoked seems in broad terms one which is sensitive to a gender analysis, although one could quibble with the detail. McGlynn[214] chastises the Court for its maternalist thinking in focusing upon the responsibilities of *women*, and indeed in the previous paragraph of the judgment the Court assumes that those (83 per cent of the total) who choose to job-share in order to combine 'work and family responsibilities' are doing so because this will '*invariably* involve caring for children'. This ignores the tremendous responsibilities taken by many women for caring for elderly relatives and indeed spouses. But the slipperiness of such a concept, and the inconsistency of the Court's approach to reasoning its judgments, comes through if one compares *Hill and Stapleton* with the more recent case of *Gruber*.[215] Here the Court rejected an argument from the applicant that resigning her post in an undertaking because of the absence of adequate child care arrangements was the equivalent of one of the 'aggravated' reasons for leaving which gave rise to an increased termination payment. The Court's reasoning is somewhat perfunctory, and does not invoke the principle which appeared to carry weight in *Hill and Stapleton*. The contrast between the two approaches is sharp. The language used is rather unfortunate (at least in English), because the statutory reasons which can indeed form the basis for the higher payment are described (presumably as a term of art) as those which are 'important'. In terms of individual decision-making frames regarding responsibilities for child-raising, great importance is undoubtedly ascribed to such matters by almost all of those

---

[213] At para. 42 of the judgment.   [214] Above n. 19.   [215] Above n. 109.

involved in child care decisions. Reusing the terms employed by the Court to summarize the statutorily supported 'important' reasons,[216] one could say that 'no worker can reasonably be expected to remain at work if he or she is not satisfied with the child care arrangements which he or she has made'. While this matter is not to be regarded as necessarily even a partial responsibility of the employer such as is the case with most of the 'important' reasons (although in systems with widespread socialized child care and high rates of female engagement in the labour market that point could be argued), an analogy could have been drawn with 'unfitness to work', which is one of the reasons for awarding the higher rate of termination payment which is unrelated to the conduct of the employer. The Court does not embark upon an attempt to persuade the national court to interpret the national provisions in a way which is in sympathy with the relevant EU policies, including the family-friendliness of work environments.

It can be concluded from this review that there is indeed some degree of inconsistency in the way the Court sometimes does and sometimes does not invoke wider principles to buttress arguments about 'equality', which can in turn feed different 'formal' or 'substantive' constructions of the term. Are Mancini and O'Leary right to suggest that it is wrong to expect the Court to invoke such wider principles more frequently? Indeed, when they are invoked, is it always in the service of bringing gender to the centre of the analysis? Cases such as *Schröder* and indeed *Marschall* would suggest not. The evidence presented here seems to suggest that the Court often deploys *legal* argument, including the invocation of equality and related principles, so as to demonstrate more sensitivity to the demands of governance in a complex multi-level system rather than to indicate great sympathy towards a progressive or feminist agenda promoting the relevance of using gender as a tool of analysis to help tease out fundamental societal dilemmas about the relationship between care and work.

C. The Court as Political Institution

It can be argued that the Court of Justice both develops and responds to the changing agendas which are inherent in the politics of the EU. The point here is not to suggest that there were no 'politics' visible in the cases discussed in the previous section, but to pay separate attention to peculiarly 'political' questions about chains of causation and the capacity of institutions to shape each other's behaviours. Here we can bring to centre stage the role of the Court in a wider institutional and political system. In practice, however, we can deal with this issue much more briefly than the previous question.

Unsurprisingly, the issue density in terms of case law and legislative/Treaty framework, combined with the interactions of dynamic actors including the

---

[216] At para. 32 of the judgment.

Court of Justice, some national courts, and social movements or organizations which have promoted litigation strategies, which together characterize the field of sex equality law and policy, have attracted the attention of some political scientists interested in assessing the precise role of the Court's 'judicial politics' in promoting increased 'legal integration'.[217] This is commonly defined as the degree to which there is compliance with EU law on the part of Member States and their political and legal authorities, and the general degree of 'authority' ascribed to EU law and the pronouncements of the Court of Justice.[218] Alter and Vargas have argued that this process of legal integration is also transforming the national *political* process, in so far as the development of EU sex equality law has shifted the domestic balance of power in favour of equality actors, especially the Equal Opportunities Commission in the UK, which has pursued a relatively successful litigation strategy.[219] Thus far, they have developed a hypothesis about the use of EC law as a tool by national groups which can explain cross-national variation in the impact of the Court's case law. On the other hand, shifting the focus to national groups themselves, they acknowledge that more research needs to be done to find out '*how* actors determine their interests in order to understand *when* actors will see an interest in behaving in ways that intentionally or unintentionally promote integration'.[220] More radically, they also acknowledge the need to 'open up the possibility that actors following their interests might contribute to disintegration rather than integration'.[221] In contrast, Tesoka likewise argues that the impact of EU judicial politics on modes of governance in this field is influenced by domestic mobilization, which in turn depends upon the degree of openness of the national political and judicial systems.[222]

Common to both those approaches is a rather static notion of the relevant 'judicial politics'. Tesoka posits, simply, that 'the judicial activism of the European Court of Justice is steering the Community legal order in a supranational direction'.[223] Certainly, it is unsurprising that no specific attention is paid to the particular 'politics of gender' (or absence thereof) which has

---

[217] e.g. Tesoka, above n. 100; K. Alter and J. Vargas, 'Explaining Variation in the Use of European Litigation Strategies: EC Law and UK Gender Equality Policy', (2000) 33 Comparative Political Studies 452; R. Cichowski, 'Empowerment through Supranational Venues: Women's Activism, the European Court and the Evolution of Sex Equality Policy in the EU', paper presented to the Annual Meeting of the American Political Science Association, Boston, Sept. 1998.

[218] See e.g. the approach taken by Karen Alter: 'Explaining National Court Acceptance of European Court Jurisprudence: A Critical Evaluation of Theories of Legal Integration', in A.-M. Slaughter, A. Stone Sweet, and J. H. H. Weiler (eds.), *The European Courts and National Courts: Doctrine and Jurisprudence* (Oxford: Hart, 1998).

[219] Alter and Vargas, above n. 217; see also C. Barnard, 'A European Litigation Strategy: The Case of the Equal Opportunities Commission', in Shaw and More, above n. 42.

[220] Ibid.   [221] Citing, in that context, Shaw, above n. 160.

[222] Tesoka, above n. 100 at p.25.   [223] Ibid.

influenced the reasoning and judgments of the Court of Justice. The attempt is being made to explain the interaction between different actors in terms of processes of integration and disintegration within a multi-level system, not to uncover or analyse gender issues. Yet as the previous discussion has shown, interpreting the Court of Justice in a field such as sex equality law is a minefield in itself. Even if the Court is not moved by any collective feminist vocation, elements of the principles which it invokes inevitably carry a certain type of political baggage in terms of the types of political project which feminists typically espouse. Those are precisely the elements which a litigation strategy might wish to harness, whilst downplaying those aspects of the judicial politics which are clearly more about issues of sovereignty or subsidiarity, as we have seen in our analysis. Something closer to that vision is brought out by Ostner and Lewis, who highlight the painful phenomenon—in relation to the operationalization of equality claims—of the 'two needles' eyes'.[224] Not only must a gender equality claim demonstrate a sufficiently close link to paid employment, but it must also be generated and instrumentalized in the context of a sufficiently receptive and favourable national environment, comprising a framework of legislation, case law, and other rules. This appears to give the impression that the study of national courts and the interactions with national politics has been the exclusive province of political scientists. This is certainly not the case. Wallace, for example, would emphasize the relevance of legal culture for reception of EU law, a point skipped over by Tesoka.[225] Wallace's is the approach of a comparative lawyer, who in turn does not deny that there are undoubtedly other 'non-legal' factors which structure the interactions. Kilpatrick, in turn, concentrates upon dialogues between national courts and the Court of Justice and 'European communities of courts', arguing that her empirical findings can best be located within historical institutionalist perspectives upon EU governance.[226]

The point here is not to demonstrate that one approach is right and the other is wrong, but to highlight the plurality of factors some of which may be causes and some of which may be effects, or which might perhaps better be viewed as operating in a dynamic circular and mutually reinforcing manner. As yet, as Alter and Vargas readily acknowledge and Kilpatrick warns, they are as yet insufficiently charted. Moreover, it is clear that issues of gender interpretation are merely coincidental to the endeavour of explaining these institutional interactions and dialogues. Sex equality law is, on this reading,

---

[224] I. Ostner and J. Lewis, 'Gender and the Evolution of European Social Policies', in S. Leibfried and P. Pierson (eds.), *European Social Policy: Between Fragmentation and Integration* (Washington, DC: Brookings Institution, 1995).

[225] C. J. Wallace, 'Community Sex Discrimination Law in the National Courts: A Legal Cultural Comparison', in Shaw, above n. 20.

[226] C. Kilpatrick, 'Community or Communities of Courts in European Integration? Sex Equality Dialogues between UK courts and the ECJ', (1998) 4 European Law Journal 121.

merely an area characterized by a suitable base for empirical study. Other than the importance attached to non-state actors such as lobby groups and the fact that it is an area exhibiting a number of diverse stakeholders some of whom approach litigation as the pursuit of a politics of principle and others such as employers and sometimes Member States who are protecting financial interests of the welfare benefits system or the pensions system and who thus deploy a politics of financial expediency, gender is a coincidental factor. The gendered division of labour, for example, is clearly at issue in numerous cases which come before the national courts and the Court of Justice. So far, however, as the concern is the position of these courts in the multi-level EU governance system, it is largely irrelevant what conclusion they actually draw from the material put before them.

D. Conclusions

It is clear from the discussion in this section that there is in large measure an underlying consistency between interpretations of the role of the Court of Justice which focus on its legal and political roles. As Unger has observed: 'The institutional and ideological constraints upon the judicial role in a democracy and the effort to expound the law as connected principle and policy seem to reinforce and to justify each other.'[227] In the forefront of Unger's mind is the American judicial system; the point seems apt also for the EU judicial system.

The previous section would seem to have given considerable succour to the view that the task of 'interpreting' the Court of Justice in the context of sex equality law must take as its centrepiece the various aspects of the 'institutional economy', and that indeed the injunction in Article 220 EC to 'apply the law' is a powerful shaping factor. There appears to be a powerful structural bias in the EU system which prevents gender analysis becoming an autonomous shaping factor in the evolution of the law and policy. This is to a large extent a feature that it will share with any liberal legal order. But the particular constraints imposed upon the Court of Justice in its ongoing constitutional dialogues with national courts means that at present it does not have a free hand to follow, for example, the lead of the Canadian Supreme Court in articulating and applying a substantive equality principle through its interpetation of the 1982 Charter of Rights.[228] Thus what might be termed the most 'progressive' of the Court's decisions represent a combination of setting EU standards which the national systems must follow and restricting the reach of EU law in order that where national laws themselves are more

---

[227] Unger, above n. 3 at 110.

[228] See generally More, 'Equal Treatment of the Sexes', above n. 17; Barnard, above n. 17 at 224–6.

developed, they will in fact prevail. Judgments in the sex equality field undoubtedly raise contested issues in the EU context, which deserve transparent consideration and demonstration, as Unger suggests.[229] Our review suggests, however, that the contestation is as often about the question of integration as it is about the dimensions of equality.

VI INTERROGATING THE COURT OF JUSTICE

The focus shifts in this final substantive section from 'interpreting' to 'interrogating'. It will ask two—as yet—hypothetical questions shaped by approaches to adjudication which step away from the 'classical-plus' model of the institutional environment of the Court of Justice which underpinned the previous section. The questions draw upon aspects of the policy and institutional contexts, as well as the possibilities of gender analysis generated within feminist scholarship, higlighted in the earlier sections of the chapter. They are variants upon 'asking the gender question'. First, we shall ask whether the predominantly masculine composition of the Court of Justice (and indeed the Court of First Instance) is likely to make a difference to judicial outcomes; second, we shall consider ways of reframing legal disputes in order to bring gender questions to the forefront of consideration in a way which extends the range of voices and points of view which can be heard. In relation to the second question, in order to make the enquiry somewhat less hypothetical, a number of examples from existing case law are used. However, to make the point about the challenges posed by what might be involved if gender is 'centred' in relation to the role of the Court of Justice, cases from outwith the field of sex equality law will be used.

Intuitively, gender-balanced public institutions would seem to suggest the presence of a fair and equitable society involving a broadly 'balanced' (in gender terms) division of labour and resources. In truth, the issues of representation and the tensions between representation and participation have often divided feminists as the search has continued for the definitive answer to the question 'why should it matter who our representatives are?'[230] In the first place, difficulties have arisen because of differences within feminist theory and feminist praxis over the desirability of representative versus participatory forms of political engagement.[231] As women have been a historically excluded category within many political systems, arguments have emerged both for *inclusion* within the existing polis and for *diversion* away from the formal

---

[229] See above n. 163.

[230] A. Phillips, 'Democracy and Representation: Or, Why Should It Matter Who Our Representatives Are?', in A. Phillips (ed.), *Feminism and Politics* (Oxford: Oxford University Press, 1998), 224.

[231] Squires, above n. 6 at 194.

structures of conventional representative politics into forms of informal participatory politics. One of the inevitable tensions in that context is that between individual and group. To support women's representation as women, the strongest arguments can be drawn from 'justice' and a type of common-sense assumption that public assemblies should be expected to evidence parity or near-parity of representation, from the historical failure of male-dominated public bodies to heed 'women's interests', and from the generalized need to revitalize democracy, suggested likewise by the tension between representation and participation identifed here.[232]

Arguments about the composition of the judiciary differ somewhat. Judges do not 'represent' the people in the conventional sense. They sit in judgment, exercising—within a democracy at least—a form of delegated power on behalf of the people. In a constitutional system, moreover, they have a particular role to play in ensuring the balance and separation of powers, and the control of the legislature and the executive according to the constitution itself embodying the rule of law. Along with other public figures, of course, they have an important 'role model' function, and in that sense the type of common-sense assumptions mustered in the previous paragraph must be equally applicable. In the national context—but less so, one might surmise, in the context of a more isolated supranational court like the Court of Justice—women judges certainly represent more specialist role models vis-à-vis the legal profession.[233]

To suggest, however, that the exercise of judgment would be different with women judges is an altogether more controversial suggestion, because it steps into historically contested territory about sexual difference, where to suggest that women reason differently from men seems to suggest an essentialized notion of sex which can be as easily used to restrict women's freedom as it is to assert that historical structures of disadvantage in the labour market, the household, and public life require transgression and dismantlement. McGlynn canvasses the case for a different 'feminine' style of judgment coming from some women, and concludes that the evidence from academic studies is equivocal.[234] It seems difficult, therefore, to escape the 'nature' question. She does so, however, by focusing on the issue of diversity rather than directly upon the role or experience which the women judge as such will bring. In other words, the case is made for 'a judiciary which is drawn from a wider range of sexes, backgrounds and ethnicities [which] will bring different experiences to bear on its judgments'.[235] Such a shift responds also to the types of concern brought to the fore by J. A. G. Griffith's celebrated studies

---

[232] Phillips, above n. 230.

[233] C. McGlynn, 'Judging Women Differently: Gender, the Judiciary and Reform', in Millns and Whitty, above n. 4 at 96–9.

[234] Ibid. 100.   [235] Ibid. 103.

The Politics of the Judiciary,[236] in terms of the narrowness of the range of background and experience of the British higher judiciary and the consequent results in terms of judicial politics and ideology. Reforms to the selection process would be needed, almost certainly, to change in a radical way the composition of the Court of Justice, if only to overcome the myth of 'the best man for the job' which so often results in perpetuating male domination of highly elite institutions where the pool for selection as well as the number to be selected is both very small and highly visible. Because the selection of the Court is not in any sense a collective process, the type of pressure exerted by Commission President (then elect) Romano Prodi on the Member States in 1999 to ensure that the number of women Commissioners at least matched that in the previous Commission cannot occur. Another associated reform might examine the possibilities for promoting the use of gender-neutral language in judicial discourse, although in a multilingual court this is an even greater minefield than it normally is at national level.

Issues of composition, however, can only take the debate so far. For the issue may be, as Minow points out, about 'reason' rather than composition. Her concern is 'points of view', and the relationships between power, privilege, and seeing the other side. She suggests that 'the more powerful we are, the less able we are to see how our own perspective and the current structure of our world coincide'.[237] The challenge, therefore, is the construction of legal disputes and the recognition of points of view. For 'otherwise, outsiders who become insiders simply define new groups as "other" '. Instead she argues for highlighting the point of view of people labelled as 'different' and 'generating vivid details about points of view excluded from or marginalized by particular institutions'. She concludes:

Seeking out and promoting participation by voices typically unheard are also crucial if equality jurisprudence is to mean more than enshrining the point of view of those sitting on the bench. The concerted and persistent search for excluded points of view and the acceptance of their challenges are equally critical to feminist theory and practice. Otherwise, feminists will join the ranks of reformers who have failed to do more than impose their own point of view.

This suggests the value of the search for ways of framing into such legal disputes, as they crystallize before the courts, something more than the legal reconstruction of the categories deemed—by reference to the law's own system of definition—to be relevant.[238] One possible approach is that suggested

---

[236] (London: Fontana, 1997).

[237] M. Minow, 'Feminist Reason: Getting It and Losing It', in K. T. Bartlett and R. Kennedy (eds.), *Feminist Legal Theory: Readings in Law and Gender* (Boulder, Colo.: Westview Press, 1991). All the quotations which follow are drawn from p. 365.

[238] See also on such questions S. Berns, *To Speak as a Judge: Difference, Voice and Power* (Aldershot: Ashgate, 1999), where one of the issues addressed is the relationship between narrative and judgment.

by 'gender mainstreaming', with its 'systematic integration of the respective situations, priorities and needs of women in all policies' and its attempt to achieve 'equality' 'by actively and openly taking into account, at the planning stage, [the] effects [of policies] on the respective situation of women and men in implementation, monitoring and evaluation'.[239] The danger with main-streaming, of course, is that with such apparent inclusiveness in fact radical challenges to the status quo may lose their capacity to disrupt received ideas about power and policy. It may involve as much 'framing out' of interests as 'framing in'. It could involve the cooption of feminist ideals into a soft-focus, family-friendly world in which choice and freedom are merely rhetorical devices rather than real experience. Does mainstreaming provide any better way of getting to the heart of a policy problem, simply because of its claim to inclusiveness? It may detract, in fact, from a better understanding of the pol-icy problem because it suggests, immediately, that the gender issue is dealt with by default. On the contrary, as the 'what's the problem' approach to pol-icy analysis advocated by Bacchi highlights, the disputes over policy initiatives not only distinguish between those in favour of and those against a particular policy, but also help in 'constituting the shape of the issues to be consid-ered'.[240] For example, issues about gender and development should not be assumed to be straightforwardly resolved because the boxes on the checklist of mainstreaming have all been ticked off. On the contrary, policy-makers should always question what representations have been assumed in the pre-sentation of a policy issue and what alternatives to taken-for-granted solutions there might be.

Applying these ideas to the judicial forum is, thus far, a rather hypothetical exercise. On the other hand, as an academic endeavour of reconstruction it has the advantage of bringing to the centre of the dispute the social or eco-nomic issue to be adjudicated upon, rather than allowing the dispute to be tri-angulated solely by reference to the received categorizations of legal orders, such as historical public/private law divides. One such bifurcation in the con-text of EU law is the separation between sex equality law and the law relating to the free movement of persons. Ackers has contributed to the literature an important empirical study which challenges received opinion about women's experience of migration—at least *within* the European Union—and thus raises new questions about the effects of the free movement rules which are the EU's contribution to regulating the socio-economic phenomenon of intra-EU migration.[241] The study explodes certain myths about the rate of female migration, as women constitute just under 50 per cent of all EU

[239] This simply repeats key parts of the Commission's definition given above at n. 136.
[240] C. L. Bacchi, *Women, Policy and Politics: The Construction of Policy Problems* (London: Sage, 1999).
[241] Ackers, above n. 42. See also H. L. Ackers, 'Citizenship, Gender and Dependency in the European Union: Women and Internal Migration', in Hervey and O'Keeffe, above n. 18.

migrants, and about the assumption that they primarily migrate to join male breadwinning partners. The interaction of the reality of migration with the free movement rules and their historic focus upon economic status, with different 'classes' of rights according to status, is equally important. These provisions can be seen as thoroughly 'gendered'.[242] Certainly, the focus on participation in the labour market as conferring legal status neatly matches the predominant concerns of the framework of sex equality law which we have already examined in this chapter. On the other hand, the establishment of a status of Citizenship of the Union by the Treaty of Maastricht (Articles 17–22 EC after the Treaty of Amsterdam) could be said to disrupt some of these categories, especially as it appears, at first sight, to confer a universal freedom of movement (Article 18). Closer inspection reveals, however, that this provision is 'subject to the limitations and conditions laid down in this Treaty and by the measures adopted to give it effect'.

It is in this context that we need to consider the case of *Martínez Sala*.[243] The Court held that a Spanish national who was long-term resident in Germany—although on what precise basis her lawful residence in that country could be deduced was not entirely clear—could rely upon the non-discrimination principle in Article 12 EC as the basis for claiming equal access to a German child-raising benefit for her newborn child. In economic terms her status might best be categorized as marginal to the labour market, but not wholly excluded. It was many years since she had worked in Germany, almost certainly as a result of child care responsibilities. The Court concluded that she could not be obliged to produce a residence permit in order to obtain the benefit, when nationals merely had to prove that they were permanently settled in Germany. Moreover, the Court held in effect that it would make no difference to her entitlement whether or not she might eventually be found by the national court to be either a worker[244] or an 'employed person' under Community social security regulations, as was possible on the constructions of 'worker' and employed person which it gave.[245] The novelty of the Court's judgment lay, however, in its invocation of Citizenship of the Union, notably Article 17(2), which 'attaches' to the citizen the rights and duties existing

[242] See H. L. Ackers, 'Women, Citizenship and European Community Law: The Gender Interpretation of the Free Movement Provisions', (1994) 16 Journal of Social Welfare and Family Law 392; see also Scheiwe, above n. 42.

[243] Case C-85/96, *Martínez Sala v. Freistaat Bayern*, [1998] ECR I-2691. For an orthodox presentation of the issues see S. Fries and J. Shaw, 'Citizenship of the Union: First Steps in the European Court of Justice', (1998) 4 European Public Law 533.

[244] This would be on the grounds that she had worked in the past, although hardly at all for more than 10 years, since when she had been drawing social welfare.

[245] Under German social welfare rules the claiming of benefits automatically protects the recipient with sickness insurance, thus bringing her under the Community social security coordination regulations as a person who is covered in respect of one of the risks included in the governing Regulation 1408/71.

under the EC Treaty. Martínez Sala could claim equality of treatment, the Court found, even if she was solely dependent upon welfare and could bring herself within the personal scope of Community law by no other means than that she is a Union citizen resident in another Member State. The only material condition was that the benefit which she claimed must fall within the scope of EU law. The Court of Justice found that it was within that scope, using its own earlier interpretation of a legislative measure which had expressly conferred social advantages on (economic) migrants and their families.[246] One interpretation of the Court's approach to the intersection of the material and personal scope of EU law, in combination with the non-discrimination principle, is that it gives something close to universal right of access to all manner of welfare benefits to all those who are Union citizens and who are lawfully resident in a Member State.

This (orthodox) interpretation of the case is taking for granted the Court's reading of the categories which frame the case, i.e. citizenship and free movement rules. Consider, instead, the approach of Moebius and Szyszczak.[247] For them, *Martínez Sala* was not the opening of the new chapter marked 'citizenship', but the continuation of a process of historic exclusion, in which the Court has refused to recognize 'care work' as a 'proper' form of work for the purposes of interpreting the Treaties. Its failure is as acute in the context of sex equality law as it is in relation to the free movement rules, where its interpretation of the notion of 'worker' includes only those engaged in some form of 'economic' activity. Only that will generate a conception of citizenship which is not the narrow legalistic formulation of the Treaty, but one rooted in the development of social rights as well as legal market rights.

The second example addresses the question of the effects of policies (and legal rules). In 1996 the United Kingdom sought the annulment, by means of a judicial review action brought under what is now Article 230 EC, of the Commission's decision to fund a series of projects aimed at combating social exclusion within the EU.[248] The context in which the action was brought was the failure of the Council—because of opposition by the UK and Germany—to agree a programme of work for 1994–9, including financial support for projects, following on from three earlier programmes aimed at alleviating some of the effects of poverty. The effect of the UK's challenge was to cast doubt upon all manner of funding for social exclusion projects, without doubt having a significant effect upon the 'third sector' of voluntary organizations, non-governmental organizations, and church groups which have come to rely upon programmes of EU funding to support their activities. It put 'a spanner in the works', as it were. In view of the evidence on women's pay in comparison to men's, and the prevalence of female-headed single-parent households, there

---

[246] Article 7(2) of Regulation 1612/68.   [247] Moebius and Szyszczak, above n. 19.
[248] Case C-106/96, *Commission v. United Kingdom (Poverty 4)*, [1998] ECR I-2729.

can be little doubt about the impact of such actions upon women in particular.

Of course, the issue of the Commission's role in implementing the EU budget, and the need for a so-called 'dual legal basis' for spending involving an entry in the budget and secondary legislation authorizing the expenditure, is no mere technical and dry issue. The resignation of the Commission in March 1999 under the shadow of strong accusations about fraud, mismanagement of budgets, and nepotism is ample evidence of that point.[249] In the event, the Court found for the UK, concluding that the Commission lacked the competence to commit the expenditure under the budget as per its plans. Its judgment comprises technical legal argument—which is hardly surprising. The question remains: were a gender mainstreaming approach to be adopted in such circumstances, would a different approach (e.g. to the expeditiousness with which the action was heard thus limiting its effect) be adopted?

VII CONCLUSIONS

The approach of this chapter has been hybrid. It is part description and analysis, part speculation upon possible alternative arguments, and part reflection upon the relevance of gender to the evolving EU polity. In relation to the analysis of sex equality law, the point should be re-emphasized that the Court's position within a semi-federal system of multi-level governance is as significant to its 'politics' as its sometimes supposed feminist credentials in promoting a relatively progressive framework of discrimination provisions. To bring out this point, the dual vision of a Court with a *legal* and *political* role to play in the EU governance system has been especially important. In EU governance work the Commission is often characterized as a 'purposeful opportunist'.[250] The description seems equally apt for the Court of Justice in the context of 'gender', as it has cloaked itself in something akin to a feminist cloak almost always only where some gain can be obtained in terms of reinforcing its own legitimacy within the system. Elsewhere, the bare realities of legal interpretation have tended more often than not to reassert themselves, leaving the highly formal legacy of an equal treatment principle based on notions of comparison rather than structural disadvantage and societally based inequity.

---

[249] T. K. Hervey, 'Casenote on Poverty 4', (1999) 36 Common Market Law Review 1079.
[250] e.g. by L. Cram, *Policymaking in the EU* (London: Routledge, 1997).

5

Turning Remedies Around: A Sectoral Analysis of the Court of Justice

CLAIRE KILPATRICK

I PRIVATE ENFORCEMENT AND REMEDIES

In the journey taken by the Court of Justice to constitutionalize the Treaties, the promotion of the private enforcement of Community law has been a lodestar, pointing the Court along the road ahead. Direct effect and supremacy, combined with the preliminary reference procedure, provided the basic tool-kit for getting Community law into the parts of national systems other international law regimes reached much less often. This tool-kit placed Community law in the hands of private parties which could use its provisions 'at home' to provide tangible, applicable, enforceable results. This functional, effectiveness-related aspect of the transformative capacity of private party enforcement was melded with a second, symbolic aspect. The private party in Community law could be presented as, and importantly sometimes actually was, a real flesh-and-blood individual. This provided both impetus and justification for the Court of Justice's development of the private enforcement model. Protection of the rights of individuals—the triumph of rights over goals, principles over policies—provides a convincing mandate for the judicial development of a new legal order. In the private enforcement model, of course, the functional desire for greater effectiveness conveniently pointed in the same direction as the symbolism of effective judicial protection of the rights of individuals in the construction of this new community.

Part of the genetic code of the private enforcement model is its dependence on dialogue between the Court of Justice and national courts. As a result, it was always going to depend on ongoing accommodation between courts. It would just as inevitably be subject to processes of adjustment, as changes effected at national and supranational level would throw up new possibilities of challenge leading in turn to evolution or mutation of the pre-existing status quo.

Placing these three elements side by side it could be said that they represent three distinctive, and crucial, imperatives for the Court of Justice: the imperatives of effectiveness, effective judicial protection, and judicial cooperation.

It is in the light of these remarks on the private enforcement model that I wish to focus more specifically on remedies within the private enforcement model. It is unsurprising that this issue has fascinated scholars. Caught in a uniquely unstable position between these three institutional imperatives of the Court of Justice, remedies within the private enforcement model provided an exquisitely challenging puzzle. The puzzle was how to find, *and hold onto*, a remedial configuration which would adequately satisfy these three institutional imperatives. The Court's jurisprudence supplied ample material to tease through for those straining to resolve the private enforcement remedies puzzle.

A remarkable degree of consensus has been reached on how the Court of Justice has tried to solve the puzzle though there is some dissent as to whether the appropriate balance between the institutional imperatives has now been achieved. The consensus on the development of remedies in the private enforcement model is based on a chronological and global assessment of the case law of the Court of Justice relating to this issue. It can be summarized in the following way.[1]

In the beginning, the Court of Justice set out a division of remedial competences which recognized the inevitable reliance of the Community legal order and the Court of Justice on national courts and remedies in the private enforcement model. Rights or substantive issues concerning Community law were for the Court of Justice, while remedies and procedural issues concerning the enforcement of EC law rights were for the national legal orders and the national courts. This was encapsulated in the recognition of national procedural autonomy. However, national procedural autonomy came accompanied by two safeguards for Community law rights: the 'practically possible' proviso and the 'equivalence' proviso. The former indicates, broadly speaking, that it should not be impossible for an individual either to assert Community law rights before a national court or to obtain redress for violation of such rights. The latter indicates that EC law rights should not be subject to worse treatment in the national procedural and remedial environment than equivalent or comparable domestic law rights.[2]

In a second, bolder phase, the Court departed from this deferential stance towards national remedies and procedures concerning Community law rights. In a series of preliminary references, the Court substituted national procedural autonomy for Community-controlled remedial and procedural

---

[1] This draws on pp. 1–9 of my chapter in C. Kilpatrick, T. Novitz, and P. Skidmore (eds.), *The Future of Remedies in Europe* (Oxford: Hart, 2000).

[2] Case 33/76, *Rewe v. Landwirtschaftskammer für das Saarland*, [1976] ECR 1989, esp. para. 5. See also Case 45/76, *Comet v. Productschap voor Siergewassen*, [1976] ECR 2043, paras. 12–16.

competence when it perceived that 'gaps' existed in remedial protection within the private enforcement model. An early 'activist' precursor was *Simmenthal*, where the Court required disapplication of an Italian rule which did not make protection of EC law rights 'practically impossible' but delayed their protection by reserving to the Italian Constitutional Court the power to set aside national laws which were incompatible with Community law.[3] Between 1986 and 1993 commentators marvelled at the 'momentous work in progress'[4] as the Court scaled dizzy heights of effectiveness and effective judicial protection with regard to remedies in the private enforcement model. Hence, in *Johnston* an ouster clause in national law was struck down because it excluded judicial protection of EC law rights.[5] *Factortame I* obliged the House of Lords to issue interim injunctions against the Crown, even where such power did not exist in national law, in order to protect EC law rights.[6] *Emmott* decided that time would not begin to run against individuals in the national legal orders until Member States had properly implemented their obligations in Community directives.[7] *Francovich* created a new Community law remedy in all the national legal orders of state liability for failure to properly apply EC law.[8] Last but not least, in *Marshall II* the Court of Justice decided that a national ceiling on compensation contravened EC law, as it did not provide an effective remedy to a victim of gender discrimination.[9]

We are now in a third phase in which the Court, in a new wave of references related to remedies, has drawn back, in some instances significantly, from full-blooded application of this activist, second-phase, case law. This is exemplified in the spectacular demise of *Emmott*, now firmly confined to its facts. Most interestingly, there has been a sustained effort, spearheaded by Advocate-General Jacobs, to read certain 'activist' decisions as being in reality

---

[3] Case 106/77, *Amministrazione delle Finanze dello Stato v. Simmenthal*, [1978] ECR 629. This decision is better explained by giving fuller prominence to the institutional imperative of judicial cooperation. The Court's hopes for developing the links promised by the 'come one, come all' approach to national courts in Article 234 (ex 177) EC required opening the use of Community law to all national courts. See also Case C-312/93, *SCS Peterbroeck Van Campenhout & Cie v. Belgium*, [1995] ECR I-4599, and Cases C-430–431/93, *Van Schijndel & Van Veen v. Stichting Pensioenfonds voor Fysiotherapeuten*, [1995] ECR I-4705, which can be differentiated according to the threat the Court perceived they presented to the institutional imperative of judicial cooperation.

[4] R. Caranta, 'Judicial Protection Against Member States: A New *Jus Commune* Takes Shape', (1995) 32 CMLRev. 703.

[5] Case 222/84, *Johnston v. Chief Constable of the RUC*, [1986] ECR 1651. See also Case 222/86, *Heylens v. UNECTEF*, [1987] ECR 4097.

[6] Case C-213/89, *R v. Secretary of State for Transport, ex parte Factortame Ltd and others*, [1990] ECR I-2433.

[7] Case C-208/90, *Emmott v. Minister of Social Welfare*, [1991] ECR I-4269.

[8] Cases C-6 and 9/90, *Francovich and Bonifaci v. Italy*, [1991] ECR I-5357.

[9] Case C-271/91, *Marshall v. Southampton & South West Area Health Authority*, [1993] ECR I-4367.

merely applications of the 'practically impossible' proviso to the unchanged status quo of national procedural autonomy in extraordinary fact situations.[10]

The third phase has also been characterized by caution and reflection with regard to other remedial developments. Hence, the conditions for State liability have been carefully fleshed out with an eye to the conditions for Community liability in Article 288(2) EC.[11] The Court has also probed further the meaning of the two provisos to national procedural autonomy.[12] This was particularly important with regard to the 'equivalence' proviso, which was not considered by the Court until very recently.[13] Many consider that, in this

[10] See esp. the Court of Justice in Case C-188/95, *Fantask*, [1997] ECR I-6783, para. 51, explaining *Emmott* on these grounds. For detailed analysis see Flynn, 'Whatever Happened to Emmott? The Perfecting of Community Rules on National Time-limits', in Kilpatrick et al., *The Future of Remedies in Europe*, 51. See also *Simmenthal* explained on these grounds by AG Jacobs in *Peterbroeck*, above, n. 3, para. 43 of Opinion. For a rather different kind of rationalization of the Court's remedies jurisprudence, see the extrajudicial comments of Judge Kakouris, who argues that national procedural autonomy is a misnomer and that the Court's case law on remedies has consistently been about the effectiveness of the Community legal order: 'Do the Member States Possess Judicial Procedural "Autonomy"?', (1997) 34 CMLRev. 1389.

[11] Esp. in Cases 46/93 and 48/93, *Brasserie du Pêcheur SA v. Germany, R. v. Secretary of State for Transport, ex parte Factortame Ltd and others*, [1996] ECR I-1029.

[12] See *Peterbroeck* and *Van Schijndel*, above, n. 3. For extended comment on the implications of these twin cases, contrast G. de Búrca, 'National Remedies for Breach of EC Law: The Changing Approach of the ECJ' with F. Jacobs, 'Enforcing Community Rights and Obligations in National Courts: Striking the Balance', both in J. Lonbay and A. Biondi (eds.), *Remedies for Breach of EC Law* (Chichester: Wiley, 1997), 13 and 25. See also now the decisions in Case C-246/96, *Magorrian & Cunningham v. EHSSB & DHSS*, [1997] ECR I-7153, Case C-326/96, *Levez v. T. H. Jennings (Harlow Pools) Ltd*, [1998] ECR I-7835 and Case C-78/98, *Preston*, judgment of 16 May 2000 discussed in detail below.

[13] The first sustained discussion is found in relation to the analogous conditions imposed in relation to state liability in Case C-261/95, *Palmisani*, [1997] ECR I-4025. Here the national court asked whether a national rule fixing a one-year limitation period for state liability actions flowing from belated implementation of a Directive was 'comparable' with three other types of procedural rule which could be considered as 'similar'. The Court stated that domestic actions pursuing the same 'objective' could be regarded as similar domestic actions. It considered that the ordinary system of non-contractual liability pursued a similar objective. But it went on to state that 'in order to establish the comparability of the two systems in question, the essential characteristics of the domestic system of reference must be examined'. This task was for the national court. See further the opposing views of AG Mancini in Case 199/82, *Amministrazione dello Stato v. San Giorgio*, [1983] ECR 3595—favouring a broad application of the 'equivalence' proviso—and AG Jacobs in Case C-62/93, *BP Supergas v. Greece*, [1995] ECR I-1883—favouring no engagement by the Court of Justice in the 'difficult and somewhat artificial task of seeking a comparable claim under national law'. The Court had to confront the issue in a series of references from Italian courts on time limits imposed on restitution of charges levied contrary to EC law: see, esp. Case C-231/96, *Edis v. Ministero delle Finanze*, [1998] ECR I-4951, and Case C-228/96, *Aprile Srl v. Amministrazione delle Finanze dello Stato*, [1998] ECR I-7141. See now *Levez* and *Preston*, above n. 12, discussed below, Section VI. For comment pre-*Preston* see A. Biondi, 'The European Court of Justice and Certain National Procedural Limitations: Not Such a Tough Relationship', (1999) 36 CMLRev. 1271.

third phase, the Court of Justice has finally struck the appropriate balance between the institutional imperatives of effectiveness, effective judicial protection, and judicial cooperation,[14] though others urge moves towards greater emphasis on one or other of these imperatives.[15]

II SECTORAL ANALYSIS

The analysis in this chapter aims to turn remedies around by examining them in two distinct ways. Both of these stem from gazing at the Court of Justice from a national labour law angle.

I turn first to the labour law angle. One cannot help noticing that many of the Court's most important remedial judgments, indeed, more generally its judgments on various aspects of the private enforcement model, have concerned labour law and/or gender equality. *Francovich* concerned the protection of employees in insolvency situations. The congruence between key 'constitutionalizing' decisions and gender equality, in the sphere either of employment or of social security, is striking. *Defrenne No. 2, Von Colson, Harz, Johnston, Marshall I* and *II*, and *Foster*[16] all spring to mind with regard to gender equality in employment while *Cotter & McDermott* and *Emmott*[17] concerned gender equality in the field of statutory social security schemes. It is worth observing that EU lawyers will be on first-name terms with many of these litigants: Andrea Francovich, Gabrielle Defrenne, Sabine Von Colson, Dorit Harz, Marguerite Johnston, Helen Marshall, Theresa Emmott. It struck me that this link between bold decisions and the subject matter might not be mere coincidence.[18] Because of that, it was worth investigating further what light could be cast on the development of the private enforcement model by pursuing a sectoral analysis focused on gender equality. One key element of that model is the provision of remedies for breaches of Community law.

[14] See e.g. T. Tridimas, 'Enforcing Community Rights in National Courts: Some Recent Developments', in Kilpatrick et al., *The Future of Remedies in Europe*, 35, and Jacobs, above n. 12.

[15] For arguments in favour of more effective judicial protection see B. Ryan, 'The Private Enforcement of European Union Labour Laws', in Kilpatrick et al., *The Future of Remedies in Europe*, 141. For arguments in favour of more national procedural autonomy see Biondi, above n. 13.

[16] Case 43/75, *Defrenne v. Sabena II*, [1976] ECR 445; Case C-188/89, *Foster v. British Gas*, [1990] ECR I-3313. For discussion of the other cases see below, Section III.

[17] See ibid.

[18] See also P. Craig and G. de Búrca, *EU Law: Text, Cases and Materials*, 2nd edn. (Oxford: Oxford University Press, 1998), 884: 'it is worth noting how many of the cases on remedies have arisen in the specific sphere of sex discrimination.'

Hence, the standard account of remedies in the private enforcement model is a move *from* an initial baseline position of national procedural autonomy *towards* effectiveness and effective judicial protection followed by recent, unclear steps back in the direction of national procedural autonomy. What happened to the standard account, derived from overall assessment of the case law, if focus was placed exclusively on gender equality cases instead?

The mirror image of the standard account appears. The move in gender equality cases is most accurately characterized as a move *from* a starting position of effectiveness and effective judicial protection *towards* national procedural autonomy.

However, this analysis becomes more accurate if the gender equality category is subdivided into employment on the one hand and social security on the other. While in both instances the move was from effectiveness to national procedural autonomy, the move happened much later in the employment cases (not until *Magorrian* in 1997 followed by *Levez* and *Preston*)[19] than it did in the social security cases (in 1993 in *Steenhorst-Neerings* and in 1994 in *Johnson No. 2*).[20] The disjuncture in the timing of the moves away from effectiveness created difficulties for the Court of Justice. In both instances the move away from effectiveness was traumatic and problematic.

Looking at the Court of Justice from a *national* perspective required a second shift of perspective from that found in the standard account of remedies in the private enforcement model. The national courts enter the picture as fully formed, three-dimensional protagonists. In the standard account, the national courts risk being effaced in two ways. First, there is always the risk that they are reduced to being mere reference fodder. Second, though one of the variables in explaining why the Court of Justice initially pursued, and recently returned towards, national procedural autonomy is the need to preserve the institutional imperative of judicial cooperation within the private enforcement model, this was underpinned by an untested assumption that the best way of pursuing judicial cooperation is to give national courts what they must want—the maximum possible national procedural autonomy. But this was not what all national courts were seeking at all times in gender equality cases.

It seemed therefore that closer analysis of the development of remedies in gender equality cases, which was sensitive both to its subject matter and to the role of national courts, was apt to help us understand better a number of issues. In particular, as gender equality case law constituted a significant chunk of the standard account's examples both of activist, second-phase jurisprudence (cases such as *Von Colson, Johnston, Emmott, Marshall II*)[21] and of the third phase of retraction and refinement (cases such as *Steenhorst-*

---

[19] See below, Section VI.   [20] See below, Section IV.
[21] See below, Section III.

Neerings, Johnson No. 2, ex parte Sutton,[22] *Magorrian, Levez, Preston*),[23] digging deeper into this seam might enhance our understanding of remedies in the private enforcement model both with regard to gender equality and more generally. The chapter proceeds to investigate this in the following way. Section III considers why the Court of Justice initially opted for effectiveness in the area of gender equality rather than national procedural autonomy. Section IV discusses why, having opted for effectiveness in the area of gender equality, the Court subsequently decided partially to abandon it. In this regard, it ponders why the Court stored up so many problems for itself by abandoning effectiveness in the gender equality in social security field at precisely the moment when it reached the high-water mark of remedial effectiveness in the field of gender equality in employment (in *Marshall II*). In Section V, I trace and evaluate the roles played by national courts, in particular with regard to the subsequent move from effectiveness to national procedural autonomy in the employment cases as well. Section VI examines what impact the late meeting of gender equality with national procedural autonomy has had on the meaning of the latter. The chapter concludes by using this analysis to look afresh at the standard account and at the meaning and interplay of the institutional imperatives of effectiveness, effective judicial protection, and judicial protection.

III EFFECTIVENESS—WHY?

Before going on to consider why the Court of Justice opted for effectiveness rather than national procedural autonomy in the area of gender equality, it is necessary to demonstrate that that is what in fact it did. The analysis is separated into employment and social security cases, as the reasoning, though effectiveness-oriented in both instances, is not identical.

The first cases in which the Court considered remedies with regard to gender equality at work are *Von Colson* and *Harz*. The Court was asked whether the remedy provided by the paragraph of the German Civil Code for gender discrimination in recruitment was compatible with Community law. The remedy provided had become known as 'the postage paragraph', as all it awarded was the out-of-pocket expenses incurred which, in recruitment cases, tended to involve only the costs involved in posting the application.[24]

---

[22] See below, Section IV.   [23] See below, Section VI.

[24] Case 14/83, *Von Colson and Kamann v. Land Nordrhein-Westfalen*, [1984] ECR 1891; Case 79/83, *Harz v. Deutsche Tradax*, [1984] ECR 1921. See further, for more detailed analysis of the German provisions, C. Kilpatrick, 'Gender Equality: A Fundamental Dialogue', in S. Sciarra (ed.), *Labour Law in the Courts: National Courts and the ECJ* (Oxford: Hart, 2001), 31.

According to the Court's established case law on remedies in the national legal orders, it should have stated that this remedy was compatible with Community law unless it made it excessively difficult or practically impossible for the plaintiffs to obtain a remedy, or if remedies for gender discrimination were less favourable than remedies for other, equivalent German law rights. Investigation of the latter requirement would in turn have raised questions about what the appropriate comparator national law remedies could or should be: remedies for race discrimination, remedies within German labour law, or remedies in civil law, for instance.

The Court did not do this. There is absolutely no reference to national procedural autonomy or the requirements of practical impossibility or equivalence in its judgment. Instead, it stated that the remedy had to 'guarantee real and effective judicial protection' which required at least adequate compensation.

The reasoning which permitted de facto trampling over German autonomy is worth noting carefully. While the UK and Danish governments, intervening in the case, stressed that Article 189(3) (now 249) of the Treaty, which defines a directive as a Community source of law, gave Member States choice over the form and methods of implementation, the Court emphasized instead that part of Article 189(3) which states that directives are binding as to the result to be achieved. This meant that Member States had to take 'all the measures necessary to ensure that the directive is fully effective, in accordance with the objective it pursues'.[25] The Court therefore moved, as its second step, to look at the objective of the Equal Treatment Directive (ETD).[26] Article 6 of that Directive requires Member States to introduce the measures necessary to enable all putative victims of discrimination 'to pursue their claims by judicial process'. This wording implies that it requires Member States to ensure adequate access to court as well as procedural guarantees for adequately processing such claims. It does not seem to encompass qualitative evaluation of the *remedies* available in the event of a successful claim. But, according to the Court, taking its third and final step, it *did* require remedial measures such as the hiring of victims of discrimination, adequate compensation, and fines.[27] The ruling was softened somewhat by saying that Article 6 was not directly effective. However, the Court took the opportunity to introduce the doctrine of indirect effect, thereby strongly encouraging the referring German courts to read, if possible, German national law so as to provide an effective remedy.

The reason I have set out in some detail the reasoning in *Von Colson* is that it set a pattern which would be followed, and elaborated upon, in subsequent gender equality cases.

---

[25] Para. 15 of the judgment.   [26] Para. 17 of the judgment.
[27] Para. 18 of the judgment.

The first feature of this pattern was to be found in the absolute non-engagement by the Court in gender equality at work cases with its established 'national procedural autonomy' position that remedies and procedure were for the national legal orders. And this was despite attempts by significant others, such as Advocate-General Van Gerven in *Marshall II*, to apply national procedural autonomy and its two provisos to gender equality at work remedies. It was not until *Draehmpaehl* in 1997 that 'national procedural autonomy' got even a walk-on part in a gender equality at work case, and even then it was an abbreviated and subsidiary aside; the main decisional apparatus remaining firmly centred on the effectiveness of the remedial and procedural rules at stake in that case.[28]

Second, in various ways *Von Colson* was the mother and father of every single gender equality in employment case asserting remedial and procedural effectiveness which came in its wake. In *Draehmpaehl* the Court invoked *Von Colson* to hold that a three-month ceiling and aggregate limits on compensation for gender discrimination breached Community law.[29] *Dekker* raised the issue of whether a national rule requiring fault as an element in proving discrimination breached Community law. This was an issue which straddled substantive and procedural boundaries. The Court combined the substantive definition of discrimination in the ETD with the procedural effectiveness required by *Von Colson* to eliminate the national requirement of fault in discrimination cases,[30] and *Dekker* was, in turn, applied to deal in the same fashion with a fault requirement in German law in *Draehmpaehl*.[31] In *Marshall II* the Court explicitly set out again precisely the same three-step reasoning path[32] taken in *Von Colson*, with the new gloss that the requirements of effective judicial protection have to be examined in the light of the specific breach, entailing in this case either reinstatement or full compensation with interest of a victim of discriminatory dismissal. Moreover, effectiveness in relation to procedure and remedies was a top priority for the Court of Justice. *Johnston* concerned the exclusion of the plaintiff's access to court for a discrimination claim by means of a national security certificate issued by the UK government.[33] The referring court asked seven questions, the sixth concerning the access to court issue. The Court, however, turned to answer that

---

[28] Case C-180/95, *Draehmpaehl v. Urania Immobilienservice*, [1997] ECR I-2195, paras. 28–9 and 41–2 of the judgment.

[29] Ibid. See, esp. paras. 24–6 (the 3-month ceiling on compensation) and 39 and 40 (the aggregate limit on compensation).

[30] Case C-177/88, *Dekker*, [1990] ECR I-3941, paras. 22–6 of the judgment. See also the Opinion of AG Darmon in *Dekker/Hertz*, paras. 34 and 35, which is very explicit on the choice made in *Von Colson* to reject the national procedural autonomy path where the Community principle of equal treatment is concerned.

[31] Above, n. 28, paras. 17 and 18 of the judgment.

[32] Paras. 17–24 of the judgment.   [33] Above, n. 5.

question first, stating that it concerned 'the right to an effective judicial remedy'. As exclusion of access to court clearly fell more squarely inside Article 6 ETD than the remedies at issue in cases such as *Von Colson* and *Marshall II*, the Court moved directly to that provision. The Court's problem was to build a bridge from the non-direct effect of Article 6 ETD announced in *Von Colson* to the direct effect it needed to have here to bypass the public interest immunity certificate. This bridge was provided by the argument that Article 6 ETD was an expression of a broader principle of judicial control, consecrated both in the constitutional traditions of the Member States and in Articles 6 and 13 of the European Convention on Human Rights (ECHR).[34] Interpreted in the light of that principle, Article 6 ETD required that 'all persons have the right to obtain an effective remedy in a competent court against measures which they consider to be contrary to the principle of equal treatment for men and women laid down in the directive', and could be directly effective.[35] In *Marshall II* the Court took the further step of attributing direct effect to the ETD in relation to remedies (rather than judicial access as in *Johnston*) as well. The provisions of the ETD had become both directly effective and remedially effective, a potent combination.

In the field of gender equality in social security, national procedural autonomy had, if anything, an even more endangered existence. The ignoring of national procedural autonomy in the employment cases meant that it retained a real, albeit restricted status in Community law. In the social security cases, national procedural autonomy was brought out into the open and threatened more generally. Hence in *Cotter* a national rule prohibiting unjust enrichment could not be applied where it would prevent full application of the principle of equal treatment in Article 4(1) of Directive 79/7. Just as importantly, the main plank of argument preventing reliance on the national prohibition of unjust enrichment was that 'to permit reliance on that prohibition would enable the national authorities to use their own unlawful conduct as a ground for depriving Article 4(1) of the directive of its full effect'.[36] This estoppel-like argument for overriding national procedural rules reached its fullest glory in *Emmott*, decided shortly afterwards. This case concerned time limits in national law which prevented those discriminated against with regard to social security benefits from claiming those benefits. The Court drew on the first step of the reasoning in *Von Colson* to assert that Article 189(3) (now 249)

---

[34] Para. 18 of the judgment.   [35] Para. 58 of the judgment.

[36] Case C-377/89, *Cotter and McDermott v. Minister for Social Welfare and Attorney General*, [1991] ECR I-1155. Compare the treatment of unjust enrichment rules in Case 68/79, *Hans Just v. Danish Ministry of Foreign Affairs*, [1980] ECR 501 (a national rule permitting the State not to pay back levies imposed contrary to EC law where such costs had been defrayed by passing them on to consumers was compatible with EC law); see also *San Giorgio*, above, n. 13, and Joined Cases C-192 to C-218/95, *Société Comateb and others v. Directeur Général des Douanes et Droits Indirects*, [1997] ECR I-165.

of the Treaty required Member States to ensure that directives were fully effective, in accordance with the objectives they pursued.[37] It combined this with the estoppel argument in *Cotter*. Unlike the employment cases, it did start from the position that the normal position was national procedural autonomy and that therefore time limits, provided they satisfied the conditions of not making Community law rights excessively difficult or impossible in practice to exercise and did not discriminate against Community law rights vis-à-vis national law rights, would be compatible with Community law. However, the estoppel and effectiveness arguments combined meant, in the Court's view, that an exception had to be created for Directives.[38] Until a Directive had been properly transposed, individuals were suspended in a state of legal uncertainty as to the rights they possessed under Community law.

It follows that, until such time as a directive has been properly transposed, a defaulting Member State may not rely on an individual's delay in initiating proceedings against it in order to protect rights conferred upon him by the provisions of the directive and that a period laid down by national law within which proceedings must be initiated cannot begin to run before that time.[39]

It is worth clarifying the differences between the reasoning in the social security and employment cases, though both achieved the result that Community definitions of effectiveness overrode national procedural and remedial rules. First, both the objective of the ETD and the text of Article 6 of that Directive were consistently employed to back up effectiveness in the employment cases. The objective of Directive 79/7, by contrast, was extremely muted in the social security cases, while the text of its (almost identically worded) Article 6[40] was not invoked at all. Second, national procedural autonomy was explicitly dealt with in the social security cases; this is not so in the employment cases. Finally—and this is linked to the previous two points—the move to effectiveness in the social security cases was not confined to equal treatment in that sphere, but, rather, explicitly affirmed procedural and remedial effectiveness for directives in general.

Having gathered in the evidence, it is time to consider why the Court opted for effectiveness in the sphere of gender equality and not national procedural autonomy which had been proclaimed in all other substantive sectors of

---

[37] *Emmott*, above, n. 7, para. 18 of the judgment.
[38] Paras. 16 and 17 of the judgment.   [39] Para. 23 of the judgment.
[40] Article 6, Directive 79/7 provides: 'Member States shall introduce into their national legal systems such measures as are necessary to enable all persons who consider themselves wronged by failure to apply the principle of equal treatment to pursue their claims by judicial process, possibly after recourse to other competent authorities.' See also Article 6 of the Equal Pay Directive, 'Member States shall introduce into their legal systems such measures as are necessary to enable all persons who consider themselves wronged by failure to apply to them the principle of equal treatment within the meaning of Arts 3, 4 and 5 to pursue their claims by judicial process after possible recourse to other competent authorities.'

Community law. In other words, how might this sectoral aberration be explained?

Many have relied on the textual base of Article 6 of the equality Directives to explain why the Court could, and did, act differently in this area. In my view, while this is not wrong, its explanatory power is weak. We have seen both that the wording of Article 6 ETD had to be considerably stretched to cover remedies and that Article 6 of Directive 79/7 was not even invoked in the social security cases. Article 6 was therefore merely a useful justificatory resource in the creation of effective remedies; not its source. Two other reasons seem more convincing. Both concern the unique position gender equality occupied in Community law. One deals with the impact of this in the building of the private enforcement model, while the other concerns the difference between national and supranational judicial operating environments.

I turn first to the private enforcement model. It is no secret that the Court preferred Community law to develop through private, rather than public, enforcement,[41] as it provided opportunities to build dense links with the peoples and courts of the Member States and make good its proclamation in *Van Gend en Loos*[42] that a qualitatively new legal order was in the making. Building that model required national judicial cooperation and effectiveness. One of the chief links between these two imperatives was the third imperative, effective judicial protection of individuals. The championing of the rights of the individual against the State provides a persuasive and distinctive rationale for both judicial cooperation and judicial activism. However, the Court of Justice, which needed to rely on effective judicial protection more than other, better established courts in legal systems of longer standing, had a problem in making this rationale persuasive which not all other courts share. This is that the 'individuals' in cases before it are very rarely real people with problems that can be generally identified with. The only personality most private parties had was legal, and their problems were rarely heart-rending.[43] From this point of view, labour law cases in general provided the Court with a vital supply of bona fide individuals in vulnerable, understandable situations. It is easier to think that a man left without wages owed because his employer is insolvent and the State has failed to comply with its obligation to set up the fund to provide him with those wages should have an effective remedy[44] than to extend our

---

[41] G. F. Mancini, 'Labour Law and Community Law', (1985) 20 Irish Jurist 1. See also P. Craig, 'Once upon a Time in the West: Direct Effect and the Federalization of EEC Law', (1992) 12 OJLS 453.

[42] Case 26/62, [1963] ECR 1.

[43] See further C. Harding, 'Who Goes to Court in Europe? An Analysis of Litigation against the European Community', (1992) ELRev. 105; R. Rawlings, 'The Eurolaw Game: Some Deductions from a Saga', (1993) Journal of Law and Society 309; T. de la Mare, 'Article 177 in Social and Political Context', in Craig and de Búrca, *EU Law*, 215.

[44] *Francovich*, above, n. 8.

sympathies in quite the same way to a UK abattoir[45] or a French brewery.[46] Labour law cases were, therefore, important in giving the Court opportunities to establish bold principles which were then (at least potentially) available for application in other non-labour law cases.

Gender equality cases were even better. These cases provided the Court with an abundance of individuals the State was clearly trying to short-change.[47] Moreover, these cases had the added value of having fundamental rights cachet. This both insulated the Court (up to a point) from having to be overly sensitive about the costs of its jurisprudence for Member States and boosted its reputation as a Court built on principle and rights,[48] establishing real European citizenship rights for the women and men of Europe. That the gender equality at work at cases were all equal treatment, rather than equal pay, cases further helped to insulate the Court from cost concerns.

Secondly, the very uniqueness of gender equality in combining vulnerable individuals, fundamental rights, and state non-compliance with Community law made it safe for the Court. The Court was able to view gender equality remedies as a neatly demarcated island precisely because the historical development of EC social policy has meant that, until very recently, gender equality has actually been an isolated island of protection for workers suffering discrimination.[49] For this reason, it could happily depart from national procedural autonomy in that area without creating uncomfortable disparities in the supranational corpus of law which might create pressures to move further away from national procedural autonomy than it wished to go in other areas. At appropriate moments the Court could, however, use gender equality cases as a launching pad for more ambitious moves in the direction of procedural and remedial effectiveness; it did this in the social security cases but not in the employment cases.

---

[45] Case C-55/94, *R v. Ministry of Agriculture, Fisheries and Food, ex parte Hedley Lomas*, [1996] ECR I-2553.

[46] *Brasserie*, above n. 11.

[47] By State we mean here Germany, Ireland, the Netherlands, and the UK, as these were the Member States in which litigation leading to preliminary references on procedural and remedial issues occurred.

[48] 'The argument in favour of anti-discrimination statutes, that a minority has a right to equal respect and concern, is an argument of principle': R. Dworkin, *Taking Rights Seriously* (London: Duckworth, 1977), 82.

[49] Protection under the Social Security Directive (79/7) only applies to those with a nexus to the paid labour market. It is also true that workers have been protected from the Treaty of Rome onwards against discrimination on grounds of nationality—however, the pressing issues in this area have predominantly concerned expansive interpretation of the substance of entitlements (or the non-application of criminal law) and not remedial issues. Where the latter issues have arisen, the Court has applied national procedural autonomy: see Case C-394/93, *Alonso-Pérez v. Bundesanstalt für Arbeit*, [1995] ECR I-4101. Procedural issues concerning free movement have focused on *access* to courts. See *Heylens*, above n.5.

The 'island mentality' with regard to gender equality had one particularly dangerous supplement. While gender equality might be isolated in the supranational judicial operating environment, it was clearly not so isolated in the national legal environments. *Von Colson*, for example, provoked a long discussion among German courts as to whether remedies relating to recruitment could or should be greater than those for unfair dismissal. These debates awoke in the UK when, after *Marshall II*, it became clear that the ETD required full compensation and was directly effective. This immediately raised questions about the viability of the similar limits on compensation for race discrimination in UK law as well as limits relating to gender discrimination concerning pay and other terms and conditions of employment in the Equal Pay Act 1970. This disparity in national and supranational judicial operating environments both permitted effectiveness to be pursued in relation to gender equality remedies and made that pursuit a riskier game than the Court seems to have realized. Of course, there was no guarantee that the Court would be called to account for the way it had played the remedies game. Luck plays a significant role in judicial fortunes. We shall see that the Court's luck with regard to remedies turned in 1993–4, in both supranational and national legal environments. It tried to save its hand by abandoning one part of its jurisprudence. This strategy proved unviable, chiefly because the Court could not see the cards being dealt to the national courts or know how and whether they would be played against it.

IV THE PARTIAL ABANDONMENT OF REMEDIAL EFFECTIVENESS IN GENDER EQUALITY CASES

It gradually dawned on the Court that its noble dream in *Emmott* that time would not begin to run against individuals until a Directive had been properly transposed could be problematic and, if unchecked, would become a nightmare. The noble dream ignored the fact, clear from gender equality cases themselves, that often the meaning of a Directive only came into existence when the Court decided what that meaning was going to be. This made the estoppel argument look very weak indeed as a general principle in this context. Unlimited periods for taking cases threatened pandemonium before the national courts with problems of gathering proof and of finding the defendant, potentially long after the alleged breach of Community law had come to light. In other words, expansive interpretation of the meaning of Directives by the Court would, if *Emmott* were maintained, continually exacerbate the problems associated with open-ended liability, especially given the extremely wide definition of the State for the purposes of Community law.

The Court began a salvage operation in the Dutch case of *Steenhorst-Neerings* and the UK case of *Johnson No. 2*.[50] These were both cases concerning social security benefits which had not been paid to these two women because of discrimination in breach of Directive 79/7. If the Directive had been properly implemented they would have received these benefits from 1984. Instead, when they were finally able to claim, they were awarded, because of a national rule limiting arrears of benefits to one year from the date of claim, benefits only from 1987 and 1986 respectively. They argued that, as in the previous social security cases, the State's failure to effectively transpose Directive 79/7 meant it should not be able to rely on this national rule to prevent full redress. The Court's judgment in *Steenhorst-Neerings* recited the conditions for national procedural autonomy and then flatly asserted, without any supporting reasoning, that those conditions *were* met in the case of these limits on arrears of benefits. Only after this did it proceed to explain why *Emmott* did not apply. Two distinctive sets of reasons emerge from the judgment. First, the nature of the limit at issue was invoked. The Court argued that time limits for taking proceedings were different from limits which did not bar taking proceedings but merely limited the retroactive effect of claims; while the former affected the very assertion of a right, the latter permitted full assertion of a right and simply limited its effects. A second set of arguments was related to the structure of social security benefits and the aim of arrears limits. Arrears limits ensured that the claimant was in fact eligible for the benefit in question for the period for which she was making her claim. Furthermore, in contributory schemes arrears limits were necessary to ensure financial balance in the scheme. In *Johnson No. 2*, which concerned an arrears limit where the second set of arguments did not apply, as her eligibility was clear and it was a non-contributory scheme, the Court refused her claim on the basis of the first set of arguments and would not enter into reasoned discussion about the second set of arguments.

Why did the Court abandon effectiveness in *Steenhorst-Neerings* and *Johnson No. 2*? In my view, the Court returned to national procedural autonomy in these cases, not because of the institutional imperatives of maintaining a relationship with courts (effectiveness, effective judicial protection, judicial cooperation) but because of the need to maintain a relationship with national governments, in particular with regard to budgetary expenditure. Levels of spending on social security are a sensitive issue at national level, and social welfare, linked to a taxing power, is a strongly national competence. In other words, the Court's stance in these particular cases, though probably politically well judged, was underpinned neither by principle nor by coherent

---

[50] Case C-338/91, *Steenhorst-Neerings v. Bestuur van de Bedrijfsvereniging voor Detailhandel, Ambachten en Huisvrouwen*, [1993] ECR I-5475; Case C-410/92, *Johnson (No. 2) v. Chief Adjudication Officer*, [1994] ECR I-5483.

legal reasoning. It simply wished to avoid the application of its principled analyses in previous gender equality cases to situations presenting a significant challenge to national budgetary autonomy. It did this by saying that arrears limits (in these cases) were not the same as time-limits for bringing proceedings (in *Emmott*).

This motivation led to the abandonment of effectiveness in gender equality cases being only partial in two senses. First, *Emmott* retained its place with regard to limits for taking proceedings.[51] Second, effectiveness retained, and indeed strengthened, its position in gender equality at work cases, as illustrated by the decision in *Marshall II*, as well as *Draehmpaehl*.[52] Unsurprisingly, many thought that perhaps these cases indicated that gender equality in social security cases were, somehow, to be treated as severable, and different, from gender equality at work cases. This thinking was given further sustenance by a decision of the Court in 1997 in a third social security case from the UK, *ex parte Sutton*,[53] decided, significantly, on the same day as *Draehmpaehl*. The value of Sutton's claim for social security benefits she was entitled to as a result of the application of the equal treatment principle in Directive 79/7 had been reduced by the effluxion of time. In *Marshall II*,[54] the Court of Justice had found that an effective remedy to compensate discrimination at work required the awarding of interest to ensure full compensation. Sutton, backed by a UK anti-poverty campaigning organization (the Child Poverty Action Group), argued that Article 6 of Directive 79/7, like its textual sister in the ETD,[55] required interest to be awarded in social security cases as well. The Court rejected her claim on the grounds that where the sum owed as a result of discrimination claimed was compensatory in nature, interest on the sum owed formed an inherent part of the right. By contrast, where the sum owed as a result of discrimination was receipt of a benefit for which the claimant was eligible, receipt of that benefit was in itself full realization of the right and there was no need to award interest. In 1997 the Court also decided *Fantask*,[56] in which *Emmott* was finally and definitively laid to rest,

---

[51] See para. 22 of *Steenhorst-Neerings*: 'The time bar resulting from the expiry of the time-limit for bringing proceedings serves to ensure that the legality of administrative decisions cannot be challenged indefinitely. The judgment in *Emmott* indicates that that requirement cannot prevail over the need to protect the right conferred on individuals by the direct effect of provisions in a Directive so long as the defaulting Member State responsible for those decisions has not properly transposed the provisions into national law.' And see the more cautious statement in para. 26 of *Johnson No. 2*: 'it is clear from the judgment in *Steenhorst-Neerings* that the solution adopted in *Emmott* was justified by the particular circumstances of that case, in which a time-bar had the result of depriving the applicant of any opportunity whatsoever to rely on her right to equal treatment under the Directive.'

[52] Above n. 28.

[53] Case C-66/95, *R v. Secretary of State for Social Security ex parte Eunice Sutton*, [1997] ECR I-2163.

[54] Above n. 9.   [55] Above n. 40.   [56] Above n. 10.

having never been applied by the Court of Justice in any case other than *Emmott* itself. Hence, by 1997 the push towards effectiveness in gender equality social security cases was well and truly over.

The lack of principled analysis and coherent reasoning in these three social security cases would soon come back to haunt the Court. As *Sutton* demonstrates, interested observers examining the Court's jurisprudence began to notice the absence of reasoning establishing a principled separation of remedies for gender equality at work and in social security. A clear illustration of the difficulty of drawing such a distinction, given the reasoning in the gender equality at work cases, is provided by Advocate-General Darmon's Opinion in *Steenhorst-Neerings*, which occupies the distinctive location of being at the tip of the crest of gender equality effectiveness before the beginning of the crash in the Court's judgment in that case. His Opinion speaks eloquently for itself.

If the right to equal treatment for men and women, which has been enshrined as a fundamental principle of Community law, particularly in the *Defrenne III* judgment, has existed for individuals since 23 December 1984, can it be restricted by a procedural provision of national law? [para. 13]

The legal classification of the time-limit in the domestic legal system of the Member State matters little in so far as it is necessary to take into consideration only the effects of applying the time-limit with regard to the principle of equal treatment. [para. 30]

In other words, while the Court could easily backtrack, when it saw that that was necessary, from *Emmott outside* the area of gender equality, it was extremely difficult for it to justify departure from effectiveness *inside* gender equality without admitting that pragmatic policy considerations had trumped its much-vaunted attachment to the fundamental principle of equal treatment. Being understandably reluctant to take that step, the Court invented distinctions as the cases came along so that arrears limits were not like time limits and compensation was not like monies owed. But these very distinctions created new potential problems because of the lack of a principled distinction between different sub-areas of gender equality. Unfortunately for the Court, the distinction between social security and employment did not map precisely the distinction between arrears limits and time limits or between compensation and monies owed in national legal environments. No better example of this can be found than section 2(5) of the UK Equal Pay Act 1970, which the Court was soon to repeatedly encounter in various guises. This states that women who have successfully proved a breach of their right to equal pay

[s]hall not be entitled . . . to be awarded any payment by way of arrears of remuneration or damages in respect of a time earlier than two years before the date on which the proceedings were instituted.

V THE IMPOSSIBILITY OF PARTIAL ABANDONMENT:
NATIONAL COURTS AND LEAKY BOUNDARIES

It is time to switch our attention from the Court of Justice to the national courts. How were the national courts reacting to, and participating in, this rather turbulent supranational remedial environment? The analysis which follows focuses on the UK courts for the simple reason that this is undoubtedly the national judicial environment where the most exciting interactions with gender equality remedies have occurred.[57]

Pre-*Emmott* gender equality remedies were not a central issue for the UK courts. Because *Von Colson*[58] had both stated that Article 6 of the ETD was not directly effective and required only that remedies for gender equality be adequate, there seemed little a proper application of EC law could do to change remedial gender equality provisions in UK law. These provisions were not capable of being reread, and some courts thought that they were in any event adequate. *Johnston* was an isolated instance of the State blocking access to court.[59] *Marshall II* proceeded through the entire UK tribunal and court hierarchy. It would not be decided by the Court of Justice until August 1993.

In the Employment Act 1989, the UK legislature removed the difference in treatment in UK law between men and women with regard to redundancy payments for those approaching, or who had reached, the age of 60 (the retirement age for women) with effect from 16 January 1990.

In the wake of *Emmott*, women in the UK, excluded prior to this Act from redundancy payments for those aged around 60, came before the UK courts to claim those payments. In a number of cases, their claim was blocked by the three-month time limit for making claims under the UK Sex Discrimination Act 1975. Post-*Emmott* and pre-*Marshall II* and other developments in 1993 and 1994, the UK courts happily applied *Emmott* to disable this time limit until 16 January 1990, the date the UK legislature had placed its national law in conformity with Article 119.[60] Hence *Emmott* was applied teleologically and generously by applying it to a Treaty article (119) in these cases, rather than confining it to directives as the judgment in *Emmott* indicated. In other words, the UK courts were also happy to play the effectiveness game, at least with regard to gender equality in employment.

In 1993–4 three distinct and explosive sets of developments, both in the UK and at supranational level, utterly transformed the gender equality remedies stakes in the UK. The three developments were the decision of the

---

[57] For what happened in Germany see Kilpatrick, above n. 24.
[58] Above, Section III.   [59] Ibid.
[60] *Cannon v. Barnsley Metropolitan Borough Council*, [1992] IRLR 474; *Rankin v. British Coal Corporation*, [1993] IRLR 69.

Court of Justice in *Marshall II*,[61] the decision of the House of Lords in *ex parte EOC*,[62] and the decisions of the Court of Justice in *Vroege* and *Fisscher*.[63]

In *Marshall II*, as we have seen,[64] the Court of Justice decided that the ETD required not merely adequate compensation but full compensation plus interest for, in this case, discriminatory dismissal. Moreover, Article 6 ETD was now, unlike in *Von Colson*, found to be capable of direct effect. This decision created a series of reverberations in the UK. First, the upper limit on compensation in the Sex Discrimination Act (SDA) 1975 was removed.[65] Second, the uncomfortable disparity this created between remedies for gender and race discrimination led to the removal of the latter limit.[66] Third, in the light of the Court of Justice's decision in *Dekker*[67] that pregnancy discrimination was direct non-comparative discrimination, the UK Ministry of Defence had conceded liability for its policy of automatically dismissing pregnant servicewomen; the advent of *Marshall II* meant that over 5,000 dismissed ex-servicewomen came before the UK courts to claim full (and often very significant) compensation. The UK government paid out well over £50 million in compensation. Fourth, though the UK legislature took no action, *Marshall II* immediately cast doubt on the two-year limit for gender pay discrimination in the UK Equal Pay Act (EqPA) 1970.

In *ex parte EOC*, the House of Lords found that provisions of UK employment law which excluded part-time workers from unfair dismissal and redundancy payments contravened Community law because they indirectly discriminated against women. Though the UK legislature subsequently removed the offending provisions,[68] many part-time workers who had been excluded from these rights prior to *ex parte EOC* came before the UK courts to claim these rights. The key case, *Biggs*,[69] illustrates the issues before the UK courts perfectly. Here the issue was whether a part-time worker who had been dismissed in August 1976 could bring an unfair dismissal claim in 1994 within three months of the decision in *ex parte EOC*. The dispute focused on the effect of *Emmott* and the wording of the UK unfair dismissal time limit,

---

[61] Above n. 9. [62] *R v. Secretary of State ex parte EOC*, [1994] IRLR 176.

[63] Case C-57/93, *Vroege v. NCIV Instituut voor Volkshuisvesting BV and Stichting Pensioenfonds*, [1994] ECR I-4541; Case C-128/93, *Fisscher v. Voorhuis Hengelo BV and Stichting Bedrijfspensioenfonds voor Detailhandel*, [1994] ECR I-4583.

[64] Above, Section III.

[65] The Sex Discrimination and Equal Pay (Remedies) Regulations (SI 1993/2798), made by the Secretary of State for Employment under s. 2(2) of the European Communities Act 1972. See also the removal of s. 66(3) SDA, which effectively excluded compensation for indirect discrimination in the Sex Discrimination and Equal Pay (Miscellaneous Amendments) Regulations 1996 (SI 438/1996).

[66] The Race Relations (Remedies) Act 1994. [67] Above n. 30.

[68] The Employment Protection (Part-Time Employees) Regulations 1995 (SI 1995/31).

[69] *Biggs v. Somerset County Council*, [1996] IRLR 203.

which required examination of whether it had been 'reasonably practicable' for Ms Biggs to have brought her claim within three months.

In *Vroege* and *Fisscher*, the Court of Justice clarified the relationship between its judgments on occupational pensions in *Bilka* and *Barber*.[70] It held that the temporal limitation it had placed on its judgment in *Barber* did not apply to discrimination against women (part-timers) concerning the right of *access and membership* to occupational pensions rather than the right to *benefits* under such schemes. The former were covered by *Bilka* and were therefore not subject to the *Barber* limitation. Time limits and arrears limits for occupational pension discrimination in the UK are the same as those in the EqPA 1970: six months and two years.[71] Over 60,000 part-time workers who had been excluded from membership of occupational pension schemes brought claims in the *Preston* litigation, arguing that the time limits and arrears limits applied to their claims contravened Community law.

The UK courts stared as a body at this appalling vista of tens upon tens of thousands of litigants before them with claims potentially stretching back to 8 April 1976 (the date *Defrenne II*[72] was decided) or 9 August 1978 (the date for ETD transposition), and possibly requiring full compensation with interest. Immediate, decisive, and united action was required to close these gaping flood-gates.

The UK courts went straight into national procedural autonomy mode with regard to anything not strictly covered by *Marshall II*.[73] *Emmott* was immediately dumped, on the ground that it did not apply to Treaty articles. The UK courts also realized fast that unless the two provisos to national procedural autonomy were given the meanest of interpretations, they could also pose problems for time limits and arrears limits in these cases. A highly restrictive approach to these two provisos was duly adopted.

In the post *ex parte EOC* cases, the UK courts refused to allow time to run from the date of that judgment or the date of the amending legislation in

---

[70] Case 170/84, *Bilka-Kaufhaus GmbH v. Weber von Hartz*, [1986] ECR 1607. Case C-262/88, *Barber v. Guardian Royal Exchange*, [1990] ECR I-1889.

[71] See, pre-1995, Reg. 12 of the Occupational Pension Schemes (Equal Access to Membership) Regulations 1976 and the equivalent Regulations for Northern Ireland; see now Reg. 5 of the Occupational Pension Schemes (Equal Treatment) Regulations 1995 and the equivalent Regulations for Northern Ireland. The effect of these Regulations is to apply the EqPA to occupational pensions, subject to the modifications in the Regulations themselves. Hence the 6-month time limit in s. 2(4) EqPA applies. With regard to arrears limits, Reg. 5 amends s. 2(5) EqPA. Hence a person's right to be admitted to an occupational scheme shall have effect only for the 2 years before the institution of proceedings.

[72] Above n. 16.

[73] Hence the UK courts did, though with some reluctance, accept *Marshall II* in the context of the dismissed ex-servicewomen's claims. Cf. *Ministry of Defence v. Cannock*, [1994] IRLR 509, and *Ministry of Defence v. Hunt*, [1996] IRLR 139.

1995.[74] Two main reasons were offered. First, it was 'reasonably practicable' for the plaintiffs to have presented their claims within three months of their dismissal. The fact that the House of Lords did not decide *ex parte EOC* until 1994 could not be taken into account as a ground for arguing that it was not 'reasonably practicable'. Second, Community law did not require the UK courts to disapply the time limit on the ground that it made their claim excessively difficult or impossible in practice. *Emmott* applied only to Directives and not to Treaty articles. This position, though convincingly imposed by the UK courts, was achieved only by misreading both UK and Community law. UK courts had a more nuanced position on whether mistakes of law could make it 'reasonably practicable' to extend time in unfair dismissal claims.[75] With regard to Community law, there was no discussion of the principle of effectiveness in gender equality at work cases. The discussion of national procedural autonomy cursorily addressed only the 'practical impossibility' proviso, and did not even acknowledge the existence of the principle of equivalence.

In the cases addressing the six-month time limit and two years arrears' limit applying to occupational pensions and pay, the courts exhibited the same determination to batten down the hatches.[76] Once again, effectiveness was ignored. The courts identified the issue to be addressed as being how to apply the national procedural autonomy provisos of 'practical impossibility' and 'equivalence'. They found that neither the time limit nor the arrears limit made it 'practically impossible' to bring a claim on the ground that no legal bar to proceedings had ever existed. More inventiveness was required to avoid the application of the principle of equivalence, as both the time limit and the arrears limit were clearly stricter than several other potential contenders in UK labour legislation. The courts stated that, in order to find out whether the Community law claim under Article 141 EC had been treated less favourably than domestic law right to equal pay, it was necessary to compare it with similar domestic law rights. The Community law claim under Article 141 EC was subject in the UK context to a time limit of six months (because of section 2(4) EqPA) and an arrears limit of two years (because of section 2(5) EqPA). The similar domestic law right to equal pay, according to the courts, was subject to section 2(4) and section 2(5) EqPA. As these contained a time limit of six months and an arrears limit of two years, there had been no discrimination against the Community law right, and therefore the principle of equivalence had not been breached. This, of course, is no comparison at all,

---

[74] *Biggs*, above nn. 69, 62, and 68. See also *Setiya v. East Yorkshire Health Authority*, [1995] IRLR 348, and *Barber v. Staffordshire County Council*, [1996] IRLR 209.

[75] See e.g. the Court of Appeal's decision in *Riley v. Tesco Stores*, [1980] IRLR 103.

[76] *Preston and others v. (1) Wolverhampton Healthcare NHS Trust (2) Secretary of State for Health; Fletcher and others v. Midland Bank plc*, [1996] IRLR 484 (EAT); [1997] IRLR 233 (CA).

as a thing (sections 2(4) and 2(5) EqPA here) can never be compared with itself. The courts also held that comparison with remedies under the Race Relations Act[77] (which covers both pay and treatment) was not appropriate.

If this close-down had been watertight, all might have been well for the Court of Justice. Given patterns of referral to the Court of Justice, and national litigation on gender equality, this stance by the UK courts would in turn have insulated the Court of Justice from ever confronting the incoherence of its gender equality remedies case law.

However, legal boundaries are leaky. Here, two types of boundary proved permeable: judicially drawn doctrinal boundaries and national judicial boundaries. The stability of the doctrinal boundaries constructed by the Court of Justice in these cases was particularly difficult to achieve, given the fact that, whatever way one looked at it, the Court's jurisprudence left key questions unanswered. Approaching it from the effectiveness angle, the questions requiring discussions with the Court of Justice were whether time limits and arrears limits in equal pay cases demanded the effective remedies approach to be applied, for the distinctive reasons given in the equal treatment at work cases and *Emmott*. Approaching it from the position that national procedural autonomy should apply in the equal pay context, probing questions arose about how to interpret the requirements of practical impossibility and equivalence in the context of gender equality at work claims. The complete suppression of these enquiries was, however, pursued with the greatest vigour by UK courts, and almost worked.

With regard to national judicial boundaries, total close-down of a system of national courts and tribunals is generally difficult to achieve with regard to the use of Community law and, in particular, the preliminary reference procedure. Here, three courts got away, each for different reasons. The first reference, in *Magorrian*, had already escaped from an Industrial Tribunal in Belfast before the full-scale exercise in suppression in Great Britain had become apparent across the Irish Sea. It asked the Court of Justice whether the effectiveness approach was correct in relation to arrears limits applied to occupational pensions. The second reference in *Levez*, by contrast, was an active and unique act of rebellion. The reference was a result of the two lay members on the tripartite Employment Appeal Tribunal outvoting the judicial President to send a reference to the Court of Justice on the meaning of national procedural autonomy, in particular the principle of equivalence in the context of the two-year arrears limit in section 2(5) EqPA.[78] This was a deliberate challenge both to the incoherence of the Court's jurisprudence and to the unsatisfactory reasoning being deployed by the UK courts to suppress further enquiry into what national procedural autonomy might mean.

[77] See above, text accompanying n. 66.
[78] *Levez v. T. H. Jennings (Harlow Pools) Ltd*, [1996] IRLR 499.

The UK judicial acceptance of the structure of the preliminary reference procedure itself led to the eventual referral of *Preston* to the Court of Justice. Though the challenge to UK time limits and arrears limits on the basis of national procedural autonomy was rejected at every level of the UK court system, the House of Lords felt obliged to admit that the Community law position was unclear and that, therefore, as a court of last instance, it had no discretion not to make a preliminary reference.[79]

After 1993–4, there was genuine instability in the doctrinal boundaries created by the Court. This combined with the presence of institutionally backed[80] litigants, represented by highly expert counsel, for whom the stakes were high in suggesting a new coherence which suited their case. In these circumstances, the operation of the preliminary reference procedure made it difficult to foreclose further enquiry. This is true, as this example vividly illustrates, even when the Court of Justice and the national courts *agree* that close-down is the most desirable option. Both the Court of Justice and the UK courts would have to deal with three cases asking how time limits and arrears limits in equal pay cases should be dealt with in the light of both effectiveness and national procedural autonomy.

VI THE UNSAFE HAVEN OF NATIONAL PROCEDURAL AUTONOMY

It is arguable that the Court was not fully aware pre-*Magorrian* of the extent to which the chickens produced by its earlier gender equality case law were well and truly coming home to roost.[81] *Magorrian*[82] was assigned to a small chamber of the Court. It was only when that Chamber narrowly escaped disaster that the Court woke up and saw what was approaching. For this reason both *Levez*, involving tiny sums of money, and *Preston* were decided by the Full Court.

---

[79] *Preston and others v. Wolverhampton Healthcare NHS and others; Fletcher and others v. Midland Bank plc*, [1998] IRLR 197.

[80] See e.g. *Levez*, backed by the Equal Opportunities Commission and the backing by the trade union UNISON for many of the applicants in *Preston*.

[81] The Court of Justice had shown some awareness of the problems which might arise in full-scale application of procedural and remedial effectiveness to equal pay and occupational pension cases when it indicated in *Fisscher* (above, n. 63) at para. 39 that national time limits could operate in such cases, subject to the application of the 'practical impossibility' and 'equivalence' provisos. However, this is best seen as the Court distancing itself from *Emmott* rather than as a fully thought-out consideration either of how this sat with the effectiveness position in gender equality at work cases or of the implications of applying national procedural autonomy to time limits in gender equality at work cases.

[82] Above n. 12.

Taken together, these three cases provide a fascinating insight into the functioning of remedies in the private enforcement model. Like the apostle Peter, the Court was confronted three times with cases pinpointing with painful accuracy the multi-faceted incoherence of its remedies jurisprudence—the cases allow us to trace how it dealt with this. Moreover, the functioning of its relationships with the national courts is further illuminated. The best way to illustrate these two linked themes is to examine very carefully the preliminary references and rulings in these three cases as, here, the denial lies in the detail.

The reference in *Magorrian* assumed—and with extremely good reason, given all the Court's previous decisions on gender equality at work—that remedial effectiveness would apply to the two-year limit on occupational pension backdating in UK law. The wording of its question implies that the tribunal referred because it wanted explicit confirmation of that from the Court before it disapplied national law:

Where the relevant national legislation restricts backdating entitlement in the event of a successful claim to a period of two years prior to the date on which the claim was made, does this amount to the denial of an effective remedy under Community law and is the industrial tribunal obliged to disregard such provision in domestic law if it feels it necessary to do so?

As I have already pointed out,[83] the Regulations applying to occupational pensions were explicitly intended to operate in the same way as the EqPA, subject to modifications necessary to reflect the specific nature of occupational pensions. Time limits were not at issue in *Magorrian*, as both plaintiffs were still in employment when they claimed. Regulation 12, like section 2(5) EqPA, was intended to limit the remedy for the right to full occupational membership to backdated entitlement for two years.

The scheme at issue in *Magorrian* had one distinctive feature. It contained a requirement that to obtain certain benefits under the scheme a minimum of twenty years' scheme membership was required. Additional requirements of this sort could, *theoretically at least,* lead to section 2(5) EqPA and Regulation 12 falling out of kilter in this type of scheme. This will be the case if Regulation 12 is interpreted as a limit to be applied *before* (rather than *after*) calculating what a woman's pension entitlement should be. The result of this interpretation in schemes requiring minimum membership would be that a UK part-time worker who had been excluded from such a scheme could *never* qualify for any benefits under the scheme as she could only ever be credited with a maximum of two years' backdated membership of the scheme (rather than the twenty required for qualification). For convenience, this will be called the 'nuclear' interpretation of Regulation 12. For our purposes, it is important to note that none of the UK participants in the case before the Court of Justice—the national court, the plaintiffs, and the UK govern-

[83] Above n. 71.

ment—thought that the 'nuclear' interpretation was correct.[84] The Court's judgment belied both assumptions of the referring court. First, it did not apply remedial effectiveness. Second, it decided the case on the assumption that the 'nuclear' interpretation was correct. How and why did this occur?

First, paragraph 37 of the Court's judgment marks the break with the Court's previously unbroken record of applying effectiveness in gender equality at work cases. For the first time the Court went straight to national procedural autonomy, stating that the two-year limit would be compatible with Community law provided it complied with the two standard provisos. Not only is effective remedies not used as the principal decisional framework in *Magorrian*, it is not even referred to in the judgment. Like the UK courts, the Court of Justice decided that the cost and legal certainty implications of applying effective remedies in equal pay cases were too great. It was time to abandon effectiveness in gender equality at work cases (at least, those concerning equal pay) as well. Like the crew of a small boat escaping rough waters for warm and calmer shallows, the Sixth Chamber in *Magorrian* zoomed away from 'effective remedies' towards 'national procedural autonomy', only to find that what had looked like calmer waters from afar promised to be just as turbulent and dangerous as those it had just left.

Second, the dangers of national procedural autonomy explain why the Court adopted the 'nuclear' interpretation of UK law. This had been offered to it, not by any of the UK participants, but by the ultimate repeat player before the Court, the Commission.[85] In particular, the Court badly needed to avoid considering the application of the equivalence proviso. It raised the very uncomfortable issue of whether the two-year arrears limit in national equal pay law was 'like' remedies in national equal treatment law and therefore, in the wake of the effects of *Marshall II*[86] in the UK, incompatible with Community law. Or was the arrears limit in national equal pay law 'like' arrears limits in UK social security law and, therefore, on the authority of *Johnson No. 2*,[87] compatible with Community law? And what factors should

---

[84] Hence the Belfast Industrial Tribunal would not have referred to 'backdating entitlement *in the event of a successful claim*' if the 'nuclear' interpretation had been seen as a possibility, as there would no chance of any successful claims if that interpretation prevailed. See also, in the Report of the Hearing, the women claimants' view: 'restricting the service which may be taken into account to service performed during the two years prior to the date of the claim being lodged has, or may have, the effect of preventing the applicants from obtaining equal pay or *at least significantly reducing their entitlement to equal pay*', and the UK government: 'a rule which permits a court or tribunal to take into account only the two years prior to the commencement of proceedings *when awarding a worker in the applicants' position additional benefits* under the scheme' (emphases added).

[85] On the Commission's influence in preliminary reference proceedings see F. Snyder, 'The Effectiveness of European Community Law: Institutions, Processes, Tools and Techniques', (1993) 56 *MLR* 19 at 30–1.

[86] Above n. 9.   [87] Above n. 50.

determine which it was more 'like'? Dealing with the equivalence proviso was a deeply unappealing prospect for the Court.

The only escape route was to find that the arrears limit did breach the other proviso to national procedural autonomy—'the practical impossibility' or 'excessively difficult' proviso. But this path looked equally difficult. The arrears limit did not prevent the women making their claim, it merely limited the value of a successful claim. This was precisely the reasoning the Court had used in both *Steenhorst-Neerings* and *Johnson No. 2* to say that arrears limits did not make it 'excessively difficult' or 'impossible in practice' to get a remedy.

The 'nuclear' interpretation allowed all these difficulties to be avoided. By adopting it, the Court was able to claim that the arrears limit, with regard to this particular scheme, would make it 'practically impossible' for the claimants to assert their rights, as they would never be able to acquire the requisite twenty years' service.

> Thus, whereas the rules at issue in . . . *Steenhorst-Neerings* and in *Johnson* merely limited the period, prior to commencement of proceedings, in respect of which back-dated benefits could be obtained, the rule at issue in . . . this case prevents the entire record of service completed by those concerned after 8 April 1976 until 1990 from being taken into account for the purposes of calculating the additional benefits which would be payable even after the date of the claim.
>
> Consequently, unlike the rules at issue in the judgments cited above, which in the interests of legal certainty merely limited the retroactive scope of a claim for certain benefits and did not therefore strike at the very essence of the rights conferred by the Community legal order, a rule such as that before the national court in this case is such as to render any action by individuals relying on Community law impossible in practice.[88]

The Court's Houdini-like abilities with national law and its own case law were also amply demonstrated in the *Levez* case.[89] The reference seemed to confront the Court head-on with the question it had just managed to dodge in *Magorrian*—how the principle of equivalence applied to the two-year arrears limit in national equal pay legislation. This was not an occupational pensions case, and therefore the option of waving the magic wand of special scheme rules to make the principle of equivalence disappear was not available. This was a straightforward equal pay case. Belinda Levez could not recover all the pay owed to her as a result of discrimination by her employer because of the two-year arrears limit. Nothing could have looked more like the equal pay equivalent of *Marshall II*. Yet the need not to apply straightforwardly the principle of equivalence was even more pressing than in *Magorrian*, given that *Preston*, with 60,000 litigants, was moving with slow determination in the direction of the Court of Justice.

---

[88] Paras. 43 and 44 of the Court's judgment.   [89] Above n. 12.

Worse still from the Court's point of view, the EAT's preliminary reference almost exclusively focused on how the 'equivalence' proviso of the Court's baseline position was to be applied. The EAT told the Court of Justice that more favourable rules were applied to other employment law claims, giving the examples of claims in respect of breach of the contract of employment, racial discrimination in pay, unlawful deductions from wages, and sex discrimination in matters other than pay. It asked the Court how 'similar domestic actions' were to be identified and evaluated under this test.

One part of one question tangentially addressed the 'practical impossibility' proviso—the Court of Justice was told that under section 2(5) EqPA the national court had no discretion to extend the two-year period in any circumstance, even where a claimant was delayed in bringing her claim because her employer deliberately misrepresented to her the level of remuneration received by men performing like work to her own.

The Court, in a highly imaginative (and incorrect)[90] extrapolation from this latter point, asserted that Levez had been 'deceived' in the legal sense of the tort of deceit by her employer. This idea, picked up from the UK government, allowed complete reformulation of all the questions posed by the EAT in order to deal with what had been transformed by the Court into an exceptional fact situation.

The general issue of principle—how to apply the 'equivalence' limb to section 2(5) EqPA—which the referring court had explicitly identified as central, became secondary.[91] In this new 'deceit' scenario, the chief question to be answered was whether the fact that the arrears limit rule vested the national tribunal with no discretion to alter that rule, even where the employer had deliberately misrepresented pay, made it 'practically impossible' to enforce the Community right to equal pay.

It stated that in 'normal' cases reasonable limitation periods for bringing proceedings would not make the exercise of Community rights 'practically impossible', even if the expiry of such periods necessarily entailed the partial or complete rejection of the claim.

Consequently, a national rule under which entitlement to arrears of remuneration is restricted to the two years preceding the date on which the proceedings were instituted was not in itself open to criticism.[92]

However, in the 'special' circumstances prevailing in Ms Levez's case, where the delay in bringing proceedings had occurred because of deliberate

---

[90] See the EAT in *Levez No. 2*, [1999] IRLR 764: 'on the evidence, it would appear that [deceit] was not the explanation for her delay in bringing the claim.'

[91] See para. 18 of AG Léger's Opinion: 'the Employment Appeal Tribunal took the view that "[t]he point of principle is, however, an important one. A decision in favour of Mrs Levez could have far-reaching implications for many other cases."'

[92] Para. 20 of the judgment.

misrepresentation by the employer of relevant pay information, a national non-discretionary arrears limit failed the 'practical impossibility' limb.

The Court stated that this finding on the 'practical impossibility' limb would mean that it would not usually need to proceed to examine whether the national rule complied with the 'equivalence' principle as well. In other words, because it was 'practically impossible' for Levez to assert her Community law rights, the national remedial rule failed the Community criteria for national procedural autonomy.

However, the Court had to proceed to examine the 'equivalence' principle because of the 'deceit' in this case. This was because, although it was 'practically impossible' for the applicant to assert her Community law rights through an EqPA claim before an Industrial (now Employment) Tribunal, as a victim of deceit she had a way of fully enforcing her EC law rights—through an action on the EqPA and the tort of deceit before the County Court. In other words, the existence of the County Court route meant that it was not 'practically impossible' for a deceived individual to enforce her EC law rights.

Given that the County Court route was 'practically possible', the Court of Justice moved to examine whether an action before the County Court on equal pay and the tort of deceit was less favourable than other similar domestic actions. This meant that the Court of Justice did not address equivalence in the manner requested by the national court. The EAT asked the Court to examine whether the two-year arrears limit under section 2(5) EqPA in an action before an Employment Tribunal was less favourable than other similar domestic actions, not whether an action before the County Court on the EqPA and the tort of deceit was less favourable than other similar domestic actions, which is the issue the Court in fact addressed.

What guidance did the Court give on the application of the 'equivalence' principle? It usefully dispensed with the argument accepted by the UK courts in *Preston*[93] and other cases such as *Biggs*[94] that claims under the EqPA were 'comparable' to Article 141 EC claims, and that, therefore, the time limit under section 2(4) and the arrears limit under section 2(5) were lawful, by pointing out that this was tautologous.

Did the Court of Justice provide any help on how to make these comparisons? While leaving it up to the national court to apply the 'equivalence' principle, it gave some indications of its stance. These built on the foundations it had begun to lay with regard to the 'equivalence' principle in *Edis*, a non-gender equality case concerning time limits for restitutionary claims in Italian law decided three months previously.[95] The Court also drew on its recent case law, in which it had developed the 'practical possibility' proviso into a qualitative evaluation of the role played by the challenged rule in the national

---

[93] Above n. 76.   [94] Above n. 69.   [95] See *Edis*, above n. 13.

procedural fabric.[96] From these cases the Court in *Levez* drew up a series of principles to be taken into account by national courts. It was for the national court 'which alone has direct knowledge of the procedural rules governing actions in the field of employment law' to apply the 'equivalence' principle. In deciding what a similar domestic action might be, the national court should look to the purpose and the essential characteristics of allegedly similar domestic actions. Moreover, in deciding whether a rule was 'less favourable' than rules governing similar domestic actions, the Court indicated, by analogy with its recent case law on the 'practical possibility' proviso, that the national court must take into account the role played by that provision in the procedure as a whole, as well as the operation and any special features of that procedure before the different national courts. The Court, however, insisted that the 'equivalence' principle was not to be interpreted as requiring Member States to extend their most favourable rules to all Community actions brought in a particular field of national law—here 'in the field of employment law'.[97]

How can we explain and evaluate what the Court of Justice does in *Levez*? Looked at from the Court's point of view, *Levez* is a subtle and calculated judgment. By the time *Levez* was heard by the Full Court, the Court knew that *Preston*—the case 'behind' *Levez*—was on its way, and was starting to feel its way towards a solution. By pulling out of the hat the alleged deceit of the employer and the related County Court claim on the EqPA and the tort of deceit, it achieved three goals simultaneously.

First, as in *Magorrian*, it avoided making any operative ruling on the compatibility of arrears limits in gender equality at work rules with Community law. Second, by looking at the County Court action in the context of the 'equivalence' principle, it was able to give some strong indications that Levez herself would win her case. But, through discussing the background to Levez's case, it started to sketch out for itself how the principles of 'equivalence' and 'practical possibility' might operate in 'standard' equal pay cases. This both provided some authority for its forthcoming decision in *Preston* and gave it an outline which it could work on and modify. The Court made *Levez* become its own dress rehearsal for the one it needed to get right—*Preston*.

Before looking at *Preston*, it should be stressed for the avoidance of any doubt that I am not trying to suggest in any way that the Court was acting in bad faith. This would, in any event, be both almost impossible and of limited utility to demonstrate. Rather, the handling of these cases demonstrates a

---

[96] *Van Schijndel*, above at n. 3.

[97] Having set out these principles, the Court gave some indication of how they might be applied in working out whether the claim before the County Court to enforce a Community right was less favourable than other similar domestic actions. The Court indicated that if other similar domestic rights could be enforced through an Employment Tribunal action which is simpler, quicker, and, in principle, cheaper, then the County Court right could be regarded as 'less favourable'.

subtler but more interesting set of points, about the operation of the preliminary reference procedure.

First, preliminary references do not arrive at the Court in a vacuum—the rest of this chapter has tried to show how references are enmeshed in both a sequential (the previous case-law on remedies) and sectoral (in specific areas of Community policy) context. Because of this enmeshing, *Magorrian, Levez,* and *Preston* were undoubtedly 'hard cases' for the Court of Justice.

Second, these cases show what a crowded stage a preliminary reference can become before the Court of Justice. Particularly in hard cases, many participants with distinctive views become apparent. In these circumstances, the bilateral modelling of the preliminary reference procedure as a dialogue between the national court and the Court of Justice is more likely to become a multilateral process of discourse in which the national court becomes one among many.[98] In neither *Magorrian* nor *Levez* was the national court the main voice listened to by the Court.

Third, the Court of Justice will also be more tuned into multiple voices in 'hard cases'. It will want to fashion the response, after examining the competing interpretations on offer which, in its view, best fits with and justifies its previous practice(s), and hence permits it to maintain its institutional integrity. In *Magorrian,* this was the Commission's 'nuclear' interpretation; in *Levez,* the UK government's.

Fourth, the national court, on receiving strange messages from the Court as a result of a preliminary reference in a hard case, may decide to sort the matter out for itself in line with its greater expertise in national law. This may remove the hard case from circulation in the judicial system. This is precisely what happened when the *Levez* reference was applied by the EAT.[99] It was heard with another case which was explicitly designed to test what would happen to the two-year limit in cases where 'deceit' was a complete non-runner. The EAT decided that the two situations could not be distinguished: 'Either s. 2(5) is in conflict with European principles or it is not.' It went on to find that section 2(5) EqPA did breach the principle of equivalence by being less favourable than the following rights which the EAT considered to be similar domestic law rights: claims for monies due under a contract, for unlawful deductions from wages, and race and disability discrimination claims. It concluded in the following fashion:

---

[98] On the dialogue/discourse metaphors with regard to preliminary references see de la Mare, above n. 43 at 240 ff., and S. Sciarra, 'Integration Through Courts: Article 177 as a Pre-federal Device', in Sciarra (ed.), *Labour Law in the Courts: National Courts and the ECJ* (Oxford: Hart, 2001).

[99] *Levez v. T. H. Jennings (Harlow Pools) Ltd (No. 2)*; *Hicking v. Basford Group Ltd,* [1999] IRLR 764.

s. 2(5) is a restriction on the right to have a full and effective remedy for breach of Article 119 and the Equal Pay Directive. It is a breach of the principle of equivalence.[100]

The EAT therefore acted unlike the Court of Justice in two ways. First, it did apply the principle of equivalence to a standard equal pay case. Second, it did not clearly distinguish between the 'effective remedies' position and the national procedural autonomy position.

In *Preston*,[101] the Court had to deal with how national procedural autonomy applied to both the six-month time limit in section 2(4) EqPA and the two-year arrears limit in the context of occupational pension schemes which did not contain a requirement, such as that in *Magorrian*, of twenty years' minimum membership.

The Court in *Preston* drew on previous strands in its case law to start stabilizing a more coherent position in the field of remedies. Nowhere is this more evident than in the treatment of the 'practical impossibility' proviso. This has been rechristened as the 'effectiveness' principle. This renaming began in *Fantask*,[102] the 1997 case in which *Emmott* was definitively buried. In that case, its purpose was to meld the practical impossibility proviso with the special circumstances prevailing in *Emmott*. In *Levez* and *Preston*, the process of renaming served to associate linguistically the 'effectiveness' previously pursued in gender equality at work cases with the 'practical impossibility' proviso and national procedural autonomy. Hence, the two 'effective remedies' strands in gender equality case law[103] have been merged into a linguistic association with the national procedural autonomy position.

The 'effectiveness' principle, as thus rechristened, was applied to the six-month time limit. Unsurprisingly, it was found not to breach that principle, the main interest of the *Preston* judgment being the utter airbrushing of *Emmott* from the Court's repertoire.[104]

More interesting is the application of effectiveness (née practical impossibility) to the arrears limit. The Court had created two different spaces for this in *Levez* and *Magorrian* without directly applying it to a standard case. Hence, in *Levez* it had indicated that, while in standard equal pay cases a two-year limit would pass muster vis-à-vis this requirement,[105] the 'special' circumstances prevailing meant that it failed this limb of national procedural autonomy. In *Magorrian*, by contrast, the Court employed a special interpretation of the scheme challenged to find that, in those specific circumstances, it was not practically possible to obtain a remedy. Given that none of the

---

[100] Ibid. 768.   [101] Above n. 12.   [102] Above n. 10.   [103] Above, Section III.
[104] '[I]t is settled case-law, *and has been since Rewe* [above, n. 2] . . . that the setting of reasonable limitation periods for bringing proceedings satisfies that principle. [para. 33] . . . Such a limitation period does not render impossible or excessively difficult the exercise of rights conferred by the Community legal order [para 34].'
[105] Above n. 92.

occupational pension schemes in *Preston* contained the features which had distinguished *Magorrian*, it seemed that the Court would rely on its dictum in *Levez* and find that the two-year limit did not contravene the practical impossibility proviso. It did not, however, do that. Instead, it stated that, as in *Magorrian*, the object here was to claim retroactive membership of the scheme rather than retroactive arrears of benefits under the scheme.[106] It then stated that the rule here was 'essentially identical' to that at issue in *Magorrian*, and therefore, similarly made it practically impossible to obtain a remedy. But the 'rule' in *Preston* precisely lacked the feature which the Court had stated in *Magorrian* allowed it to find that it was 'practically impossible'. Women are not absolutely excluded on any interpretation from occupational pension membership by the two-year arrears limit—its effect is to limit their entitlement to backdated membership to two years. Hence the Court in *Preston* decided, unlike its decision in *Magorrian*, that in standard occupational pension cases, the two-year arrears limit on membership breaches the practical impossibility/effectiveness principle.[107] It did not use the option it had left open in *Levez* to say that the two-year arrears limit never made it practically impossible to enforce Community law rights (although it is still potentially available to distinguish pay from occupational pensions in future cases).

The strategic deployment of *Magorrian* in *Preston* to find that the arrears limit did make it practically impossible to enforce Community rights meant, of course, that once again the Court did not investigate whether the arrears limit complied with the principle of equivalence. Like St Peter, therefore, the Court of Justice has thrice denied this issue.

This left open only the issue of whether the six-month time limit in section 2(4) EqPA satisfied the principle of equivalence. The Court reiterated its generic, and not especially helpful, guidance in *Levez*, in essence sending a strong message to national courts that they should and would have to deal with equivalence themselves.

One final feature of note, given what was said earlier about the principled analysis sustaining the 'effective remedies' position in the substantive sector of gender equality at work, is that legal certainty has been elevated to the status of a 'fundamental principle'.[108] As any student of Dworkin could tell the Court, while principles must always trump policies, competing principles have to be weighed in order to obtain the right answer in any given case. This,

---

[106] Para. 37. This constituted an unacknowledged distinguishing of *Steenhorst-Neerings* and *Johnson No. 2*; see above, Section IV.

[107] Note the significant play on the double meaning of the 2-year rule preventing 'the *entire* record of service . . . from being taken into account' in para. 43. In *Magorrian*, 'entire' meant that 'none' of their service would be taken into account (according to the 'nuclear' interpretation); in *Preston*, 'entire' had the very different meaning of 'not all' their service.

[108] Para. 33 of the judgment. See also *Palmisani*, above n. 13, para. 28.

then, is a useful resource for handling future cases where fundamental rights, such as gender equality, come up against procedural and remedial limits.

VII REASSESSING REMEDIES IN
THE PRIVATE ENFORCEMENT MODEL

In this chapter, it has been shown that the Court of Justice, guided by effective judicial protection considerations, opted for effective remedies in the sector of gender equality rather than national procedural autonomy. It has also demonstrated how two kinds of straying away from a principled sectoral approach led to the abandonment of effectiveness in gender equality cases. First, in *Emmott*, the Court extended effective remedies extra-sectorally. Second, in the subsequent social security cases, it abandoned its principled effective remedies analysis within the sector of gender equality for policy-oriented reasons. The lack of explicit reasoning about either principle or policy led the Court instead into a set of ad hoc and often factually tenuous distinctions in the areas of equal pay and social security which disposed of the cases before it without providing any satisfying, long-term coherence. This created a difficult and unglorious period for all European courts dealing with remedies. The relationship between effective remedies and national procedural autonomy in the sphere of gender equality remains unclear. In particular, are equal treatment and equal pay at work subject to the same analysis?

In my view, a more explicit and principled commitment to sectoral coherence by the Court in the area of gender equality would have better preserved institutional integrity. Gender equality *is* unlike many of the issues the Court deals with. However, the Court of Justice did not explicitly admit this for two reasons.

First, it wanted to retain gender equality as a launching pad for the promotion of effectiveness in other areas of Community law where effective judicial protection arguments are less resonant. However, if the Court's commitment to gender equality was more explicitly and resolutely principled, and therefore sectorally bounded, it would not risk that particular principled analysis for pragmatic, effectiveness-related gains in other areas.

Second, it may have considered that explicit attachment to a sectorally coherent position would have given it insufficient manoeuvring space to make room for policy considerations inside gender equality. However, it is arguable that, on the contrary, more explicit attachment to a sectorally coherent position would have given it a stronger position from which to justify both non-departures and exceptional departures from this principled analysis. Imagine how different the tale recounted in this chapter would be if the Court had admitted in *Steenhorst-Neerings* (as it did in *Defrenne II* and *Barber*)[109] that,

---

[109] Above nn. 16 and 70.

because of exceptional cost implications, it was modifying, for *specified* and *limited* reasons, its usual analysis in gender equality cases.

Moreover, sectoral coherence would allow, and would have allowed, the courts to decide together what remedies should be available for breach of fundamental rights. This does not necessarily mean that full compensation or open-ended time limits is the optimum solution. What is required is careful evaluation of existing legislative choices. Sectoral coherence in the sphere of gender equality would also place the courts of the Community in a stronger position to handle properly the new generation of discrimination rights emanating from Article 13 EC.[110]

Finally, if we look back at the standard account of remedies, what would happen if we removed the gender equality cases on the ground that they constitute a sectorally distinct development? We might then examine the other, not numerous, 'effectiveness-led' remedies decisions to see if, for example, *Factortame I*[111] can be justified by reference to a special balance of the three institutional imperatives identified at the outset of this chapter. For the great bulk of cases, even non-believers in right answers may think that national procedural autonomy is not only an accurate description of the case law but an appropriate judicial response.

---

[110] See Directive 2000/43/EC (implementing the principle of equal treatment between persons irrespective of racial or ethnic origin) and Directive 2000/78/EC (establishing a general framework for equal treatment in employment and occupation).

[111] Above n. 6.

6

The Jurisdiction of the Community Courts Reconsidered

PAUL CRAIG

This chapter will reconsider the jurisdiction of the Community courts. The inquiry is timely given the need to think more generally about the Community's institutional structure in the light of expansion. There have also been two important papers which directly address key issues concerning the Community's judicial architecture. One has been written by those currently in the ECJ and CFI,[1] and will be referred to hereafter as 'the Courts' paper'. The other was produced by a Working Party composed largely of former judges of the ECJ at the behest of the Commission.[2] The Chairman was Olé Dué and it will be referred to as 'the Dué Report'.

The discussion will be structured in the following manner. There will be an analysis of the central attributes of the present judicial system. This will be followed by a review of the reasons for the increasing caseload borne by the Community courts, and the techniques presently available to limit the number and type of case which they hear. The focus will then shift to the aims which should underlie reform of the Community's judicial structure. The bulk of the chapter will analyse the proposals made in the two papers, drawing out the broader implications and consequences of particular jurisdictional reforms. The discussion will conclude with the reception of these proposals by the IGC, and the changes actually made in the Nice Treaty.

I CENTRAL ATTRIBUTES OF THE PRESENT SYSTEM

Discussion of the proposals for reform of the Community judicial system requires an understanding of the central attributes of that system.

---

[1] *The Future of the Judicial System of the European Union (Proposals and Reflections)* (May 1999) (hereafter *FJS*).

[2] *Report by the Working Party on the Future of the European Communities' Court System* (Jan. 2000) (hereafter *RWP*).

A. The Community Courts

It is clear that properly understood we have three types of Community Court, not just two: the ECJ, the CFI, *and* national courts. It is important not to forget the latter when we think of the structure of the Community judicial system. The rationale for inclusion of national courts in this respect is of course that they are enforcers of Community law in their own right, and have been ever since the seminal decisions in *Da Costa*[3] and *CILFIT*.[4] National courts will apply EC law to cases which come before them, either where the ECJ/CFI have already decided the point of law in question or where the matter is *acte clair* in the sense articulated in *CILFIT*. The ECJ in an earlier paper characterized national courts 'as the courts with general jurisdiction for Community law',[5] and this characterization was repeated in the Courts' more recent paper.[6]

The *Da Costa* decision served to enhance the authority of the ECJ's rulings, in the sense that national courts were told to regard such rulings as authoritative on the issues contained therein. This altered the original conception of the relationship between national courts and the ECJ, from one which was essentially bilateral, in which rulings were only of relevance to the national court which requested them, to one which was essentially multilateral, in which ECJ rulings would have an impact on all national courts. It provided the foundation from which the ECJ could construct a more authoritative system of Community law. The decision in the *CILFIT* case meant that those rulings were now to have authority for situations in which the point of law was the same, even though the questions posed in earlier cases were different, and even though the proceedings in which the issue originally arose differed. National courts became enforcers of Community law in their own right. Once an issue of Community law had been determined by the ECJ, national courts could then apply that law without further resort to the ECJ. National courts became part of a Community judicial hierarchy with the ECJ at the apex of the network.

The ECJ's treatment of *acte clair* fits with the preceding analysis. The Court in *CILFIT* could have chosen to deny any place for the *acte clair* doctrine in EC law. This was the view espoused by Advocate-General Capotorti.[7] The Court chose not to follow this approach, and instead gave the doctrine

---

[3] Cases 28–30/62, *Da Costa en Schaake NV, Jacob Meijer NV and Hoechst-Holland NV v. Nederlandse Belastingadministratie*, [1963] ECR 31.

[4] Case 283/81, *Srl CILFIT and Lanificio di Gavardo SpA v. Ministry of Health*, [1982] ECR 3415.

[5] *Report of the Court of Justice on Certain Aspects of the Application of the Treaty on European Union—Contribution of the Court of First Instance for the Purposes of the 1996 Intergovernmental Conference* (May 1995) (hereafter *RCJ*), para. 15.

[6] *FJS*, 24.   [7] Case 283/81, [1982] ECR 3415, at 3439.

limited support, albeit hedged about with a range of restrictions. Commentators have taken differing views as to what the ECJ intended by casting its judgment in these terms. Some contend that the real objective was to deal a death blow to the concept, through the very range of restrictions imposed thereon. Others argue that the Court's purpose was to legitimate the concept, but to make the national courts more responsible when using it. The effect of the decision was, however, to leave cases which met the ECJ's conditions to be decided by the national courts. For such clear-cut cases, the national courts functioned as the delegates of the ECJ for the application of Community law, thereby allowing the latter to utilize its time in the resolution of more problematic cases.

In drawing up a list of Community judicial organs we should not forget the seminal role played by the Commission. It may well be argued that, in strict doctrinal terms, the Commission is not a court at all, but more akin to an agency which exercises adjudicative functions. This picture of the Commission is reinforced by its very susceptibility to judicial review. This may well be accepted, but it should not be allowed to mask the underlying reality. If the Commission when exercising its judicial functions is to be regarded as an agency, then it is an agency which has enormous power and responsibility within certain key areas of EC law. It is the Commission which has the front-line responsibility for competition policy and state aids. If it did not exercise initial judicial power over these areas then this would have to be reassigned either to another specialist agency or to the CFI. The latter is not a viable option, given the workload entailed by initial decision-making in the areas of competition and state aids. Indeed, this very workload has been problematic for the Commission itself, which has encouraged national courts to take an ever more prominent role in the enforcement of competition law, leaving the Commission time to adjudicate on those cases which raise new issues of principle, or which are especially difficult.

B. The Division of Responsibility between the ECJ and the CFI

We shall consider in due course the possibility of reforming the jurisdictional competence of the ECJ and the CFI in order to make it more rational and efficient. For the present it should be recognized that the division of jurisdictional responsibility between the two courts has been largely ad hoc. It is well known that the CFI was created to ease the workload of the ECJ. It was therefore natural to assign it certain types of case which by their very nature had a heavy factual quotient which took up too much time of the ECJ itself. It was for this reason that competition and staff cases were assigned to the CFI. The extension of jurisdictional competence to the CFI over direct actions brought by individuals under Articles 230, 232, and 288 was a further move to ease the workload of the ECJ. The same motive, combined with the idea that the

CFI had built up expertise in the areas of competition and intellectual property, led to cases concerning the Community trade mark being assigned to the CFI.

C. The Division of Responsibility between the ECJ/CFI and National Courts

The division of responsibility between the ECJ/CFI and national courts has been coloured by a number of different factors, two of which stand out and are to some extent in tension.

The main objective has been to confer a broad power on national courts to enforce Community law, since this enhanced the overall effectiveness of EC law in the manner considered above. Hence the encouragement given to national courts to apply Community precedent in cases which come before them without recourse to the ECJ unless there was need to do so. Hence also the ECJ's insistence that any national court must be able to apply EC law in a case which came before it, and its insistence also that national rules should not be able to hinder or impede this.

This has been tempered by the desire to preserve the uniformity of application and interpretation of EC law. This was the rationale for the *Foto-Frost* decision:[8] while national courts have the ability to declare EC norms to be valid, and whilst they must treat ECJ decisions that a Community norm is invalid as having *ergo omnes* effect,[9] they cannot themselves declare a Community norm to be invalid, although they can of course now provide some interim relief.[10]

D. The Division of Responsibility between the ECJ/CFI and the Commission

We have considered thus far the factors which have affected the division of responsibility between the ECJ and CFI, and between both of these courts and national courts. A number of considerations have affected the allocation of power as between the ECJ/CFI and the Commission.

We have already seen that the Commission itself has been under considerable pressure because of its workload, hence the desire to enlist the further support of national courts. The volume of work in areas such as competition and state aids meant that it would have been impossible for either the ECJ or the CFI to exercise original jurisdiction. Expertise was a further reason for

---

[8] Case 314/85, *Firma Foto-Frost v. Hauptzollamt Lubeck-Ost*, [1987] ECR 4199.

[9] Case 66/80, *International Chemical Corporation v. Amministrazione delle Finanze dello Stato*, [1981] ECR 1191.

[10] Cases C-143/88 and 92/89, *Zuckerfabrik Suderdithmaschen AG v. Hauptzollamt Itzehoe*, [1991] ECR I-415.

according power to the Commission over such areas. Competition policy involves difficult economic concepts. At the inception of the Treaty it would not have been an easy task for a generalist court, such as the ECJ, to develop the expertise to enable it to flesh out the bare bones of Articles 81 and 82 of the Treaty. There is moreover a less obvious, but important, advantage of according power over these matters to the Commission. Policy in an area such as competition or state aids can be developed through either adjudication or rule-making. Other things being equal, there is clearly an advantage in according power to a body which has the ability both to adjudicate and to make rules, since this thereby maximizes the freedom of choice as to how best to develop policy in that particular area. The Commission possesses this dual capacity. It will make the initial adjudication in a competition or state aids case, and can use this as the vehicle through which to develop its thinking about, for example, oligopoly. The Commission can also make rules which have a profound effect on the reach of Articles 81 and 82, as exemplified by the block exemptions which it has made on matters such as exclusive distribution and exclusive dealing.

E. The Central Importance of Preliminary Rulings within the EC Judicial System

The ECJ and CFI possess jurisdictional competence over actions brought before them in a number of different ways, including direct actions under Articles 226, 230, 232, and 288. There is, however, little doubt that it is the ECJ's jurisdiction over preliminary rulings under Article 234 which is regarded as the jewel in the crown of the existing regime. The preliminary reference procedure enshrined in this Article has been of seminal importance for the development of EC law. There are three reasons why this is so.

First, preliminary references have been the procedural vehicle through which key concepts such as direct effect and supremacy have developed. This is graphically captured by Mancini and Keeling:[11]

If the doctrines of direct effect and supremacy are . . . the 'twin pillars of the Community's legal system', the reference procedure laid down in Article 177 must surely be the keystone in the edifice; without it the roof would collapse and the two pillars would be left as a desolate ruin, evocative of the temple at Cape Sounion— beautiful but not of much practical utility.

Secondly, preliminary rulings have not only been the procedural vehicle through which direct effect and supremacy have developed. The very existence of this procedure has been part of the justificatory argument for the existence of direct effect itself. The ECJ has drawn on the existence of the Article

---

[11] F. Mancini and D. Keeling, 'From *CILFIT* to *ERT*: The Constitutional Challenge Facing the European Court', (1991) 11 YBEL 1, at 2–3.

234 procedure to justify the substantive doctrine of direct effect and to justify the extension of that doctrine. This is readily apparent from the ECJ's reasoning in *Van Gend* itself.[12] The ECJ held that the existence of Article 177 indicated that a point concerning the interpretation of EC law could be raised before a national court. There was nothing in the wording of the Article to suggest that the matter could not be raised by an individual litigant, even though the decision whether to refer the matter would of course be made by the national court itself. This said, the ECJ provided further evidence that individuals could derive rights from Community law which they could invoke in the national forum. A decade later the ECJ invoked the same argument to justify the extension of direct effect to directives in *Van Duyn*.[13]

Article 177, which empowers national courts to refer to the Court questions concerning the validity and interpretation of all acts of the Community institutions, without distinction, implies furthermore that these acts may be invoked by individuals in the national courts.

Thirdly, preliminary rulings have been the mechanism through which the supremacy doctrine has been 'nationalized'. This is in part because the supremacy of Community law has been developed through cases which have arisen through the Article 234 procedure.[14] It is in part because the very structure of this procedure means that the case will start and end in the national courts. To be sure, the national court must accept the basic tenets of the supremacy of EC law. However, once this has occurred the fact that the supremacy doctrine is applied by and through national courts renders it much more effective than if it had simply been attached to an Article 226 action.

F. Preliminary Rulings as a Constraint on the EC's Judicial Architecture

The preliminary ruling procedure is therefore justly regarded as the jewel in the crown of the ECJ's jurisdiction. It should, however, also be recognized that the nature of this procedure, as opposed to one which is more appellate in nature, has placed constraints on the way in which the judicial architecture of the Community has developed. It is necessary to be aware of these, since they affect the reforms which have been proposed.

The very fact that preliminary rulings take the form of a reference of a question from a national court to the ECJ, while the substance of the case remains for resolution within the national court, means that it is felt by many that

---

[12] Case 26/62, *NV Algemene Transporten Expeditie Onderneming van Gend en Loos v. Nederlandse Administratie der Belastingen*, [1963] ECR 1.

[13] Case 41/74, *Van Duyn v. Home Office*, [1974] ECR 1337, Rec. 12 of judgment.

[14] Case 6/64, *Costa v. ENEL*, [1964] ECR 585; Case 106/77, *Amministrazione delle Finanze dello Stato v. Simmenthal SpA*, [1978] ECR 629.

there must be a 'one-stop shop'. The questions referred by the national court must go to one and only one Community court. While it would be possible to have questions sent to the CFI with limited rights of appeal to the ECJ, the general thinking is that this would be unacceptable because of the delays thereby involved. Whether this is indeed such an obstacle is not so clear.[15] We shall return to this issue below.[16]

This problem is compounded by the fact that preliminary rulings vary enormously in terms of their importance. If all such cases were of real importance, then it would not matter that they should all go to the ECJ for resolution. However, many requests for preliminary rulings are of the 'turkey tail or nightdresses' character. Applicants will seek to challenge the validity of Community regulations or decisions. They find it impossible to do so through Article 230 because of the very restrictive standing rules which apply thereunder. The only way in which an applicant can seek to test the validity of such norms is through an indirect action under Article 234. A common scenario is that a national customs authority, or agricultural intervention board, will apply a Community regulation concerning the details of customs classification, agricultural levies, and the like to a particular producer. The producer feels that the goods have been wrongly classified, or that the levy is discriminatory, and therefore resists payment. The customs authority, or agricultural intervention board, takes legal action and the applicant argues before the national court that the regulation is invalid, and asks that the relevant questions be referred to the ECJ. A glance through the Community law reports for any one year reveals the number of such cases which are heard by the ECJ. It is of course right and proper that such matters are judicially resolved. It is, however, far less obvious that the ECJ should be spending its time and resources on such matters.

II REASONS FOR INCREASE IN WORKLOAD OF THE COURT

It is clear that the principal rationale for the ECJ's paper on reform of the Community's judicial system is the workload problem. It is therefore important to understand the different factors which have led to the increase in the caseload of the ECJ and CFI. Four such factors can be identified, some of which are obvious, others less so.

The first, and most obvious, such factor is enlargement of the Community. The expansion of the EC from six to fifteen States, with the real prospect of further expansion to twenty-eight, means that there is more business for the Community courts.[17]

---

[15] The Courts' paper explicitly considers the possibility of two adjudications on preliminary rulings in the context of its discussion of decentralized judicial bodies, *FJS*, 28–9.
[16] See below, pp. 206–10. [17] *RWP*, 9.

The second rationale for the increase in the caseload of the Community courts is that the areas over which the EC has competence have expanded and continue to do so. This means that the range of cases brought before the ECJ and CFI has continued to grow. A further increase in caseload is to be expected as a result of:[18] the new Title IV of the EC Treaty dealing with the external aspects of free movement of persons (visas, asylum, immigration, and the like); the legislation relating to the third stage of EMU; Title VI of the TEU concerning police and judicial cooperation in criminal matters; and the provisions of a number of Conventions concluded between the states on the basis of the new Article 31 of the TEU.

A third factor leading to the increase in the workload of the Community courts is the very success of EC harmonization initiatives. It is axiomatic that one of the main aims of the EC is to harmonize laws and thereby facilitate the creation of a truly single market. How difficult it is to get agreement on such harmonization measures depends of course upon the nature of the subject matter in question and the differences between the existing laws of the Member States. When such a measure is enacted it may well generate new work for the Community judicial system. Any new piece of legislation, whether enacted at Community or national level, will always contain important issues which require judicial clarification. Where the new legislation is of considerable scope and complexity this may well lead to a significant increase in the caseload of a court. The introduction of the Community trade mark provides a fitting example. There are approximately 100,000 such applications lodged with the Community authorities in Spain. The CFI has been assigned jurisdiction over the area and will hear challenges to decisions made by the Community trade mark authorities. It is estimated that there will be between 200 and 400 such cases coming before the CFI per annum, and this has led the CFI to ask for six extra judges, two new panels.

The final factor which has fuelled an increase in the workload of the ECJ and CFI is rather different in nature. It is the growing awareness of EC law by lawyers. At the inception of the Community few knew much about EC law, and for a long time it remained the preserve of a limited number of specialists. Taking an EC point was regarded as rather unusual, and often seen as a matter of last resort. While it is true that countries have lawyers who specialize in EC law, it is also true that most lawyers will naturally now think about whether there is an EC point in a case which comes before them.

The combined effect of these factors on the workload of the Community courts were noted in the Courts' paper and in the Dué Report. The Courts' paper stressed that the organizational and procedural framework 'must be revised to enable the Court of Justice and the Court of First Instance to shorten existing time limits and deal with further increases in the number of

18 *FJS*, 6–8.

cases brought'.[19] If this did not occur, then there would be delays on a scale which cannot be reconciled with an acceptable level of judicial protection in the Union. The Courts' paper then continued in the following vein:[20]

Furthermore, in the case of the Court of Justice, the extra case-load might well seriously jeopardise the proper accomplishment of its task as a court of last instance which, in addition, has a constitutional role. The Court would then no longer be able to concentrate on its main functions, which are to guarantee respect for the distribution of powers between the Community and its Member States and between the Community institutions, the uniformity and consistency of Community law and to contribute to the harmonious development of the law of the Union. Such a failure on the part of the Court would undermine the rule of law on which, as stated in Article 6(1) EU, the Union is founded.

III CURRENT JUDICIAL MECHANISMS FOR LIMITING CASELOAD

It is clear that there are already a number of judicial mechanisms for limiting the number of cases which come before the ECJ/CFI. It is also clear that the juristic devices which are available in this respect differ in relation to the main heads where the Community courts presently have jurisdiction.

In relation to *direct actions contesting the validity of Community norms*, standing requirements are the main control device which apply to such actions brought by private parties. Views may well differ as to whether the existing rules which are applied under Article 230 are justified or not, although it has to be said that most commentators are critical in this respect.[21] This debate is, however, only of indirect relevance here. The key point is that the existing rules on standing are very tight, and therefore it would not be possible to address the workload problem by making them any tighter, since the present rules already preclude direct actions brought by private parties in the great majority of cases.

In relation to *enforcement actions brought by the Commission before the ECJ* under Article 226, the main control mechanism which relates to caseload

---

[19] Ibid. 8.   [20] Ibid. 9. See also *RWP*, 5–8.
[21] P. Craig and G. de Búrca, *EU Law: Text, Cases and Materials*, 2nd edn (1998), ch. 11; A. Barav, 'Direct and Individual Concern: An Almost Insurmountable Barrier to the Admissibility of Individual Appeal to the EEC Court', (1974) 11 CMLR 191; H. Rasmussen, 'Why Is Article 173 Interpreted against Private Plaintiffs?', (1980) 5 ELR 112; R. Greaves, '*Locus Standi* under Article 173 EEC when Seeking Annulment of a Regulation', (1986) 11 ELR 119; C. Harlow, 'Towards a Theory of Access for the European Court of Justice', (1992) 12 YBEL 213; P. Craig, 'Legality, Standing and Substantive Review in Community Law', (1994) 14 OJLS 507; A. Arnull, 'Private Applicants and the Action for Annulment under Article 173 of the EC Treaty', (1995) 32 CMLR 7; N. Neuwahl, 'Article 173 Paragraph 4 EC: Past, Present and Possible Future', (1996) 21 ELR 17.

resides in the discretion which the Commission possesses as to whether it should take a case or not.[22] The number of cases brought under Article 226 is in any event not that great. Given that the Commission has a discretion as to whether to bring a case, and that it chooses to use its scarce resources to fight those cases which it believes to be most significant as judged by a variety of criteria, then there is no real way of alleviating the workload of the ECJ by reform in this area.

The ECJ does possess certain mechanisms whereby it can limit the number of cases brought before it for a *preliminary ruling under Article 234*. The procedure under Article 234 is based on cooperation between the national court and the ECJ. The early case law indicated that the ECJ would rarely if ever question the factual basis on which the national court referred, and it would often be willing to reformulate questions posed by national courts where these had been badly framed.[23] However in the seminal *Foglia* jurisprudence[24] the ECJ made it clear that it would make the ultimate decision as to the scope of its own jurisdiction. It was not simply to be a passive receptor, forced to adjudicate on whatever was placed before it. It asserted control over the suitability of the reference. The decision in the case itself, concerning the allegedly hypothetical nature of the proceedings, was simply one manifestation of this assertion of jurisdictional control. The principle in *Foglia* lay dormant for some considerable time, and attempts to invoke it did not prove markedly successful.[25] However from the early 1990s the ECJ used the *Foglia* principle to decline to give rulings in cases which were hypothetical, where the questions raised were not relevant to the resolution of the substantive action in the national court,[26] where the questions were not articulated clearly enough for the ECJ to be able to give any meaningful legal response, and where the facts were insufficiently clear for the Court to be able to apply the relevant legal rules.[27] The ECJ has now incorporated some of the results of its case law in

---

[22] R. Rawlings, 'Citizen Action and Institutional Attitudes in Commission Enforcement', (2000) 6 ELJ 4.

[23] Craig and de Búrca, *EU Law*, 433–6.

[24] Case 104/79, *Pasquale Foglia v. Mariella Novella*, [1980] ECR 745; Case 244/80, *Pasquale Foglia v. Mariella Novello (No. 2)*, [1981] ECR 3045.

[25] Case 261/81, *Walter Rau Lebensmittelwerke v. De Smedt PvbA*, [1982] ECR 3961; Case 46/80, *Vinal SpA v. Orbat SpA*, [1981] ECR 77; Case C-150/88, *Eau de Cologne and Parfumerie-Fabrik Glockengasse No 4711 KG v. Provide Srl*, [1989] ECR 3891.

[26] Case C-83/91, *Wienand Meilicke v. ADV/ORGA F.A. Meyer AG*, [1992] ECR I-4871; Case C-18/93, *Corsica Ferries Italia Srl v. Corpo dei Piloti del Porto di Genova*, [1994] ECR I-1783; Case C-428/93, *Monin Automobiles-Maison du Deux-Roues*, [1994] ECR I-1707; Case C-134/95, *Unita Socio-Sanitaria Locale No 47 di Biella (USSL) v. Istituto Nazionale per l'Assicurazione contro gli Infortuni sul Lavoro (INAIL)*, [1997] ECR I-195; Cases C-320, 328, 329, 337, 338, and 339/94, *Reti Televisive Italiane SpA (RTI) v. Ministero delle Poste e Telecommunicazione*, [1996] ECR I-6471.

[27] Cases C-320-322/90, *Telemarsicabruzzo SpA v. Circostel, Ministero delle Poste e Telecommunicazioni and Ministerio della Difesa*, [1993] ECR I-393; Case C-157/92, *Banchero*,

its *Guidance on References by National Courts for Preliminary Rulings.*[28] Paragraph 6 states that the order for reference should contain a statement of reasons which is succinct but sufficiently complete to give the Court a clear understanding of the factual and legal context of the main action. It should include, in particular, a statement of: the essential facts; the relevant national law; the reasons why the national court referred the matter; and a summary of the parties' arguments where appropriate. While the ECJ has therefore exerted greater control over the admissibility of references than hitherto, it has also continued to make it clear that it will only decline to give a ruling if the issue of EC law on which an interpretation is sought is manifestly inapplicable to the dispute before the national court, or bears no relation to the subject matter of that action.[29]

The ECJ also has a more indirect way of limiting caseload under Article 234, by limiting the intensity of judicial oversight. This is the classic technique used by the ECJ when reviewing cases brought to it under Article 234 to contest the validity of Community acts which cannot be challenged directly through Article 230 because of the limited standing rules. Applicants who wish to challenge the validity of Community action will often have to do so through national courts, which will then send the case to the ECJ for a preliminary ruling as to whether, for example, an agricultural measure was disproportionate and hence in breach of Article 34. The ECJ has made it clear that it will not readily find that the challenged Community norm was invalid, more especially in an area where the Commission and Council have broad discretionary power. The applicant may well have to prove that the measure was manifestly disproportionate, or very obviously discriminatory.[30] In one sense this is clearly not a method of control over caseload at all, since the ECJ will have to hear the relevant dispute, even if at the end of the day it decides that the measure is valid since the applicant has not been able to prove the requisite degree of illegality. However, in another sense low-intensity review can clearly operate as a tool for controlling caseload. Those who are thinking of challenging the validity of a measure will come to realize that they have to prove something quite extreme before they can succeed. They will therefore

[1993] ECR I-1085; Case C-386/92, *Monin Automobiles v. France,* [1993] ECR I-2049; Case C-458/93, *Criminal Proceedings against Saddik,* [1995] ECR I-511; Case C-167/94R, *Grau Gomis,* [1995] ECR I-1023; Case C-2/96, *Criminal Proceedings against Sunino and Data,* [1996] ECR I-1543; Case C-257/95, *Bresle v. Prefet de la Région Auvergne and Prefet du Puy-de-Dôme,* [1996] ECR I-233.

[28]   [1997] 1 CMLR 78.

[29]   Case C-85/95, *Reisdorf v. Finanzamt Koln-West,* [1996] ECR I-6257; Case C-118/94, *Associazione Italiana per il World Wildlife Fund v. Regione Veneto,* [1996] ECR I-1223; Case C-129/94, *Criminal Proceedings against Bernaldez,* [1996] ECR I-1829; Case C-446/93, *SEIM—Sociedade de Exportacoa de Materias, Ld v. Subdirector-Geral das Alfandegas,* [1996] ECR I-73.

[30]   Craig and de Búrca, *EU Law,* 506–10.

desist from bringing the action where it is clear to the applicant and his lawyer that the chances of proving what the Court requires is remote.

These techniques for limiting the caseload under Article 234 have not, however, served to stem the tide of references coming to the ECJ. The *Foglia* principle, and the case law based upon it, will only serve to exclude a limited number of references. Moreover, national courts will, it is hoped, learn to frame their references better, and in that sense there will over time be fewer cases which can be excluded on this ground. In any event, references for a preliminary ruling have increased by 85 per cent since 1990, and they now constitute half of the new cases brought before the ECJ.[31]

IV THE AIMS OF REFORM OF THE JUDICIAL SYSTEM

Before considering the detailed proposals it is important to have some idea of the overall aims of the reform process. The Courts' paper and the Dué Report both posit three fundamental requirements which must be taken into account when thinking of the future of the Community's judicial system:[32]

> the need to secure the unity of Community law by means of a supreme court;
> the need to ensure that the judicial system is transparent, comprehensible, and accessible to the public;
> the need to dispense justice without unacceptable delay.

These are clearly important aims in any judicial system, and they must be especially applicable in the context of the EC. There are, however, three other objectives which should also be borne in mind when thinking of reforms to the judicial architecture of the EC:

> there should be effective enforcement of Community law;
> the system should be structured to ensure that the most important points of law are decided by the ECJ, and that the ECJ is, so far as possible, not troubled by the less important cases;
> the system should, other things being equal, be as coherent and symmetrical as possible.

It may well not be possible to ensure the perfect fulfilment of all of these objectives. They should nonetheless not be lost sight of when we consider the detailed reforms themselves. It is to these that we should now turn.

---

[31] *FJS*, 5.   [32] Ibid. 18; *RWP*, 10.

V THE REFORM PROPOSALS:
AMENDMENTS TO THE RULES OF PROCEDURE

Both the Courts' paper and the Dué Report consider a number of changes which could be adopted by the Council now, without the need for the adoption of any Treaty amendment. The general objective is to 'introduce greater flexibility in the application of the Rules of Procedure, so as to enable the adaptation of the procedures to the degree of complexity and urgency of each case'.[33] These proposals are to be welcomed. While they deal with points of procedural detail, they are important nonetheless.

A. Recourse to Accelerated Procedures

The object of this proposal is to modify the existing Rules of Procedure to enable the ECJ to deal more expeditiously with cases which require speedy resolution.[34] At present neither the Statute of the Court of Justice nor its Rules of Procedure allow for such an accelerated procedure whereby the ECJ could deal with certain cases under a separate procedure. The closest that the existing rules come to providing for this is in Article 55(2) of the Rules of Procedure, which enables the President of the ECJ to order that a particular case be accorded priority over other cases. This does not, however, empower the ECJ to dispense with certain procedural steps. The proposal is therefore to include in the Rules of Procedure a provision allowing an accelerated procedure to be applied in cases of manifest urgency. This would then allow certain of the normal procedural steps to be omitted or accelerated depending on the nature of the case. A similar power would apply in relation to cases which come before the CFI.

B. Changes in the Oral Procedure

Oral hearings are valued by the parties, but they can also take up a considerable amount of time. The Court of Justice is particularly concerned to ensure that the 'hearing does not become a ritual where the parties concerned merely repeat word for word the arguments which they have already presented during the written procedure'.[35] It therefore proposes that Articles 44a and 104(4) of the Rules of Procedure should provide that a hearing is to take place 'either if the Court so decides of its own motion or if a reasoned application is made by one of those parties or one of the persons referred to in Article 20 of the EC Statute of the Court of Justice, setting out the points on which that party or person wishes to be heard'.[36]

---

[33] *FJS*, 10.   [34] Ibid. 11–12.   [35] Ibid. 11.   [36] Ibid. 12.

C. Directions and Information

The third of the procedural proposals made in the Courts' paper draws on powers possessed by the European Court of Human Rights. The ECJ wishes to have the power to issue practice directions relating to matters such as the holding of hearings and the filing of pleadings. It also advocates that the judge rapporteur, in consultation with the Advocate-General, should be able to request that the parties submit factual information or other material which is felt to be relevant to the case.[37]

D. Preliminary Rulings

We have already seen the steep rise in the number of requests for preliminary rulings. It is therefore unsurprising that the ECJ should propose procedural reforms which will serve to expedite the resolution of such cases. One such reform is an amendment to the Rules of Procedure whereby national courts could be asked to clarify matters where the questions which they have referred provide insufficient information to enable the ECJ to understand the point of law which has been raised. The other proposal is equally interesting. It is that Article 104 of the Rules of Procedure should be modified to allow the ECJ to give a preliminary ruling by order where the question raised is simple, and the answer straightforward, or where the question does not, having regard to the existing case law, raise any new issue.[38] It has moreover been suggested in the Dué Report[39] that the terms of the information note concerning preliminary references issued by the ECJ[40] should be incorporated within the Rules of Procedure, and that compliance therewith should be mandatory. Requests which did not so comply would be rejected.

E. The Power to Amend the Rules of Procedure

The proposals considered thus far are clearly sensible and could, as stated above, be accomplished without any amendments to the actual Treaties. Changes to the Rules of Procedure require unanimous approval by the Council.[41] All of the proposals set out above must therefore pass this hurdle if they are to become legally effective. The ECJ has been pressing for greater autonomy over its Rules of Procedure for some time. It repeats this call in the Courts' paper on reform of the judicial architecture of the Community. The ECJ points out that securing unanimity in an enlarged Community which has in excess of twenty members may well paralyse the process of amending

---

[37] *FJS*, 12.   [38] Ibid. 13.   [39] *RWP*, 17.
[40] *Guidance on References by National Courts for Preliminary Rulings*, [1997] 1 CMLR 78.
[41] Arts. 225 and 245 EC.

the Rules of Procedure. It proposes that the Treaty be amended to allow both the ECJ and the CFI to adopt their own Rules of Procedure. If this should prove too revolutionary a proposition for the Member States, it is proposed that the Treaty be amended so that the Rules of Procedure could be changed by qualified majority within the Council.[42]

VI THE REFORM PROPOSALS: THE COMPOSITION OF THE ECJ AND THE CFI

A. The ECJ

The expansion of the EC to a Community of fifteen Member States, with the prospect of further expansion to twenty or twenty-five, has strained the existing decision-making structure. It is accepted that institutional reform is required, and there was an expectation that this would be addressed in the Treaty of Amsterdam. This did not occur, but broader institutional reform is now being considered in detail by the Community institutions. One manifestation of the strains caused by expansion of the EC is to be found in the composition of the ECJ. While the connection between nationality and membership of the ECJ is not stipulated in the Treaty, it has always been accepted that there should be one judge from each Member State. In an earlier paper, prepared for the negotiations which led to the Treaty of Amsterdam, the ECJ addressed the two considerations which are of paramount importance in this context.[43]

On the one hand, any significant increase in the number of judges might mean that the plenary session of the Court would cross the invisible boundary between a collegiate court and a deliberative assembly. Moreover, as the great majority of cases would be heard by Chambers, this increase could pose a threat to the consistency of the case law.

On the other hand, the presence of members from all the national legal systems in the Court is undoubtedly conducive to harmonious development of Community case-law, taking into account concepts regarded as fundamental in the various Member States and thus enhancing the acceptability of the solutions arrived at. It may also be considered that the presence of a judge from each Member State enhances the legitimacy of the Court.

There is little doubt that in political terms the continuance of the status quo whereby each Member State has a judge on the ECJ represents the easiest option, quite simply because any shift from that position would require the articulation of new criteria to govern appointments. The Dué Report does indeed assume that the existing system will remain for the foreseeable

---

[42] *FJS*, 15.   [43] *RCJ*, point 16.

future.[44] It does, however, recognize that plenary sessions could not consist of all the judges of the ECJ, the suggestion being that such sessions should consist of just over half of the Court's membership.[45] The role of the Presidents of Chambers would also have to be enhanced to ensure consistency between rulings of Chambers in an enlarged ECJ.[46] A further suggestion made in the Report is that the opinion of the Advocate-General should only be sought in important cases.[47]

It may nonetheless be doubted whether the present policy could or should continue in a Community of twenty-eight Member States. Analogies drawn with the membership of the European Court of Human Rights are not particularly helpful, given the very different nature and objectives of the EC and the European Convention of Human Rights. If it were decided to limit the number of judges on the ECJ then two important issues would have to be addressed.

A decision would have to be made as to the upper limit on the number of judges in the ECJ. There would then have to be a decision as to how the judges were chosen. It would clearly be unacceptable for an existing Member State to have any 'vested right' that a judge should be appointed from its country. Various options are open in this respect. There could be a rotation system whereby a judge from a Member State was appointed for a particular period of time. There could, at the other end of the scale, be an open competition for appointments to the ECJ, with those who were successful holding office for a limited period of time. There are doubtless many other possible ways in which appointments could be made.

B. The CFI

The Courts' paper also considers the composition of the CFI. We have already seen that the workload of the CFI is set to increase as a result of cases concerning the Community trade mark. The possible attribution to the CFI of jurisdiction in the field of patents will necessitate a further increase in personnel, and this will also be necessary if the CFI does become a more general court of first instance in the manner to be discussed below.[48]

Increasing the number of judges in the CFI may raise budgetary problems within the more general Community, but it does not generate the same issues of principle as does an increase in the judges within the ECJ. This is recognized in the Courts' paper, where it is said that although the 'increase in the number of Chambers would necessitate additional measures for the co-ordination of the case-law, the intervention of the Court of Justice as the court of last instance make it possible to ensure its unity'.[49] Nor is the link between

---

[44] *RWP*, 46.   [45] Ibid. 46–7.   [46] Ibid. 47.   [47] Ibid. 48–9.
[48] See below, pp. 193–5.   [49] *FJS*, 20.

nationality and judges in the CFI as important as it is in the ECJ. In any event the number of judges required for the CFI means that it will be possible, if it is felt desirable, for there to be judges from each Member State.

The CFI works in Chambers and this can be used to accommodate the need for subject matter specialization. Such specialized Chambers operating within the CFI seems preferable to separate specialist courts. Individual members of the CFI could be assigned to a specialist Chamber for a period of time in order to gain expertise in that area, and there could be a rolling system whereby the judges start and finish date was staggered to ensure continuity.

VII THE REFORM PROPOSALS: THE CFI AS GENERAL FIRST INSTANCE COURT IN DIRECT ACTIONS?

The jurisdiction of the CFI has, as seen above, grown in an ad hoc manner. Heads of jurisdiction have been given to it primarily to relieve the workload of the ECJ itself, hence the assignment of staff and competition cases to the CFI. The transfer of all direct actions brought by non-privileged applicants was fuelled by similar concerns. The future role and jurisdiction of the CFI is of central importance to the overall judicial architecture of the Community. One objective of reform must be to achieve a system which is as coherent as possible.

It is therefore somewhat surprising that the Courts' paper is both brief and hesitant about the possible transfer of further competence to the CFI to hear direct actions. Two paragraphs are devoted to the matter. We are told that there are no grounds at present for proposing the transfer of any heads of jurisdiction over and above those whose transfer has already been proposed by the ECJ. We are then told that 'the possibility cannot be ruled out that it may become necessary, if the volume of cases continues to grow, to review the basis on which jurisdiction is allocated between the two Community courts and to transfer further heads of jurisdiction to the Court of First Instance'.[50] There may well be 'political' reasons for being circumspect about this matter, since the Member States may be resistant to suggestions that direct actions in which they are involved should be heard by the CFI rather than the ECJ.

The Dué Report is more forthcoming in this respect.[51] Its starting point is that the CFI should, as a matter of principle, be the first judicial forum for direct actions, including review for legality and compensation. The CFI's jurisdiction would include actions brought by a Member State or Community institution. This principle was then qualified in the Report such that direct actions involving matters of urgency and importance would be assigned to the ECJ.[52] Only those cases where a rapid judgment was essential

---

[50] Ibid. 21.   [51] *RWP*, 23–9.   [52] Ibid. 24–5.

to avoid serious problems in the proper functioning of the Community institutions would fall into this category.[53]

The thrust of the Dué Report's proposal is to be welcomed. There is a strong case for rationalizing the present regime and making it more coherent by transforming the CFI into a *general first instance court in direct actions*. We should move away from the idea that the CFI is a court primarily for technical or factually complex cases. We should not accept that the jurisdiction of the CFI is destined forever to remain eclectic and ad hoc. The CFI is already the first instance court for direct actions involving non-privileged applicants who seek to challenge the validity of Community norms. Its jurisdiction should be extended to enable it to hear all direct actions under Articles 230, or 232, even where the case is brought by a privileged applicant such as the Council, Commission, or a Member State, or by a quasi-privileged applicant such as the European Parliament or the European Central Bank. It would also be desirable if the CFI could operate as a first instance court in enforcement actions brought under Article 226. The Member States may, however, be particularly resistant to a change which would mean that they could be sued before the CFI for non-compliance with Community obligations, rather than before the ECJ itself. This should not dissuade us from making the CFI a general court of first instance in direct actions under Articles 230, and 232. There should of course be the possibility of appeal to the ECJ where the case raised a general point of Community law importance.[54]

The vision of the CFI as general first instance court in direct actions does moreover fit well with other developments in the general regime of Community adjudication. To an increasing extent cases which come before the Community courts will already have been the subject of some form of adjudication. This has always been the case in the context of competition and state aids, where the Commission itself will have given a formal, legally binding decision on the matter which the parties can challenge before the CFI. The development of a specialist agency in the context of trade marks is a further move in the same direction. There is now a proposal that staff cases should be handled by inter-institutional tribunals composed of lawyers plus assessors. They would be entrusted with the task of conciliation and, where necessary, of ruling on disputes.[55] Such rulings could be challenged before the CFI, with the possibility of a further, limited right of challenge before the ECJ. Any recourse to the ECJ in such cases would, however, be subject to a very strict filtering procedure. It would be for the parties to lodge an applica-

---

[53] *RWP*, 25. The Report makes it clear that actions under Art. 226 would fall within this category.

[54] A filter for appeals from the CFI to the ECJ is part of the proposals made in the Dué Report, ibid. 28.

[55] *FJS*, 17; *RWP*, 30–1.

tion which the ECJ would rule on without *inter partes* proceedings, before an appeal could be made.[56]

If we put together these ideas, a rational division of jurisdiction begins to emerge. The CFI should become the general court of first instance in direct actions irrespective of the nature of the applicant. There should be limited rights of appeal to the ECJ. The criterion suggested in the Dué Report is that there must be a point of law of major importance either for the development of Community law or for the protection of individual rights. A Chamber of three judges from the ECJ would consider requests for appeal against a ruling of the CFI.[57] In cases where there has been a prior adjudication on the matter by the Commission or some other specialist agency, then the decision of that body should be open to challenge before the CFI. The Dué Report proposes that in these areas the CFI should in principle be the final court of appeal, subject only to an appeal to the ECJ at the behest of the Commission where there was a point of general legal interest.[58]

VIII THE REFORM PROPOSALS: PRELIMINARY RULINGS

We have already seen the steep rise in the number of references for preliminary rulings which have come before the ECJ: 85 per cent since 1990, with an increase of 10 per cent in 1998 as compared with the previous year.[59] Such cases now account for more than half of the new cases brought before the ECJ, 264 references out of 485 cases. The Courts' paper carries a stark warning of the need for reform:[60]

The constant growth in the number of references for preliminary rulings emanating from courts and tribunals of the Member States carries with it a serious risk that the Court of Justice will be overwhelmed by its case-load. If current trends continue without any reform of the machinery for dealing with cases, not only will proceedings become more protracted, to the detriment of the proper working of the preliminary ruling system, but the Court of Justice will also be obliged to conduct its deliberations with such dispatch that it will no longer be able to apply to cases the thorough consideration necessary for it to give a useful reply to the questions referred.

It is highly likely that the impact of its decisions will diminish as their number increases and as they deal more frequently with questions of secondary importance or of interest only in the context of the case concerned.

The nature and scale of the problem are therefore clear. Both the Courts' paper and the Dué Report consider different ways in which this problem could be tackled.

---

[56] *FJS*, 16; *RWP*, 28–9.   [57] *RWP*. 28–9.   [58] Ibid. 29–35.   [59] *FJS*, 5.
[60] Ibid. 22.

A. Limitation of the National Courts Empowered to Make a Reference

There is clearly a 'precedent' for a reform of this kind, and it is to be found in Articles 61–9, the new Title IV of the EC Treaty, dealing with 'Visas, Asylum, Immigration and Other Policies Concerning the Free Movement of Persons'. These matters were, prior to the Treaty of Amsterdam, dealt with in Pillar 3, concerning Justice and Home Affairs. The Article 234 procedure has been modified in its application in relation to Title IV. Article 68 stipulates that a preliminary ruling can only be sought by a national court or tribunal against whose decisions there is no judicial remedy in national law, as opposed to the normal position under Article 234, whereby any such court or tribunal has a discretion to seek a reference.[61]

Notwithstanding the existence of this precedent, the Courts' paper and the Dué Report come down firmly against any general extension of this idea as a method of limiting preliminary rulings.[62] Nor is this surprising. The ability of any national court or tribunal to refer a question to the ECJ has been central to the development of Community law in both practical and conceptual terms.

In practical terms, it has been common for cases which raise important points of EC law to have arisen on references from lower level national courts. To limit the ability to refer to a court of last resort would result in cases being fought to the apex of national judicial systems merely to seek a referral to the ECJ. Many applicants might not be able to afford such lengthy proceedings at the national level, and therefore be dissuaded from persisting with the argument based on EC law. Furthermore, the 'uniform application of Community law frequently depends on the answer to a question of interpretation raised before a national court not having to await the outcome of appeal proceedings but being given by the Court of Justice at the outset, so that the case law can become established at an early stage in the Member States of the Union'.[63]

In conceptual terms, the ability of any national court or tribunal to refer has been of importance in emphasizing the penetration of EC law to all points of the national legal system. It is of course true that even if references were limited to courts of last resort, lower courts would still have the ability to apply existing precedent of the Community courts. The fact that any national court or tribunal can refer does, however, serve to emphasize that individuals can rely on their directly effective Community rights at any point in the national legal system. If the lower-level national court is unsure about the interpretation of a point of EC law it can make a reference on that issue itself without

---

[61] Art. 68(3) also provides that the Council, Commission, or a Member State can request the ECJ to give a ruling on a question of interpretation arising under Title IV, or acts of the institutions based on this Title. Such rulings do not apply to judgments of national courts, etc., which have become *res judicata*.

[62] *FJS*, 23–4; *RWP*, 12–13.   [63] *FJS*, 24.

the need for approval from any higher national court. It should not moreover be forgotten that preserving the ability of any national court to refer acts as an important safeguard against the possibility that the court of final resort might be 'conservative or recalcitrant' and hence reluctant to refer even where this is clearly warranted on the facts of the particular case.

B. The Introduction of a Filtering Mechanism

Another way in which the volume of preliminary rulings might be reduced would be to introduce a filtering mechanism which limited the types of case heard by the ECJ. There are three different variants of a filtering mechanism and these must be discussed separately, since different policy considerations apply to each.

1. A Filter Based on the Novelty, Complexity, or Importance of the Question

The Courts' paper points to two advantages of such a filtering mechanism. From the national perspective, 'such a filtering system would prompt national courts and tribunals to exercise selectivity in choosing which questions to refer, and would thus encourage them to exercise yet more fully their functions as Community courts of general jurisdiction'.[64] From the EC's perspective, 'the existence of a filtering mechanism would enable the Court of Justice to concentrate wholly upon questions which are fundamental from the point of view of the uniformity and development of Community law'.[65]

The Dué Report advocates some constraints of this kind. National courts should, it said, be encouraged to be bolder in applying Community law themselves.[66] The Report recommends amendment to Article 234 so that it is made clear that, subject to the power to refer, national courts are to be regarded as having general jurisdiction over matters of EC law. It suggests that lower national courts should consider both the importance of the question in terms of Community law and whether there is reasonable doubt about the answer, before referring. National courts of final resort should moreover only be obliged to refer on questions which are 'sufficiently important for Community law', and where there is still 'reasonable doubt' after examination by lower courts. The Report is, however, equivocal as to whether such factors should merely be taken into account by national courts in deciding when to refer, or whether they should operate as a more substantive bar on the cases which can be referred, the application of which is decided by the ECJ itself. The Report appears to incline towards the former. This reading is reinforced by the fact that the Report at a later stage comes out explicitly against giving the ECJ itself the power to select those questions which it considered were sufficiently important for Community law.[67] Whether this position is sustainable may,

---

[64] Ibid. [65] Ibid. 25. [66] *RWP*, 14–15. [67] Ibid. 21.

however, be doubted. Let us imagine that Article 234 is reformulated, as suggested in the Dué Report.[68] The 'importance issue' and the 'reasonable doubt issues' would then be factors to be taken into account by a national court in deciding whether to refer. The interpretation of these factors would then be a matter of Community law, to be decided on ultimately by the ECJ. This does indeed seem to be recognized, since the Report states it will be for the ECJ to determine the precise scope which should be given to the 'importance' or 'significance' issue.[69]

There are, however, two problems with a filtering system of this nature, one of which is immediately apparent, the other less so.

One problem is that such a mechanism might distort the judicial cooperation which has long been regarded as a central feature of the Article 234 procedure: the ECJ will answer any question referred to it. It is true that the ECJ has, through the *Foglia* ruling and the cases decided thereafter, made it clear that it will not be forced to accept any reference sent to it by the national courts. Such references must fulfil the conditions of admissibility laid down in that jurisprudence, and the Courts' paper acknowledges the continued necessity for satisfying such conditions.[70] It should, however, be acknowledged that the introduction of a filtering mechanism of the kind under consideration here would entail a limitation on the ability of the national courts to refer which has not existed hitherto. The *Foglia* ruling, important though it is, only provides the foundation for declining to hear a case where it is hypothetical, where the facts are insufficiently clear, or where the question of law does not arise on the facts of the case. Under the filtering mechanism being considered here questions which were clear, well framed, of current relevance, and backed up by adequate factual findings could be rejected on the ground that the question posed was not sufficiently important to warrant the time of the ECJ. In the Courts' paper there is a concern that 'national courts and tribunals might well refrain from referring questions to the Court of Justice, in order to avoid the risk of their references being rejected for lack of interest'[71] and that this could jeopardize the machinery for ensuring that Community law is interpreted uniformly throughout the Member States.

There is another problem with this filtering mechanism which is not mentioned in the Courts' paper or in the Dué Report. Those who are in favour of such a system commonly point to legal systems such as that in the USA, where the Supreme Court will decide which cases it is willing to hear. There is no doubt that the Supreme Court uses this power to exercise control over the size of its docket and the types of case it wants to hear. It is for this reason that commentators in the EC look with interest at such a system, since it seems to offer a way of limiting the ECJ's caseload, thereby allowing it to concentrate its energies on matters of real importance for the Community.

---

[68] *RWP*, 53–4.   [69] Ibid. 15.   [70] *FJS*, 25, para. 4.   [71] Ibid. 25.

There is much to be said for the US system. It is, however, mistaken to believe that it can be directly copied in the EC. The crucial difference is that the US is an appellate system, and the EC is a referral system. A moment's reflection will reveal why this is of such importance in this context. In the USA, if the Supreme Court declines to hear a case there will be a decision on the point of federal or constitutional law which is in issue.[72] It is precisely because the system is appellate that a decision on the case will have been reached by a lower court which one of the parties will then seek to have overturned by the Supreme Court. The situation in the EC is markedly different. The national court has not decided the case. It has referred a question which has arisen in the case for resolution by the ECJ. If the ECJ declines to answer the question on the ground that it is not sufficiently important or novel to warrant its time, then there is no decision by a Community court on the question at all. This places the national court in a difficult position. It is of course true that the national court should apply existing Community law precedent where that exists. It is true also that the national court should decide the matter for itself if the question can be regarded as *acte clair* within the confines laid down in the *CILFIT* case. The premise behind the filtering idea is, however, that the ECJ may decline to take a reference where there is no existing precedent, and where the matter is not *acte clair*. In such situations there are only two options logically open to the national court.

It could attempt to decide the matter of EC law for itself. If this were regarded as acceptable it would mean that the role of national courts as Community courts of general jurisdiction would have been expanded. We would be accepting that national courts could apply EC law in three situations: where there is a Community law precedent, where the matter is *acte clair*, or where the ECJ itself has declined to take the case.

The national court could alternatively decline to decide the EC point one way or the other. The effect on the substantive outcome of the case would be that the party who sought to rely on the point of EC law would be unable to do so, and the case would be decided on the assumption that this point was unproven. Thus, if a party sought to resile from a contract on the ground that it contravened Article 81, the claim would fail, since the national court would be unwilling to decide the legal issue in favour of the applicant, the legal consequence being that the contract was still binding.

The application of a filtering idea within the context of the referral system as it operates in the EC is therefore more problematic than it is within the context of an appellate system, more especially one where there is a tier of federal appellate courts below the supreme court. This does not mean that the idea should be ruled out. It does mean that the analogies drawn from

---

[72] This will commonly be given by a lower-tier federal court, either a federal court of appeals or a federal district court, or perhaps by a state supreme court.

appellate systems must be treated with caution. It also means that if the EC were to experiment with this idea then it would be incumbent on the ECJ to give some real guidance to the national courts as to which of the two options mentioned above they should be adopting. There are of course problems with both options. If we opt for the former, and encourage national courts to decide such points for themselves, then we risk undermining the uniformity of application of EC law. If we opt for the latter, and accept that national courts can decline to decide the EC point one way or the other, then we are de facto accepting that EC law can be ignored in such instances. While there are therefore problems with both of these options, the former is nonetheless to be preferred. It is better that EC law be applied to the instant case, albeit with the possibility that the national courts might err or differ in their view, than that EC law should be ignored. It should not, moreover, be forgotten that the dangers of lack of uniformity attendant upon this option are less dramatic than might have initially appeared. This is because the filtering mechanism is designed, as the Courts' paper makes clear, 'to weed out at a pre-liminary stage cases of lesser importance from the point of view of the uni-formity and development of Community law'.[73] Thus cases left for resolution by national courts which the ECJ declined to hear pursuant to a filtering mechanism would, by definition, be those where uniformity of view was not of paramount importance. It should also be recognized that if it transpired that differences of view between national courts on a matter which the ECJ had initially declined to hear became a reality and were problematic, then a reference in a later case could always be possible. The ECJ would, in such circumstances, be inclined to accept such a reference.[74]

2. The National Court Proposes an Answer to the Question

Another way of limiting the caseload of preliminary rulings which the ECJ has to deal with would be for the national court to include in its reference a proposed reply to the question referred. The advantages of such a system are said in the Courts' paper to be that it would 'lessen the adverse effect of the filtering mechanism on the cooperation between the national court and the Court of Justice, while the proposed reply could at the same time serve as the basis for deciding which questions need to be answered by the Court of Justice and which can be answered in the terms indicated'.[75] A similar pro-posal has been advanced in the Dué Report, which states that national courts should be encouraged, though not obliged, to include in the preliminary questions reasoned grounds for the answers which the national court con-siders to be most appropriate. Where the ECJ concurs with the national court it could reply, specifying its reasoning by reference to the reasons given by the national court.[76]

---

[73] *FJS*, 24.   [74] *RWP*, 16.   [75] *FJS*, 25–6.   [76] *RWP*, 18.

Neither the Courts' paper nor the Dué Report gives further consideration to this option. There are, however, difficulties with this proposal. Most national courts and tribunals are not specialists in EC law. It is one thing for the national court or tribunal to identify a question which it believes is necessary for the resolution of the case before it. It is another thing entirely to be able to provide an answer to that question. The latter will at the very least require an expenditure of time and resources at the national level by courts and tribunals many of whom may be ill-equipped for the type of inquiry demanded of them. It is of course true that higher-level national courts may well be able to furnish some answer to the question posed. It should nonetheless be recognized that the proposal being considered here would transform the task faced by such courts. There would have to be detailed argument before the national court of the EC issues involved in the case in order to provide the judge with the requisite material from which to give an answer to the question posed.

Nor is it clear that this proposal would in reality achieve its objective. We should remember that the objective is to relieve the ECJ of some of its caseload burden. Yet even if national courts are required or encouraged to provide an answer to the question posed, the ECJ will still have to give the matter some detailed consideration. This will be necessary in order to decide whether the question really can be answered in the terms indicated by the national court, or whether it needs to be answered afresh by the ECJ.

3. *Towards an Appellate System*

A more radical option is considered in the Courts' paper, which has the effect of transforming the present system from one which is reference-based to one which is more appellate in nature:[77]

A more radical variant of the system would be to alter the preliminary ruling procedure so that national courts which are not bound to refer questions to the Court of Justice would be required, before making any reference, first to give judgment in cases raising questions concerning the interpretation of Community law. It would then be open to any party to the proceedings to request the national court to forward its judgment to the Court of Justice and to make a reference for a ruling on those points of Community law in respect of which that party contests the validity of the judgment given. This would give the Court of Justice the opportunity of assessing, at the filtering stage, whether it needed to give its own ruling on the interpretation of Community law arrived at in the contested judgment.

Such a procedure, resembling an appeal in cassation, would facilitate the task of the Court of Justice. It would enable the Court to give its ruling on the reference in full knowledge of the national context, both factual and legal, in which the points of Community law raised in the case in question fall to be interpreted.

---

[77] *FJS*, 26.

This proposal is interesting and has far-reaching implications. The Dué Report was strongly opposed to such a change, stating that 'such a proposal would debase the entire system of cooperation established by the Treaties between national courts and the Court of Justice'.[78]

I shall begin by examining the difficulties attendant upon this change, and then consider the advantages of taking such a step.

The first point to make about this proposal is a repetition of the point made about the previous option. To require national courts or tribunals to decide the point of EC law in issue would be to impose a burden on them which many lower-tier courts or tribunals would find difficult to discharge. The second point is that the proposal is unlikely to achieve the objective of limiting the caseload of the ECJ. There would, as acknowledged in the Courts' paper,[79] always be an incentive on the party which had lost the case before the national court to seek a reference to the ECJ, if only to defer enforcement of the judgment.

Thirdly, it is clear that this proposal would require amendment to the Treaty. Article 234 is framed in terms of a national court requesting a ruling from the ECJ where the national court considers that a decision on the question is necessary to enable it to give judgment. Under the proposal set out above this criterion would, by definition, not be met. The national court would already have given its judgment, including on the points of EC law. Reference to the ECJ would happen thereafter at the behest of the parties. The very language of preliminary ruling would be inappropriate under this new regime.

Fourthly, if we take this proposal at its face value then it would seem to involve overruling *Foto-Frost*.[80] A number of the cases which arise in national courts do not seek to challenge the compatibility of national law with Community law. The object is rather to challenge the validity of Community norms which cannot be challenged under Article 230 because the applicant will not have standing. *Foto-Frost* is authority for the proposition that national courts are not empowered to declare a Community norm to be invalid, although they can find that it is valid. The proposal being considered here is framed in terms of the national court giving judgment on the case, including the points of EC law involved therein, which can then be contested before the ECJ if one of the parties so desires. Where the case does concern an indirect challenge to the validity of a Community law norm, then it would seem to follow from this proposal that the national court could, if it felt that it was legally warranted, give a judgment that the Community norm was invalid, which could then be contested before the ECJ.

---

[78] *RWP*, 13.
[79] *FJS*, 26.
[80] Case 314/85, *Firma Foto-Frost v. Hauptzollamt Lubeck-Ost*, [1987] ECR 4199.

Fifthly, there is a crucial ambiguity in the formulation of the proposal in the Courts' paper. The extract quoted above is framed in terms of a party to the proceedings 'requesting' the national court to refer its judgment to the ECJ, in order that the latter can rule on those points of Community law when the correctness of the national court's judgment is contested. Later on the same page the Courts' paper talks in terms of the parties to an action being able to 'require' the national court to make a reference.[81] This latter formulation appears to capture the essence of this proposal.

The final point to be made about this proposal is perhaps the most important. If it is adopted we should recognize that it fundamentally alters the regime encapsulated in Article 234. This is not an objection in and of itself, but we should nonetheless be cognizant of the change thereby entailed. In an appellate regime a lower court gives a decision on the entirety of the case which is binding on the parties, subject to the possibility of appeal. Appeal lies in the hands of the parties to the case, although it may be necessary to secure the leave of the court to undertake the appeal. In a reference system as presently conceived the national court gives no decision on the case or the question of EC law raised therein prior to making the reference to the ECJ. A question is referred to the ECJ, and the final decision in the case will only be given by the national court once the answer to that question is forthcoming from the ECJ. The decision whether to refer will, moreover, be in the hands of the national court.

The proposal under consideration would in effect change the regime from a reference system to an appellate one. The national court would give a decision on all aspects of the case, and it would then be for the parties to 'require' the national court to make a reference to the ECJ. It is not clear that the language of a 'reference' would be suitable any longer in such a regime. The transformation of Article 234 entailed by this procedure was acknowledged in the Courts' paper:[82]

[S]uch a procedure would involve a fundamental change in the way in which the preliminary ruling system currently operates. Judicial co-operation between the national courts and the Court of Justice would be transformed into a hierarchical system, in which it would be for the parties to an action to decide whether to require the national court to make a reference to the Court of Justice, and in which the national court would be bound, depending on the circumstances, to revise its earlier judgment so as to bring it into line with a ruling by the Court of Justice. From the point of view of national procedural law this aspect of the system would doubtless raise problems which could not easily be resolved.

It might be thought in the light of the above that we should not persist any further with this option. We should nonetheless consider the advantages of such a transformation of the status quo. An appellate system is more

---

[81] *FJS*, 26.   [82] Ibid.

characteristic of a developed federal or confederal legal system than is a reference system, and it could be argued that the EC is ready for such a change. National courts have become more familiar with EC law over the years, and it may be time to move towards an appellate regime in which the national court gives judgment on the entirety of the case, subject to appeal to the ECJ. This may well be a desirable development. We should not, however, go down this road on the assumption that it will thereby limit the caseload of the ECJ. It will not do so for the reason given above: there will always be an incentive for the loser before the national court to appeal to the ECJ. However, the move towards an appellate regime would make for greater flexibility in a crucial respect. We saw earlier that one of the perceived constraints of the reference system was what was termed the 'one-stop shop'. The national court refers a question from a case which is still undecided, and this has led many to believe that such a case can only be heard by one Community court because of the delays which would be involved if there were more than one adjudication at Community level. The shift towards an appellate system undermines this assumption. The national court has actually given judgment on the substance of the entire case, including the point of EC law involved therein. This would then open the possibility for references or appeals from such decisions to go initially to the CFI. We have already made the case for the CFI to be a general court of first instance in direct actions. It could now also act as the first instance court to hear appeals from national court decisions which arise under a modified Article 234. There would then be the prospect of appeal to the ECJ for cases which were of real importance. The judicial architecture of the Community would be coherent, and the ECJ could use its time for adjudication on the most deserving cases.

C. Conferral on the CFI of Jurisdiction to Give Preliminary Rulings

At present all requests for a preliminary ruling go to the ECJ. One way, therefore, of easing the workload of the ECJ would be to allow the CFI to give preliminary rulings. This would of course require an increase in the number of judges in the CFI, but, as we have already seen, there are fewer problems in increasing the number of judges in the CFI as compared to the ECJ. The possibility of conferring such jurisdiction on the CFI was canvassed positively, albeit cautiously, in the Courts' paper.[83] The Dué Report was, however, opposed to this change, except in a limited number of special areas. Such rulings should, said the Report, be given by the ECJ because this was the most important task for the development of Community law. It was also felt that the 'one-stop shop' problem would mean that if such rulings were to be given by the CFI there would be no possibility of an appeal to the ECJ from the CFI's rulings.[84]

---

[83] *FJS*, 27.   [84] *RWP*, 22.

There is nonetheless much to be said for the idea that the CFI should be able to give preliminary rulings. Many of the cases which currently go to the ECJ for a preliminary ruling involve indirect challenges to the validity of Community norms where the non-privileged applicants cannot satisfy the standing criteria under Article 230. The substance of such cases are therefore concerned with just the kinds of issue which would be heard by the CFI itself in a direct action under Article 230. It is therefore very difficult to argue that the CFI should not be able to hear the substance of such cases if they emerge indirectly via national courts as requests for preliminary rulings.

The more precise role of the CFI within a scheme of preliminary rulings would depend upon whether assignment of cases to it was coupled with one of the other reforms suggested above, or whether it occurred within the context of the more traditional Article 234 reference procedure. These will be considered in turn.

It would, as argued in the previous section, be possible to confer jurisdiction on the CFI to give rulings after a judgment on the case had been given by the national court. It would then be for one of the parties to the case to require the national court to refer the matter to a Community court. All such cases could initially be referred to the CFI which would give judgment, subject to appeal to the ECJ for cases raising points of particular importance. The CFI would, on this scenario, be the general first instance court for all types of case.

If, however, we preserve the more traditional reference procedure, whereby the national court refers a question of Community law prior to any judgment being given on the substance of the case, and the national court makes the decision whether to refer, then the role of the CFI might have to be somewhat different. This is because of the point made earlier about the 'one-stop shop'. If it is felt that there can only be one Community law adjudication under a traditional Article 234 reference system, and we desire some of these cases to be heard by the CFI, then there would have to be some method of allocating those cases which were to be heard by the ECJ and those which were to be heard by the CFI. Logically there are two ways in which this could be done. Either all requests for rulings could initially go to the ECJ, which would then 'delegate down' some of these cases to the CFI. Or all requests for rulings could initially go to the CFI which would 'send up' to the ECJ those which were the most important. The former is likely to be more politically acceptable, with the ECJ making the determination as to which cases it should hear and which should go to the CFI.

A third possibility would be to retain the traditional reference procedure: send all requests for preliminary rulings to the CFI with the possibility of appeal or reference to the ECJ for those cases which are of particular importance, complexity, or novelty. This would of course run counter to the 'one-stop shop' idea. The reason for nonetheless considering this possibility is that the Courts' paper itself countenances the prospect of two adjudications on preliminary rulings in the context of decentralized judicial bodies to be discussed below. If this is indeed felt to be possible, there is no reason why preliminary rulings could not go to the CFI with the possibility of further recourse to the ECJ.

D. The Creation of Decentralized Judicial Bodies

Another option for easing the ECJ's burden of preliminary rulings is to create in each Member State a judicial body responsible for dealing with such rulings from courts within their territorial jurisdiction. The Courts' paper leaves open the issue as to whether they should have the status of a Community or a national court.[85] The discussion in the Dué Report is premised on the assumption that they would be national courts.[86]

Apart from easing the burden on the ECJ, this particular regime of decentralized courts is said to have the benefit of alleviating translation costs, since it is assumed that the parties to the case will be from that country. A decentralized regime would also have the obvious advantage of bringing legal redress physically closer to citizens, who could obtain a preliminary ruling without the necessity of travelling to Luxembourg.

The Courts' paper and the Dué Report are, however, concerned that such decentralized courts would jeopardize the uniformity of Community law:[87]

Any reorganisation of the preliminary ruling procedure on a national or regional basis, regardless of whether jurisdiction is conferred on national or Community courts, involves a serious risk of shattering the unity of Community law, which constitutes one of the cornerstones of the Union and which will become still more vital and vulnerable as a result of the enlargement of the Union. Jurisdiction to determine the final and binding interpretation of a Community rule, as well as the validity of that rule, should therefore be vested in a single court covering the whole of the Union.

The Dué Report comes out against the creation of such bodies largely for this reason.[88] The Courts' paper gives greater consideration to this institutional development. To meet the concern set out above, it suggests that there should be the possibility of a case going to the ECJ from one of the decentralized judicial bodies. The proposal appears to involve a mix of reference and appeal. Thus, the decentralized judicial body should have the power to refer a matter to the ECJ where the legal issue is of more general relevance for the unity or development of Community law. There should also be provision for

---

[85] *FJS*, 28. [86] *RWP*, 20–1.

[87] *FJS*, 28; *RWP*, 21. See also *The Role and Future of the European Court of Justice: A Report of the EC Advisory Board of the British Institute of International and Comparative Law, chaired by the Rt. Hon. The Lord Slynn of Hadley* (1996), 101–4.

[88] *RWP*, 21–2.

'the possibility of appealing to the Court of Justice "on a point of general legal interest", in accordance with detailed procedures to be laid down, against preliminary rulings given by those bodies'.[89]

The creation of some form of regional courts to supplement the existing judicial architecture of the Community has been advocated in the past.[90] It is also the case that the CFI has, in earlier reports, come out strongly against the establishment of such bodies, arguing that such a development would be of no relevance or interest to the Community and would be extremely costly.[91] Any conclusion as to the desirability or not of such decentralized bodies is dependent upon a number of issues which must be discussed separately.

It is important at the outset to decide whether such bodies will be part of the *national judiciary or whether they will be Community courts operating at a national or regional level.* This issue is left open in the Courts' paper. It is surely better that they should be Community courts. The only argument in favour of their being regarded as national courts is that the financial cost might then fall on the Member States rather than the EC. This consideration must be outweighed by other factors which are more important in the long term. Such courts should be regarded as Community courts, since this best fits with the idea of building a developed Community judicial system below the ECJ, of the kind which exists within other countries such as the USA. It would be detrimental to begin this process of building a Community judicial hierarchy by placing these new courts within the national legal system, and this is so notwithstanding the fact that the national courts themselves are, as we have seen, Community courts in their own right in certain respects.

Closely allied to the matter just considered is the issue of whether the decentralized bodies should operate on a *national or regional level.* The Courts' paper is ambiguous in this respect. The primary impression which is given is that such courts will operate within each Member State. This impression is reinforced by the desire to save on translation costs, the assumption being that if the courts are organized on a national basis then all the proceedings can be in the national language. At other points the paper is framed in terms of reorganization on a national or regional basis.

A regional form of organization would be preferable for a number of reasons. In practical terms, it would almost certainly be more efficient, since a number of existing or future Member States would be too small to warrant such a court of their own. Translation costs would not be that high, since many cases would still arise between litigants who were from the same Member State. It should nonetheless be recognized that there will still be

---

[89] *FJS*, 28–9.
[90] J.-P. Jacque and J. Weiler, 'On the Road to European Union: A New Judicial Architecture: An Agenda for the Intergovernmental Conference', (1990) 27 CMLR 185.
[91] *RCJ*.

translation costs irrespective of whether such courts are organized on a regional or national basis, since the litigants will not always be from the same country. In normative terms, a regional regime is preferable to a national one, since it obviates the dangers which could flow from the latter. If the decentralized courts were organized on a national basis, then there would be a danger that differences of view between such courts would be cast as the 'German v. French view', the 'UK v. Italian', etc. This danger would be exacerbated if such courts were to be regarded as national rather than Community courts. This hazard would be avoided, or at the very least the tension would be much reduced, if the courts were to be organized regionally rather than nationally. In the USA, where a regional pattern of organization exists, there are of course differences of view between the different circuits which cover the country. These are, however, cast in just such terms: the 5th Circuit may, for example, be regarded as more liberal than the 2nd Circuit on a certain issue.

E. The Relationship between Decentralized Judicial Bodies and the CFI

Whether decentralized judicial bodies should be created depends in part upon the relationship between such bodies and the CFI. This is an interesting and difficult issue. The nature of this relationship cannot be divorced from other proposals concerning the judicial architecture of the Community which have been considered earlier. There are five possible ways in which to see this aspect of the judicial architecture of the Community developing.

1. An Appellate System with the CFI and No Decentralized Bodies

This discussion is based on the assumption that the reference system is transformed into a more appellate regime in the manner discussed earlier. National courts would be required to give judgment in cases raising matters of Community law, and it would then be for a party to the case to request or require the national court to make a reference for a ruling on those points of Community law in respect of which that party contests the validity of the judgment given. If such a system were introduced then it would, as argued above,[92] be possible and desirable for the CFI to become a general court of first instance, having initial jurisdiction not only over direct actions under Article 230 but also over indirect actions which arise under a modified Article 234. There would then be the possibility of appeal to the ECJ where the point of law raised was of particular novelty, or importance for the development of EC law. If this were to occur it would be difficult to find a place for regional or decentralized courts, since the CFI would be taking indirect actions as well as direct actions.

---

[92] See above, pp. 193–5 and 204–6.

2. An Appellate System with Decentralized Bodies and No CFI

The reference system could be transformed into an appellate regime in the manner considered above, with the possibility of further resort to the ECJ. The decentralized judicial bodies thus created would actually replace the CFI. It would be perfectly possible in theory to create such bodies and to vest them with jurisdiction over direct as well as indirect actions. On this view the CFI would cease to exist and its work would be reassigned to the decentralized judicial bodies. This would have the advantage of bringing Community law closer to the citizen. It must, however, be recognized that there is little prospect of this occurring in practical terms. The CFI is well established and would fight vigorously for its survival.

3. A Traditional Reference System with the CFI and No Decentralized Bodies

This scenario is based on the assumption that we continue with a reference system of the general kind presently enshrined within Article 234, and that we do not transform it into a more appellate regime. There may well be some filter of the kind considered above, but this would not fundamentally change the nature of the Article 234 procedure in the way that a shift from a reference to an appeal system would. Preliminary rulings could go initially to the CFI, with the prospect of further recourse to the ECJ. The further recourse to the ECJ could then be by the same mixture of reference and appeal as proposed in the Courts' paper in relation to decentralized judicial bodies.

4. A Traditional Reference System with Decentralized Bodies and No CFI

This is the converse of the option just considered. On this view decentralized bodies would be created which would give preliminary rulings in the general manner presently enshrined in Article 234. There would be the possibility of further recourse to the ECJ through the mixture of reference and appeal described above. The decentralized bodies would also be accorded jurisdiction over direct actions, and hence the CFI would cease to exist.

5. Coexistence of the CFI and Decentralized Bodies

It would of course also be possible for there to be a place within the judicial architecture for both the CFI and decentralized judicial bodies. The CFI would have its present jurisdiction, or, as advocated earlier, it would become the general first instance court for all direct actions irrespective of the nature of the litigants in the case. The decentralized judicial bodies would hear preliminary rulings, with the prospect of further recourse to the ECJ. An advantage of this model is that it achieves a blend between centralization, as represented by the CFI, and decentralization, as represented by the new national or regional bodies.

There are, however, two factors which point in the other direction. These should be borne in mind when thinking of future developments in this area.

In organizational terms, we should not create a further level of courts unless we are clear that it is necessary. It is, as we have seen above, not self-evident that we require both decentralized bodies and the CFI, and this is so irrespective of whether we persevere with a traditional-style reference system, or whether we transform it into a more appellate regime.

In substantive terms, we should not lose sight of the effect of the jurisdictional divide between the CFI and decentralized bodies entailed in the option presently under consideration. If indirect actions go to the decentralized bodies, then they will often be passing judgment on the validity of Community norms in cases where non-privileged parties are unable to bring a direct action because of the inability to secure standing. It is, other things being equal, desirable that the CFI be able to hear such cases, more particularly if it is regarded as the general first instance court for the Community in the context of direct actions. A counter to this argument would of course be that if the ECJ and CFI defined the standing criteria for direct actions less restrictively, then such cases would in any event come to them.

IX THE INTER-GOVERNMENTAL CONFERENCE AND THE NICE TREATY

The Courts' paper and the Dué Report both contain valuable analyses of the judicial architecture within the EC and its possible future development. How far these suggestions were taken up was, however, dependent on the political will of the Member States, and other institutional actors, who took part in the IGC. This is self-evidently the case insofar as reforms require Treaty amendments. Judicial reform has not, in the past, been high on the agenda of IGCs. The very fact that the 1999–2000 IGC was concerned with the institutional implications of enlargement meant, however, that there was a greater likelihood of judicial reform being considered alongside reforms of the other major Community institutions. It is necessary to consider the discussions in the IGC in order to understand the changes adopted in the Nice Treaty.

A. The IGC

What follows is based on the Feira European Council meeting.[93] The preliminary conclusions from this meeting drew heavily on an earlier note from

---

[93] *Intergovernmental Conference on Institutional Reform, Presidency Report to the Feira European Council* (June 2000).

the IGC Conference of Representatives of the Member States.[94] It is clear that all Member States accepted the need for judicial reform, and that they accepted also the need to allow for future changes to be made without going through the cumbersome process of Treaty amendment.[95]

In relation to the composition of the ECJ, almost all states agreed that the number of judges in plenary sessions should be limited in order that these did not become like an assembly, and that it should not be compulsory to have an Advocate-General's opinion in all cases. Most also agreed that there should continue to be one judge from each Member State on the ECJ.[96] New judicial boards of appeal should be created to deal with, for example, staff matters and trade marks, subject to appeal on points of law to the CFI.

There was fairly broad support, although not complete consensus, on changes to the respective jurisdictional competence of the ECJ and the CFI. There were, however, still significant issues to be resolved. This is readily apparent from the alternative formulations of the draft amendment to Article 225, which deals with the competence of the CFI. One formulation of draft Article 225(1) accorded the CFI power to hear classes of action to be defined in accordance with Article 225(3). The other accorded it power over classes of direct action referred to in the Treaty, with the exception of those that the Council, acting under 225(3), reserves for the ECJ. This latter formulation would clearly require the drawing up of a list of actions which are reserved for the exclusive competence of the ECJ.

The draft Article 225(2) was designed to give the CFI power to hear questions referred for preliminary rulings in certain specified areas. This power might be subject to the proviso that if the ECJ believed that a case within such an area raised an issue of general importance for EC law, then the ECJ would itself give the ruling. An alternative proviso was that such decisions made by the CFI would be subject to review by the ECJ, on terms to be laid down in the Statute of the Court.

The draft Article 225(3) provided that the Council, acting unanimously at the request of the ECJ, after consulting the EP and the Commission, or possibly at the request of the Commission after consulting the EP and the ECJ, should determine the classes of action referred to in Article 225(1) and the areas in which the CFI could make preliminary rulings pursuant to Article 225(2).

B. The Nice Treaty

The reforms actually adopted in the Nice Treaty built on the discussion which had taken place in the IGC. The main changes are as follows.

---

[94] *Conference of the Representatives of the Governments of the Member States, Friends of the Presidency Group (Court of Justice and Court of First Instance)* (May 2000).
[95] *Intergovernmental Conference on Institutional Reform*, above n. 93, at 39.
[96] Ibid. 40.

The Nice Treaty has modified the composition and structure of the court system in a number of ways. It has been decided that the ECJ shall consist of one judge from each state, Article 221. This had been the practice hitherto, but there was no Treaty provision requiring this to be so. The dangers of the ECJ becoming too unwieldy, and crossing the line from a court to a deliberative assembly, were felt to be outweighed by the importance of having one judge from each state. Time will tell whether this was a wise move or not. The role of the Advocate-General has been subtly altered by the amendments made to Article 222. This now provides that the Advocate-General shall make reasoned submissions on cases which, in accordance with the Statute of the Court of Justice, require his or her involvement. The composition of the CFI has also been modified. There is to be at least one judge from each Member State, Article 224(1). This has always been the case, but it was not mandated by the Treaty itself. We have already seen that the composition of the CFI is less problematic than that of the ECJ. The Nice Treaty provides, in addition, for judicial panels to take certain cases, such as those between Community and its servants.[97] A further structural reform which will be welcomed by members of both courts, is that their respective Rules of Procedure can be adopted by qualified majority in the Council, unanimity no longer being required.[98]

The Nice Treaty has also made a number of changes to the jurisdiction of the Community courts. The position until now had been that the CFI would be accorded jurisdiction over certain classes of case as a result of a determination made by the Council, albeit at the request of the ECJ. This was subject to the Treaty limitation that the CFI could not hear preliminary rulings. The Nice Treaty has modified Article 225. In Article 225(1) it is now provided in the Treaty itself that the CFI can hear actions covered by Articles 230, 232, 235, 236, and 238, with the exception of those cases assigned to a judicial panel and those reserved in the Statute for the ECJ itself. Article 51 of the Statute makes it clear that the CFI will not have jurisdiction in direct actions brought by the Community institutions, the ECB, or the Member States. These cases will continue to go to the ECJ. Article 225(1) stipulates further that the Statute may provide for the CFI to have jurisdiction for other classes of case. The judicial panels created pursuant to the Nice Treaty can be reviewed by the CFI, subject to a limited right of review by the ECJ in exceptional instances.[99] Article 225(3) accords the CFI power for the first time to hear preliminary rulings in specific areas laid down by the Statute of the Court of Justice. Where the CFI believes that the case requires a decision of principle which is likely to affect the unity or consistency of Community law, it may refer the case to the ECJ. Preliminary rulings given by the CFI can, exceptionally, be subject to review by the ECJ, under the conditions laid

---

[97] Art. 225a.   [98] Arts. 223(6), 224(6).   [99] Art. 225(2).

down in the Statute, where there is a serious risk to the unity or consistency of Community law being affected.[100] A Declaration has been attached to the modified Article 225 urging the ECJ and the Commission to give overall consideration to the division of competence between the ECJ and CFI, and to submit proposals as soon as the revised treaty enters into force. There are further Declarations concerning the nature of the review procedure which is to operate under Articles 225(2) and 225(3), the practical operation of which is to be evaluated after three years.

X CONCLUSION

The Courts' paper and the Dué Report are to be welcomed for their willingness to canvass a range of options which have a profound effect on the future shape of the Community's judicial architecture. While all of the issues raised are of interest, two matters are particularly important for the future shape of the Community judiciary. The Nice Treaty now provides some answers on these issues.

The first is whether the CFI is to be allowed to mature as the general first instance court at least for direct actions. The answer to this is unclear. Direct actions brought by Community institutions, Member States, and the ECB will continue to be heard by the ECJ. There may, however, be some rethinking of this in the future, given that the Declaration on Article 225 urges the ECJ and Commission to give overall consideration to the division of competence between ECJ and CFI 'in particular in the area of direct actions'.

The second crucial issue is whether the CFI should be given any jurisdiction over preliminary rulings. The Nice Treaty has provided an affirmative answer on this point. The significance of this change will, however, depend on the classes of case over which the CFI is given jurisdiction to hear preliminary rulings.

A number of the broader issues raised in the previous discussion have not been taken up in the Nice Treaty. These include the possibility of shifting from a reference to an appellate system, and the establishment of decentralized, regional courts. It would, however, be wrong to conclude that the Nice Treaty has failed in reform of the judicial architecture. Discussion as to the possibilities of reform prior to revision, is almost always wider-ranging than the reforms undertaken when the Treaty is actually revised. When viewed in this light, the judicial reforms embodied in the Nice Treaty are significant. These provisions, in particular the revised Article 225, allow further reform to be undertaken through amendment of the Court's Statute. The very fact that the IGC appended the Declaration encouraging the ECJ and Commission to

---

[100] See Art. 62 of the Statute of the Court of Justice.

give overall consideration as soon as possible to the division of competence between the ECJ and CFI is indicative of the fact that the door to further reform in this area remains open.

Epilogue: The Judicial Après Nice

J. H. H. WEILER[*]

The European judicial architecture may not be crumbling[1] but it is certainly in need of rethinking—not an easy project: Traditionally the custodianship of the Community legal order has been given to lawyers—a conservative bunch. What's more, the unintended genius of the system which at its core and most original combines national courts and the European Court of Justice through the Preliminary Reference procedure has produced spectacular systemic results. If it works (or appears to work) why fix it? Last, though not least, despite the urgent incentive for radical innovation in the face of pending Enlargement and the rhetoric of, no less, constitutionalism emanating from various capitals[2], the actual pace of change in recent IGCs has been lacklustre in both ambition and result, incremental rather than radical. Why expect more for the judicial branch of Union governance?

Yet, ever since the Single European Act one lives in fear that what might look like an anaemic outcome of the latest Intergovernmental Conference will,

[*] Jean Monnet Professor of Law and Director of the Center for International and Regional Economic Law and Justice at New York University School of Law. I am indebted to Imola Streho for help in the research and to Gráinne de Búrca for her comments on the first draft. The usual disclaimer applies.

[1] H. Rasmussen, 'Remedying the Crumbling EC Judicial System', (2000) 37 CMLRev 1071. In addition to Rasmussen's insightful piece see, too, the prescient J. P. Jacqué, 'L'avenir de l'architecture juridictionnelle de l'Union', (1999) 35 RTD eur. 443, and A. Arnull, 'Judicial architecture or judicial folly? The challenge facing the European Union', (1999) 24 ELRev. 516 commenting on the Community's Court Discussion paper on the future of the judicial system of the Union, May 1999 http://europa.eu.int/cj/en/pres/avemg.pdf. G. Hirsch, 'Dezentralisierung des Gerichtssystems der EU', (2000) 33 ZRP 57. I also profited from the reflection at the Colloqium on Revising the EU's Judicial System organized jointly by the CCBE and the College of Europe, Bruges, which took place on 19 and 20 November 1999. See C. Turner and R. Munoz, 'Revising the Judicial Architecture of the European Union', (1999/2000) 19 Yearbook of European Law.

[2] See e.g. the Op. Ed by Valéry Giscard d'Estaing and Helmut Schmidt, *International Herald Tribune*, 11 Apr. 2000. Then came the Fischer eruption. See generally C. Joerges, Y. Meny, J. H. H. Weiler (eds.), 'What Kind of Constitution for What Kind of Polity—Responses to Joschka Fischer' (RSC Center, EUI, 2000). For a more honest discussion by a leading public figure admitting the statal implications of the new construct see G. Federico Mancini, 'Europe: The Case for Statehood', (1998) 4 European Law Journal, 29–42, and Harvard Jean Monnet Working Paper 6/98. Romano Prodi is also known to favour a constitutional exercise. Jürgen Habermas may be considered a public figure too. See 'The European Nation-State and the Pressures of Globalization', *New Left Review*, no. 235 (May 1999), 46–59, and, earlier, 'Die Einbeziehung des Anderen, Chapter III "Hat der Nationalstaat eine Zukunft?"', (Frankfurt: Suhrkamp 1996) 128–91.

in fact, turn out to be a lion in a sheepskin. After the disappointment of Amsterdam, Nice was meant to provide the final opportunity of grasping firmly the nettle of Enlargement and allowing the governments of the Member States to make the structural changes necessary for a Union of twenty-five and more. The outcome, which ostentatiously lists the number of votes the likes of Romania will have in the Council, is, however, more like a sheep in the skin of a lion. Once again the truly hard decisions have been postponed. The original Community system received its nth coat of new paint but it is still the old Commission–Council–Parliament engine creaking beneath the bonnet.

When it comes to reform of the judicial architecture the picture is more complex. The beauty of Nice is, as ever, in the eyes of the beholder. Driven by the results of a high-powered consultative committee of insider-outsiders and by indirect input from the Courts themselves[3] and concerned mostly by the mismatch between a heavy caseload and a finite number of judges, i.e. by a concern for efficiency in the administration of justice, Nice introduces some important innovations which hold the potential for a significant inroad into the perennial problem of logged dockets and delayed justice at least in as much as direct actions are concerned.[4]

Most notable is the new Article 220,[5] which in conjunction with Article 225a provides for the possibility of introducing 'judicial panels', in effect a new, first-instance tier, appealable to the Court of First Instance to hear and determine 'certain classes of action or proceeding brought in specific areas'. For its part the Court of First Instance becomes the 'default' jurisdiction for most direct actions, excepting cases reserved to the Court of Justice and those eventually to be reserved to the Judicial Panels.

There are additional improvements designed to streamline the functioning of both Courts, notably the revamped system of chambers, Grand Chamber, and a Full Court[6] and the sanctioning of disposing of a case without a submission from the Advocate General.[7] These innovations are in line with

---

[3] See Report by the Working Party on the Future of the European Communities Court system (January 2000) Five of the seven members of the Committee set up by the Commission to advise it on reform were former Members of the Court. Another was a former high-ranking member of the Commission. The last was a high government official. For this and other details on the work of the Working Party, see H. Rasmussen, op. cit., n.1, p. 1086 and seq.

[4] Whilst heavy workload is not the only concern it figures significantly in the Report by the Working Party, in H. Rasmussen, at pp. 1079–83 and *passim*.

[5] The Court of Justice and the Court of First Instance, each within its jurisdiction, shall ensure that in the interpretation and application of this Treaty the law is observed. In addition, judicial panels may be attached to the Court of First Instance under the conditions laid down in Article 225a in order to exercise, in certain specific areas, the judicial competence laid down in the Treaty.

[6] See Article 16 of the Protocol on the Statute of the Court of Justice SN 1247/1/01 REV 1, 14 February 2001.

[7] See Article 20 of the Protocol on the Statute of the Court of Justice see reference above n. 6.

improvements already introduced prior to Nice in the internal operation of the Court.

But Nice goes further. In relation to the judicial branch the IGC, with the input of the Dué Committee and the two Courts, may indeed already have taken two crucial steps which at least potentially open the way to the more radical change necessitated by Enlargement.

First, though Nice, in a measure constitutionalizing practice, stipulates one judge per Member State for the Court of Justice, it provides for *at least* one judge per Member State for the Court of First Instance.[8] The way has been opened for a Court of First Instance which contains more judges than the Union contains Member States and in which the principle of parity of 'representation' is no longer applicable.

Second, of huge future importance is the opening of the door, at least a crack, in Article 225(3)

The Court of First Instance shall have jurisdiction to hear and determine questions referred for a preliminary ruling under Article 234, in specific areas laid down by the Statute.[9]

The potential cumulative impact of these innovations are on a par with the introduction of the Court of First Instance itself.

But these are harbingers for the future. The actual outcome of the Conference in this area too, as with the political institutions, is an inability to break away from the scheme of the original Treaties. At the core of this architecture, and its most important feature by any perspective one may care to adopt, is the Preliminary Reference and the Preliminary Ruling. This procedure has remained substantially unchanged for half a century. A Court of First Instance with new-found dignity, Judicial Panels and all the rest notwithstanding, Europe continues to drive in its rusty and trusted 1950 model with the steering wheel firmly in the hands of the Court of Justice.

Put differently, the IGC was not willing to engage in either profound rethinking or profound re-engineering of the judicial function in view of a much changed polity to the one in which the current system was set. Indeed,

---

[8] Article 221 and Article 224 respectively of the EC treaty as modified by the treaty of Nice SN 1247/1/01 REV 1.

[9] Article 225(3) also provides for the possibility of the CFI referring a Preliminary Reference to the Court of Justice in important cases which require a decision of principle likely to affect the unity or consistency of Community law. This strikes me as an unfortunate idea to have enshrined in the Treaty. As I shall argue below one of the weaknesses of the classical Preliminary Reference procedure is that the Court of Justice is the first and last instance to decide issues of Community law. Especially in cases such as that, it would be good to have a decision of the Court of First Instance and then to invoke the second provision in Article 225(3) which allows review by the Court of Justice. The Article permits such a result since the transfer of the case to the Court is facultative and not obligatory for the Court of First Instance.

perhaps not surprisingly, the Court(s) themselves, who provided the principal intellectual input into the reform effort, were unable fully to grasp either some inherent weaknesses in their positioning or the significance of the current constitutional moment. It is part of human nature to screen oneself from one's own weaknesses. They opened the door but did not walk in. Perhaps that is the wisdom of judicial prudence.

And yet the context in which the judicial system is situated has changed radically in the last fifty years. The increase of size from six Member States to a potential of twenty-six is really only part of the problem, and possibly not even the most important part. Not a limited jurisdiction over some technical areas but a complex polity with jurisdiction ranging from human rights to monetary policy to difficult aspects of immigration and even citizenship.[10] Not a world dominated by the Cold War but one afflicted with very hot transnational and transcontinental trade disputes and rivalries—squarely within the jurisdiction of that Community and Union.

And then the Court itself: no longer an instance for dispute settlement, but a judicial giant which has successfully positioned itself at the constitutional centre of Europe, a Europe in which national legal orders suddenly feel under threat.[11] In this respect the Court is a (lucky) victim of its own spectacular success.

It is against these changes that the problems of the stasis at the core of the European judicial function must be assessed. The architecture that served well the Community at its foundation and consolidation phases would merit rethinking and reform *even if the Community were not to enlarge.*[12]

The matter is complicated since big chunks of what needs to be changed are not a matter for the IGC but for the Court and the other actors which play a part in shaping its composition and role.

I want to begin by raising three issues which are considered by some as taboo in the debate on the future Judicial Architecture. The tasks of the Court, the qualifications of the judges and the nature of the judicial conversation between the European Court and National Courts.

---

[10] H. Rasmussen op. cit above n. 1, pp.1077–8, also G. Hirsch op. cit above n. 1, p. 58; J-P. Jacqué op. cit., above. n. 1, p. 444 and C. Turner and R. Munoz op. cit., above n. 1, Section I. Cf. P. Craig, 'The Jurisdiction of the Community Court Reconsidered' [in this volume] section II.

[11] This is most notable in the area of private law, see D. Caruso, 'The Missing View of the Cathedral: The Private law Paradigm of European Legal Integration', (1997) 3 European Law Journal 3. But also in areas of public law: see generally the Member State Reports in A.-M. Slaughter et al. *The European Court and National Courts—Doctrine and Jurisprudence* (Oxford: Hart, 1998).

[12] G. Hirsch op. cit., above n. 1, p. 58.

My theses here are simple:

a. The Court cannot effectively discharge its duty with its present tasks and present composition. This is not just a question of workload—a problem which may to some extent be addressed by the Nice changes. It is also a question of competences and credibility.

b. The style of judicial decisions is outmoded, does not reflect the dialogical nature of European Constitutionalism, and is not a basis for confidence-building European constitutional relations between the European Court and its national constitutional counterparts.

Any discussion of the judicial architecture must start with the preliminary reference procedure, one of the most remarkable and successful dimensions of the European legal order and European constitutionalism.

Its success, however, has come with some costs.[13]

Barring the very few cases of 'inappropriate' references, the ECJ is obliged to deal with a growing number of references—a number expected to rise with Enlargement.[14] The reference procedure is the equivalent of almost *all* cases pending before national courts going to the national constitutional court before they can be disposed of at lower instances. The new system of chambers and the streamlined provisions may ease the backlog but cannot eliminate the root cause. It also means that the ECJ has to answer questions on all aspects of European law. One day a most specialized issue of agricultural law, the next day a complex issue of product liability and, increasingly, other aspects of private law and on day three, most critically, profound issues of constitutional law which engage the highest courts and the deepest legal values of the Member States.

Couple these two features together and the trajectory becomes one of implosion.

The issue of workload is not simply the delays which the heavy load on both Court and Tribunal create—justice delayed is justice denied. It is, and this is usually only whispered, an issue of quality of justice. Even a cursory examination of the timetable of a Court of Justice judge reveals that between meetings and deliberations and actual hearings the workload is such that judges have very little time to think deeply about many of the cases—especially those for which they are not the Reporting Judge—which they

---

[13] Cf. J. H. H. Weiler, 'The European Court, National courts and References for Preliminary Rulings—The Paradox of Success: A Revisionist view of Article 177 EEC', in Article 177 EEC: Experiences and Problems, H. Schemers et al., North-Holland (Asser Instituut 1987), 366 and J-P.Jacqué, J. H. H. Weiler, 'On the Road to European Union—A New Judicial Architecture', (1990) 27 CMLRev 187 ff.

[14] H. Rasmussen, op. cit., above n. 1, p. 1072.

eventually have to decide.[15] This has various consequences, one of which concerns the role of Legal Secretaries. In the United States the question of the appropriate role and influence of judicial clerks has been discussed intensely. I believe that similar questions may legitimately be raised about the role and influence of Legal Secretaries at the ECJ. This is not meant in any way to impugn the integrity of the process but simply to bring arithmetic to bear on the problem. The year has so many days, the day has so many hours, the Court has so many judges, the judges have so many cases (indeed many)— time to think, to reflect, to deliberate is the most scarce resource of the Institution. Justice delayed is justice denied, but so is hurried justice, scantily deliberated justice, justice in which Legal Secretaries write and judges merely approve. The fault is not that of the Court. We ask too much of it.

The success of the Preliminary Reference also makes us forget the fact that in this procedure, the ECJ is court of both first and last instance—in principle a very unsatisfactory situation in itself constituting a violation of a fundamental principle of justice. This fact alone would call at least for the most careful and deliberative process in each and every case—since there is no appeal—but this is exactly what we do not allow the Court to do because of the heavy burden we place on it.

But the matter does not end simply with workload and time burden. Strangely, even paradoxically, the ECJ concept follows more the Anglo-American model of a plenary court supposedly competent in all areas of law rather than the continental model of specialized courts—as we find in different ways in Germany, Italy, France, Greece, and other countries. There is the general issue of specialization, and the most delicate one is the functioning of the ECJ when it sits as the Constitutional Court of the Union.[16] One of the peculiarities of the European system is that its most decisive constitutional issues depend, as a matter of legal realism, on a relationship of trust, confidence and credibility between the European Court and its national counterparts. The European Court can pronounce on the supremacy of Community law, or on the Francovich principle of Member State liability all it wants, so to speak. These doctrines become effective only when accepted and practised by national courts under the guidance of the highest courts in each Member State.

It is no secret that the 1990s have seen a certain erosion in the relationship. The German 'Maastricht Decision' in which the German Constitutional Court declared, in defiance of established case law of the ECJ, that national

---

[15] H. Rasmussen, op. cit., above n. 1, p. 1080, and see also J-P.Jacqué, J. H. H.Weiler, op. cit., above n. 13, p. 188.

[16] In some respects, every time it is called upon to interpret the Treaty it could be said to be sitting as the Constitutional Court since the Treaty is the Union's constitution. I mean, instead, when it sits on matters that would be considered of a constitutional nature in the legal cultures of most Member States.

authorities may disregard European law measures if they fall outside the competences of the Community as understood by German State organs, is notorious.[17] Less well known are a number of decisions by other high courts in various Member States that display similar defiance. The Italian Constitutional Court declared that it did not regard itself in most cases that come before it as a Court or Tribunal in the sense of Article 177 (now 234) and, thus, considered itself outside the duty to make preliminary references. Troubling decisions have come out of Denmark, Belgium, and possibly Spain.[18]

It should not surprise us, even if this is rarely spelt out in good company, that there is a certain credibility issue. The members of the ECJ are jurists of the highest quality. But only a few of them are constitutionalists. When European law and the European Court demand subordination even of the most important constitutional principles of a Member State (such as the protection of fundamental human rights) to European law, it is critical that such decision emanate from a tribunal which is capable, *and seen to be capable* of comprehending the constitutional sensibilities of the Member State at issue and communicating that comprehension to its national counterparts. Without this we can only expect more Maastricht Decisions. The same can be said, of course, regarding decisions of the Court on complex economic matters such as intellectual property, competition, and the like. I focus on the constitutional dimension because it is politically the most sensitive and it touches often on legal values which go to the very identity of the Member States. The position of the European Court is different from that of the Supreme Court of the United States and even of the House of Lords. Its relationship with, and dependence on, national courts is far more delicate and sensitive.

In thinking about the future of European law, consideration must be given to whether finally the European Court system should become European (rather than Anglo-American) and see the establishment of specialized jurisdictions, among them a European Constitutional Court composed of judges whose qualifications and expertise would be mostly in this field.

Après Nice is meant to be a reflection of what really ought to be done with Enlargement and a growing jurisdictional reach of the Union in place. Tony

[17] German Constitutional Court, judgement of 12 Oct. 1993, 89 BverfGE 155, English translation 33 ILM 388 (1994).

[18] Italian Constitutional Court 15 Dec. 1995, no. 536, Rac.uff. corte cost. V.118, 1995, p. 729; Danish Supreme Court, case no I 361/1997, Judgement of 6 Apr. 1998, UfR 1998.800 H, English translation [1999] 3 CML Reports 854; Cour d'arbitrage arrêt no 12/94 of 3 Feb. 1994, Moniteur Belge 1994, pp. 6137–47; cf. Spanish Tribunal Constitucional case, Declaration of 1 July 1992, English translation [1994] 3 CML Reports 101 see on this point A. Estella de Noreiga, 'A Dissident Voice: The Spanish Constitutional Court Case Law on European Integration', (1999) 5 EPLaw 269.

Arnull once wrote, tongue in cheek, that the back of an envelope would suffice to jot down a blueprint for the reform of Europe's judicial system.[19] He may have exaggerated. The back of a postal stamp on that envelope could do the job just as well. Here, then, are my two bits to the discussion of what a new architecture may look like—a concept car rather than a prototype.[20]

The proposed new architecture has two limbs too—the process at the level of the ECJ and the CFI and the process at the level of national courts.

At the heart of the system would be a reversal of our habitual positioning of the Court and the Court of First Instance. It is the Court of First Instance which is to become the centrepiece of the judicial system, its workhorse, with the Court of Justice standing at the hierarchical apex as its own brand of Supreme Court of the Union.[21] Nice, as noted, already opens the door: Article 220 provides that the 'Court of Justice *and the Court of First Instance,* each within its jurisdiction, shall ensure that in the interpretation and application of this Treaty the Law is observed' (emphasis added). This is an important symbolic empowerment which has important potential implications for the future. There are three crucial elements in this concept. The first is that Preliminary References would, in most cases be addressed to the Court of First Instance.[22] As noted, Article 225(3) provides that the Court of First Instance shall have jurisdiction to hear and determine questions referred for a preliminary ruling under Article 234, in specific areas laid down by the Statute. This crack should be opened fully. One has to get rid once and for all of the fetish that it is somehow non-functional or disrespectful or in any other way inappropriate that national jurisdictions should turn to the CFI rather than the ECJ for a Preliminary Ruling. As we shall see, however, in this con-

---

[19] A. Arnull, op. cit., above n. 1, p. 516.

[20] Most of the proposals have already been outlined in two papers delivered by me in 1999 at the Walter Hallstein Institute of European Law at the Humboldt University of Berlin and at the Institute of International Economic Law at Helsinki. I thank both institutions for the opportunity to present my ideas and to receive some feedback. Cf. 'The Function and Future of European Law' in Veijo Heiskanen & Kati Kulovesi (eds.), *Function and Future of European Law: Proceedings of the International Conference on the Present State, Rationality and Direction of European Legal Integration* (Helsinki: Institute of International Economic Law, 1999).

[21] The nomenclature would, of course, be of some significance. 'Supreme Court' and 'Constitutional Court' are two terms probably to be avoided because they carry a set of associations which might be politically unwelcome. The 'European Court' and the 'European High Court' perhaps?

[22] H. Rasmussen, op. cit., above n. 1, p. 1098 ff., also that the author is recognizing the advantages of 'partial renationalization of the EC's judicial architecture' and envisages 'national "preliminary judicial body" ' as proposed by the Working Party, p. 1111; see also on this issue G. Hirsch, op. cit., above n. 1, p. 59 who suggests rather a 'Dezentralisierungsmodelle' which is 'stärkere Europäisierung' preferable to 'Renationalisierung', p. 60. Both authors recognize the advantages of this reform in terms of saving time and costs. Cf. J-P. Jacqué, op. cit., above n. 1, pp. 447–9. See also C. Turner and R. Munoz, op. cit., above n. 1, Section V.

cept a special privileged relationship is foreseen for the highest courts of the Member States.

Judicial Panels are very important for discrete areas of specialized jurisdiction and they should remain so under any future scenario. But in that future it would have to be the Court of First Instance which, modelled on the experience in most European countries, should have its own functional chambers or divisions. A General Chamber and several specialized chambers. Without being exhaustive one can imagine specialized chambers in matters of Customs Law including Antidumping and other Safeguard Measures; Competition, Social Security, Agriculture. Matters not falling within the jurisdiction of a specialized chamber would fall within that of the General Chamber.

The second crucial element in the new concept is that the number of judges of the Court of First Instance would be decided on a purely functional basis.[23] Here, too, Nice already opens the door as indicated above. It may thus be that the Customs Law Chamber would have twelve members because of the number of cases it has to deal with and the Agriculture Chamber only six. The General Chamber too could have more judges than the number of Member States so as to ensure a reasonable burden on each panel and a reasonable timescale in rendering decisions. The General Chamber would have a plenary forum (one judge from each Member State) for important cases and could also sit *en banc* for very important or complex cases very much in line with the provisions of Nice for the jurisdiction of the Court of Justice sitting as a 'full' court.

Specialized chambers would be composed of judges selected on the basis of their expertise from a Community-wide pool. Critically, and this is the third element, as the Community enlarges, the principle of parity will eventually have to yield. Here, prior practice at the Court and Nice already chart the way with its model of Full Court, Grand Chamber and other chambers in which, perforce the principle of nationality is suitably differentiated. For reasons of coherence, any specialized panel of judges hearing a case in a chamber could always include one judge from the General Chamber too. Of course the full apparatus of the Advocates General, if this office is to be maintained, will also be transferred to the CFI. The present situation would be inverted, the presence of the Advocates General would be the rule at the CFI level and the possibility to call upon one would be open at the ECJ level.[24]

As noted above, according to this suggestion, the CFI (for which a more suitable name could be found) would have plenary jurisdiction under the existing jurisdiction of the ECJ—i.e. it would entertain both direct actions and preliminary rulings under the existing rules and procedures established by

[23] J-P.Jacqué op. cit., above n. 1, p. 445 and Craig, 'The Jurisdiction of the Community Court Reconsidered' [in this volume] section VI.B

[24] See H. Rasmussen op. cit., above n. 1, p. 1080.

the Treaty.[25] But its elevated number of judges would mean that the current delays associated with turning to the European Court would be eliminated.

This architecture would ensure both a balance between the specialized and generalized judge, it would substantially expedite the administration of justice and, because of the combination of specialization and reduction in docket burden, would also improve the deliberative quality of the decisions rendered. And yet the advantages of the classic European system of preliminary references and direct actions will be maintained—the best of both worlds.

The European Court of Justice would become, under this vision, a kind of European supreme court. It would have primarily Appellate Jurisdiction from decisions of the Court of First Instance in direct actions, on the same principles that govern the relationship between the two courts today. In cases involving the legality of acts of the Institutions and of failure of Member States to fulfil their obligations under the Treaty, the institutions and Member States would have an automatic right of appeal. Individuals would have leave to appeal if the Tribunal itself certified that the matter was of such interest that it should be heard by the European High Court or if they petitioned the High Court and it itself decided to hear such an appeal.

The European High Court would, however, have one new jurisdiction— the appeal from Preliminary Rulings. These, I propose, would be taken by a reference made by the highest courts in the national jurisdictions—either in dealing with a case that came to them on appeal from a lower national court where a reference had already been made in the matter at issue, or, if the first reference was made by the highest national court itself, it could re-refer the matter to the European High Court if it were not satisfied by the decision of the Court of First Instance.

I would also suggest that when a reference was made from the highest courts of the Member States to the Court of Justice, to underscore the importance of the matter and the national interest in the case and to ensure the fullest possible consideration of all national sensibilities, the deciding Panel should always include one judge of the national Court making the reference, though not from the actual group of judges deciding the case—in other words a national ad hoc judge from the highest court of the Member State in those cases where the highest court makes a reference or appeal to the European High Court. One should not gasp. The notion of ad-hoc judges is not novel and in the face of an ever more complicated relationship between the ECJ and national jurisdictions some such provisions merit consideration.

The composition of the recast ECJ should reflect its more 'august' responsibilities. Member States should reflect much harder on the candidates they send. It would be worth reflecting whether European High Court judges

---

[25] Subject, of course, to any improvement in that system. Cf. P. Craig, 'The Jurisdiction of the Community Court Reconsidered' [in this volume].

should not come normally from the highest courts of the Member States. Particularly, the experience of the judges in constitutional matters should become far more relevant than it is today. Though not a constitutional court in the formal sense, it would be in practical terms just that.

The final issue derives from the same special relationship and dependence between the ECJ and its national counterparts. Whereas in relation to the architecture I think the model should be less Anglo-American and more Continental, as regards the style of judgments, I think the Court should abandon the cryptic, Cartesian style which still characterizes many of its decisions and move to the more discursive, analytic, and conversational style associated with the common law world—though practised by others as well, notably the German Constitutional Court. As noted above, especially in its Constitutional jurisprudence, it is crucial that the Court demonstrate in its judgments that national sensibilities were fully taken into account. And it must amply explain and reason its decisions if they are to be not only authoritarian but also authoritative.[26] The Cartesian style, with its pretence of logical legal reasoning and inevitability of results,[27] is not conducive to a good conversation with national courts. In the same vein I would argue for the introduction of separate and dissenting opinions.[28] One of the virtues of separate and dissenting opinions is that they force the majority opinion to be reasoned in an altogether more profound and communicative fashion. The dissent often produces the paradoxical effect of legitimating the majority because it becomes evident that alternative views were considered even if ultimately rejected.

As a precondition for these changes in the style of ECJ decisions, the Member States in the next IGC would have finally to eliminate a continuous affront to the integrity of the European legal system, namely the renewability provisions for sitting judges on the Court. The European Parliament has proposed, twice, in its input to two successive IGCs that judges on the ECJ be appointed to one non-renewable term of office, thus removing any appearance of dependence on a Member State. (Whilst we are at it, the same should be true also for Commissioners who are meant to be independent.)[29] The refusal of the Member States to accede to that request is simply unacceptable.

---

[26] See J. Vining, *The Authoritative and the Authoritarian* (Chicago: University of Chicago Press, 1986).

[27] Cf. Lasser, 'Judicial (Self-)Portraits: Judicial Discourse in the French Legal System', (1995) 104 Yale LJ 1325.

[28] C. Turner and R. Munoz, op. cit., above n. 1, Section VII—Finding the Solutions—More Fundamental Revisions to the Judicial Architecture, II. Changes to the system of adoption of judgements: Dissenting judgements.

[29] A. Arnull, op. cit., above n. 1, p. 522. The author is particularly concerned by the issue of transparency in relation to the nomination of the judges and advocates general. See also C. Turner and R. Munoz, op. cit., above n. 1, Section VII, I.

Once this elementary anomaly is corrected, the conditions for dissents and separate opinions would be open.

The new Architecture should also address issues at the national level. The main recommendation here is to encourage a more proactive style of relationship between the national courts and their European counterparts. National courts must be encouraged to move away from the model that to be a good European Court is to make Preliminary References to the European Court of Justice and to say Amen to the pronouncements of the Court. To be a good European Court is to engage the European Court of Justice in a continuous conversation such that it is not only the parties and the Commission which inform the sensibility of the European Courts but also the judicial branch of national judiciary. Right now we have two models: Lower Courts (with some notable exceptions like the formidable Finanzgericht of Hamburg) simply frame questions for the European Court and follow the Rulings. By contrast, some of the most august Higher Courts regard themselves as the custodians of national constitutional values, the gatekeepers whose task is to make sure that core values of the national polity are not compromised by European norms. They do not regard themselves as part of a European constitutional conversation whose object would be to both shape European constitutional values and reshape national ones. The stand-alone attitude of the Italian and German Constitutional Courts both of which to date have never made a Reference despite decisions which clearly should have been the subject of References is not only not conducive to the Rule of Law but compromises the very interest and integrity of their own constitutional order.

A new style of conversation should encourage Member State courts at all levels not simply to ask the question but to propose what they think ought to be the correct Ruling and, most importantly, inform the European Court in the Reference itself of the constitutional and other concerns that the national legal order has when referring the question to the European Court of Justice.

Europe's judicial branch does not simply require the application of oil to creaking cogs designed to allow the system to cope with the quantitative burden of Enlargement. It requires a recasting of roles and relationships to meet an altogether more complex political and legal challenge.

Index